Your Undergraduate Degree in
PSYCHOLOGY

To my parents, who taught me that work is good—that work,
however menial or elevating, teaches.
—Paul Hettich

Dedicated to psychology majors everywhere, working to make a
positive difference in the world.
—Eric Landrum

Your Undergraduate Degree in
PSYCHOLOGY

FROM COLLEGE TO CAREER

PAUL I. HETTICH

DePaul University

R. ERIC LANDRUM

Boise State University

Los Angeles | London | New Delhi
Singapore | Washington DC

Los Angeles | London | New Delhi
Singapore | Washington DC

FOR INFORMATION:

SAGE Publications, Inc.
2455 Teller Road
Thousand Oaks, California 91320
E-mail: order@sagepub.com

SAGE Publications Ltd.
1 Oliver's Yard
55 City Road
London, EC1Y 1SP
United Kingdom

SAGE Publications India Pvt. Ltd.
B 1/I 1 Mohan Cooperative Industrial Area
Mathura Road, New Delhi 110 044
India

SAGE Publications Asia-Pacific Pte. Ltd.
3 Church Street
#10-04 Samsung Hub
Singapore 049483

Acquisitions Editor: Reid Hester
Editorial Assistant: Sarita Sarak
Production Editor: Laureen Gleason
Copy Editor: Megan Granger
Typesetter: Hurix Systems Pvt. Ltd.
Proofreader: Jen Grubba
Indexer: Karen Wiley
Cover Designer: Glenn Vogel
Marketing Manager: Lisa Brown
Permissions Editor: Karen Ehrmann

Printed in the United States of America

Library of Congress Cataloging-in-Publication Data

Hettich, Paul I.
Your undergraduate degree in psychology: from college to career / Paul I. Hettich, DePaul University, R. Eric Landrum, Boise State University.

pages cm
Includes bibliographical references and index.

ISBN 978-1-4129-9931-1 (pbk.: alk. paper)

1. Psychology—Vocational guidance.
I. Landrum, R. Eric. II. Title.

BF76.H488 2014
150.23—dc23   2012031487

This book is printed on acid-free paper.

13 14 15 16 17 10 9 8 7 6 5 4 3 2 1

Contents

Preface   vii

About the Authors   xi

About the Contributing Authors   xii

PART I. GET READY FOR YOUR TRANSITION TO THE WORKPLACE   1

1. Meet the New Workplace Realities (and Your Paperback Mentors)   3

2. Yes! You Can Succeed in Life With a Bachelor's Degree   15

3. Make the Most of Your Opportunities—Now!   35

PART II. KNOW THYSELF—BETTER!   57

4. What Is the Secret of Excellent Career Planning?   59
   by Camille Helkowski

5. Your Journey Through Psychosocial Development Continues Long After Graduation   77

6. Know the Skills You Need to Succeed (Course Content is No Longer the Focus)   95

7. Jump-Start Your Job Search   113
   by John Jameson

PART III. ONBOARDING TO WORK   **141**

8. Why Are Attitudes, Motivation, and Work Centrality Important?   143

9. Your First Real Job? It's Primarily About Communicating   165

10. Avoid False Expectations: Onboarding and Your First 90 Days   185

PART IV. I GRADUATED AND GOT A JOB: WHAT'S NEXT?   **207**

11. Your Personal Life Changes After College   209
    by Abby (Wilner) Miller

12. From Know Thyself to Manage Thyself   227

13. Prime Yourself for More Transitions   245

14. What Lies Ahead?   261

Author Index   **281**

Subject Index   **285**

Preface

It was the best of times, it was the worst of times, . . . it was the spring of hope, it was the winter of despair.

—Charles Dickens (1812–1870)

Excerpted from the opening lines of Dickens's *A Tale of Two Cities,* these words ring true for many college students today. Arguably, the need for, promises of, and access to higher education have never been greater than in the second decade of the 21st century. In this respect, it is the best of times to be a college student. Yet the challenges students encounter while forging their college education into a satisfying career are daunting. Many students may face three crises as they graduate. The first is overwhelming *loan debt,* with repayment typically beginning 6 months after they leave college whether or not they are employed. The second crisis is *unemployment* or *underemployment* in an unstable national and global economy where countless jobs continue to be outsourced, replaced by technology, or simply terminated. The third crisis, nurtured in part by the first two, is that of (returning to Dickens) *great expectations.* Students are conditioned from elementary school to believe that a college degree will place them on a fast track to personal success in a secure and satisfying career. Yet competition for the best postgraduate opportunities continues to be fierce: In 2009–2010, there were 97,216 recipients of a bachelor's degree in psychology in a total graduating class of 1.65 million baccalaureate recipients (National Center for Education Statistics, 2011). So these may also be the worst of times for college students and, for some, times filled with despair or frustration but little hope.

Teachers are concerned about the world their baccalaureate graduates must enter. Psychology educators are passionate about dispersing psychological science, but they may not be experts in the current job market or in how to help psychology students choose and succeed in a career. For example, to what extent are their students aware of the clashing cultures of corporate and college organizations and of the particular skills and behaviors they need to succeed? Do students know how to market themselves effectively amidst the competition and subsequently adapt to the workplace once they are hired?

Our goal in writing *Your Undergraduate Degree in Psychology* is to help students enter the workforce during and after college cognizant of the issues and prepared for the challenges they will encounter. We strongly believe that teachers can be highly influential partners in this goal. There are no quick and easy solutions to these issues and challenges, but we introduce them for serious discussion and share ideas, insights, and recommendations we believe will help build competence and confidence for a student's journey after college. The salient features of this book include the following.

Many "careers in psychology" books focus primarily on occupations requiring baccalaureate or graduate degrees and the skills students should learn. We approach the college-to-career transition for what it truly is—a diverse and interactive combination of dynamic intrapersonal, interpersonal, and environmental career-shaping experiences. Specifically, we encourage students to engage in systematic self-assessment; exploit campus opportunities that enhance self-reflection and career development; establish transferable skills employers seek; heighten awareness of their continuing journey through psychosocial development; master job-search skills; recognize the critical roles that organizational culture, communications, motivation, and self-management occupy in entry-level job success; and prepare for changing relationships and further life/career transitions. We know of no other resource in psychology that examines these dimensions to the extent we do.

Our focus is on individuals who enter the labor market immediately after graduation, including students who delay entry to graduate or professional school for 1 or more years to gain experience, earn money, and solidify goals. So welcome also, you graduate-school–bound students!

Your Undergraduate Degree in Psychology may be read as part of a course, such as Careers in Psychology, Orientation to the Psychology Major, or Introduction to the Psychology Major. It is also intended as supplementary reading for internship and capstone courses. Even if this book is not part of a specific course, the key is for students to critically examine the information it reveals and act on the recommendations we present. Ultimately, students *need* to know the answers to the questions, "How can I be best prepared to stand out from other new graduates entering the world of work?" and "How can I succeed in my first jobs?" Those are the types of questions we can help with!

To accomplish our goal of helping students prepare for work and career, we provide a forum in which students and teachers interact with one another and with us—as "paperback mentors" of sorts—as we explore the crucial issues that influence successful entry into contemporary workplaces. Having engaging interaction with a book and its ideas is a challenge, but it can be done. We designed this book to help students actively think about the world of work and career choices; frequent and meaningful self-reflection can lead to a strategic plan to help students pursue their life goals. The features we embedded in this book to facilitate self-reflection include "Time Out" sections inserted periodically in our narrative: "Time Out: Reflective Questions" and "Time Out: Exercise." At the end of each chapter are "Getting Involved" activities that include "Journal Starters" and diverse and often research-oriented projects that teachers may want to assign as is or modify to fit their specific goals. The "Additional Resources" component of each chapter enables students to dig further into a particular topic by consulting websites or other print sources. Each chapter ends, of course, with a list of the references we consulted for the topics we addressed.

College-to-workplace preparedness and transition is a major topic of growing importance in today's world of work, but it is not widely researched in psychology. Consequently, we invited colleagues with expertise exceeding our own in specific critical areas to guest-author chapters on career planning, job search, and post-college relationship changes. In addition, an important segment of our literature is drawn from outside of mainstream psychological research; this portion derives from surveys or reports of job-related issues originating from such organizations as the Collegiate Employment Research Institute and the National Association of Colleges and Employers, as well as from popular but reliable print and electronic sources. Finally, we illustrate several concepts using examples based on the experiences of former students and actual events.

No book project of this magnitude thrives without excellent advice. We are very grateful to many individuals who have been helpful and supportive throughout our journey. This has clearly been a team effort. In the editorial department at SAGE, Christine Cardone was our starting pitcher and Reid Hester came in as the closer. We are very thankful for Sarita Sarak, who kept us, in her firm but friendly manner, on track each step of the way and batted 1.000. Our team contains other valuable members. For the breadth and depth they shared on crucial topics, we thank our guest authors Camille Helkowski, John Jameson, and Abby (Wilner) Miller.

For their critical reviews of the manuscript and the invaluable insights and comments they shared, we are very grateful to William Addison, Eastern Illinois University; Ruth L. Ault, Davidson College; Bernard C. Beins, Ithaca College; Kristie Campana, Minnesota State University, Mankato; Phil Gardner, Michigan State University; Jane S. Halonen, University of West Florida; Meera Komarraju, Southern Illinois University, Carbondale; Beth M. Schwartz, Randolph College; Randolph A. Smith, Lamar University; and Annette Kujawski Taylor, University of San Diego.

Behind the scenes at SAGE were others who shared their expertise, including marketing manager Lisa Brown, permissions editor Karen Ehrmann, production editor Laureen Gleason, copy editor Megan Granger (our extra special thanks!), and cover designer Glenn Vogel. In addition, we appreciate Jon Keil's critical reading of several chapters and his helpful suggestions, as well as the gracious assistance of the DePaul University Library staff. We thank Robert Shelton and

Nakware Howard for their helpful suggestions for Chapter 7 ("Jump-Start Your Job Search").

To mix our metaphors, it takes a village to win a game, and we are thankful for every member of the team that made for our cumulative game-winning effort. And, last but not least, we as coauthors have grown in knowledge and wisdom from our mutual collaboration.

Reference

National Center for Education Statistics. (2011). *Digest of education statistics 2011*. Washington, DC: U.S. Department of Education. Retrieved from http://nces.ed.gov/programs/digest/d11/tables/dt11_286.asp

About the Authors

Paul I. Hettich, PhD, earned his degrees in psychology from Marquette University, New Mexico State University, and Loyola University Chicago. He served as an Army personnel psychologist at the Fort Jackson, South Carolina, Armed Forces Examining and Entrance Station (now the Military Entrance Processing Station); as a program evaluator at Cooperative Educational Research Laboratory in Northfield, Illinois; and as applied research scientist at the Intext Corporation in Scranton, Pennsylvania.

These positions created a "real-world" foundation for a 35-year academic career at Barat College (Lake Forest, Illinois). In addition to full-time teaching, he chaired the psychology department; served as academic dean; and directed institutional research, grant writing, and community college articulation. He was Barat's first recipient of the Sears-Roebuck Foundation award for teaching excellence and campus leadership. He taught at St. Clare's College in Oxford (England) and at the University of Stirling (Scotland). At Stirling, he subsequently served as an online tutor for the master's program in Lifelong Learning and on the editorial board for the *Journal of Adult and Continuing Education*. Following DePaul University's acquisition of Barat College, he continued to head the psychology program and retired with the rank of Professor Emeritus.

Hettich is a Fellow in Division 1 (Society for General Psychology), Division 2 (Society for the Teaching of Psychology), and Division 52 (International Psychology) of the American Psychological Association. He has more than 90 professional presentations and has authored or coauthored more than 25 refereed publications, including two books and three book chapters. He writes the quarterly column "Wisdom From the Workplace" for *Eye on Psi Chi*. His interest in workplace transition originates from graduates and employers who have revealed a major disconnect between university and workplace expectations, cultures, and practices.

R. Eric Landrum is a professor of psychology at Boise State University, receiving his PhD in cognitive psychology from Southern Illinois University, Carbondale. His research interests center on the educational conditions that best facilitate student success as well as the use of SoTL (Scholarship of Teaching and Learning) strategies to advance the efforts of scientist-educators. He is responsible for more than 300 professional presentations at conferences, more than 20 published books/

book chapters, and more than 70 professional articles in scholarly, peer-reviewed journals. He has worked with more than 275 undergraduate research assistants and taught more than 12,500 students in 20 years at Boise State. During summer 2008, he led an American Psychological Association working group at the National Conference for Undergraduate Education in Psychology, studying the desired results of an undergraduate psychology education.

Eric is the lead author of *The Psychology Major: Career Options and Strategies for Success* (4th ed., 2009) and also authored *Undergraduate Writing in Psychology: Learning to Tell the Scientific Story* (2008) and *Finding Jobs With a Psychology Bachelor's Degree: Expert Advice for Launching Your Career* (2009). He coauthored *An EasyGuide to APA Style* (2012) and *You've Earned Your Doctorate in Psychology . . . Now What?* (2012), and was lead editor for *Teaching Ethically: Challenges and Opportunities* (2012) and coeditor of *Assessing Teaching and Learning in Psychology: Current and Future Perspectives* (2013). He served as vice president for the Rocky Mountain region of Psi Chi (2009–2011). He is a member of the American Psychological Association, a fellow in the American Psychological Association's Division 2 (Society for the Teaching of Psychology, or STP), served as STP secretary (2009–2011), and will serve as the 2014 STP president.

About the Contributing Authors

Camille Helkowski, MEd, NCC, LCPC, is associate director of Loyola University Chicago's Career Development Center. She has been involved in higher education for more than 30 years, and her roles have included counselor, administrator, and instructor. She currently teaches an undergraduate course in career and life planning and a graduate course in career counseling, and supervises counseling practicum students throughout the academic year. Cam is the coauthor of several articles and books about college students, including *Connect College to Career: A Student's Guide to Work and Life Transitions* with Paul Hettich and *The College Student Counseling Treatment Planner* with Chris Stout and Art Jongsma. She is also a highly evaluated speaker who has presented at conferences throughout the United States and Canada. Her life outside of Loyola includes spending several hours a week in her private counseling practice and sharing as much time as possible with her very large family.

John Jameson is a seasoned higher-education, talent management, and job transition consultant. He recruited diverse talent for CNA Insurance and General Growth Properties in campus, lifecycle, and sourcing roles. He served as a career advisor at Robert Morris University and, in 2009, founded Connecting Insights, where he enables job seekers to interview with confidence through video mock-interview programs. He is a board member of the DePaul University ASK (Alumni Sharing Knowledge) organization and president of Alpha Kappa Psi business fraternity's Chicago Alumni Chapter. John enjoys collaborating with student organizations in the areas of recruitment and leadership development, and he has facilitated various interviewing, résumé writing, and networking workshops. John received a bachelor's in industrial and organizational psychology from DePaul University and lives in Chicago.

Abby (Wilner) Miller conducts and manages research focusing on low-income, first-generation college students for The Pell Institute for the Study of Opportunity in Higher Education. At the time of publication, Abby was transitioning from her role as research manager for the Pell Institute to a position as consultant in higher-education policy at JBL Associates. She is also the coauthor of the bestselling *Quarterlife Crisis: The Unique Challenges of Life in Your Twenties* and *Quarterlifer's Companion: How to Get on the Right Career Path, Control Your Finances, and Find the Support Network You Need to Thrive.* She has provided commentary on the transition from college to the workforce for media outlets including *Today, Oprah,* CNN, MSNBC, *The Washington Post,* and *The New York Times.* Abby also created and maintains the website quarterlifecrisis.com, an online community for twentysomethings. Abby holds a bachelor's degree in psychology from Washington University in St. Louis and a master's degree in educational policy and leadership from the University of Maryland.

PART I

Get Ready for Your Transition to the Workplace

Meet the New Workplace Realities (and Your Paperback Mentors)

Forewarned; forearmed. To be prepared is half the victory.

—Miguel de Cervantes (1547–1616), writer

Reality Check: Becoming a Freshman in the 21st Century Workplace

We believe that life is about transitions. We are in a constant state of change, and perhaps change is the only constant; we start over and reinvent ourselves all the time. Think about your transition from elementary school to middle school—it was a chance to start over. Or the transition from middle school to high school—you started over as a freshman. And then the transition from high school to college—you were a freshman (again). Starting over and starting fresh are not just recurring themes in the educational world but also in our personal lives, whether it be with friends, intimate relationships, and so on. Since there will be so many times in your life when you will become a freshman again, your abilities to adapt and be flexible are key for your future success.

You may not wish to admit that entering the "real world" after college is becoming a freshman again, but that is the case. You will begin *again* in a new organization at a low, perhaps the lowest, level of the hierarchy and in an organizational culture vastly different from college. You will be assigned new and different tasks and must master new skills. You will work with persons as coworkers (not classmates) and supervisors (not teachers), many of whom are older than you. You may have to move to a new location and establish new friendships. Life will be very different, because the transition from college to workplace represents a demarcation—a break—far more drastic than your transition from high school to college. If you read this book carefully and take our advice seriously, you will know what you need to do to maximize your chances for success during your freshman year in the 21st century workplace.

What Does the 21st Century Workplace Look Like?

Your workplace in the 21st century may not resemble the typical scenario experienced in the latter half of the 20th century. Cappelli (2009) reminded us that before the 1980s, applicants were often hired based on their potential. Entry-level positions were just that—entry level—and employers expected to provide additional detailed training, sometimes following an apprenticeship model when it took years beyond the bachelor's degree to acquire the requisite skills and knowledge to be truly successful in the specialized workplace. However, there is less employer-based education and preparation today (Cappelli, 2009), and according to some employer surveys, fewer than half the employers surveyed provide any training at all.

So your future workplace may not even resemble the workplaces of your parents and grandparents, which is just another reason why students need mentoring to transition successfully from college to career. For some, that transition may include a stop-off in graduate school, but the master's or doctoral student in psychology typically also wants a career. Let this book serve as one of your mentors—specifically, your "paperback mentor" (more on this concept later).

So what does the future hold? Well, change is inevitable. According to a U.S. Bureau of Labor Statistics (BLS) longitudinal study currently underway (as cited in Bialik, 2010), workers from ages 18 to 42 in this particular study have averaged 10.8 different jobs. In the BLS study, changing jobs was defined as a change in job title, either within the same company or to a different company. If you think about how you might advance in your profession or career, changing jobs would be a good indicator because promotions ideally mean more responsibilities and benefits, and perhaps a new job title. What about changing careers? In the same article, Bialik also reported that no good data support the typical adage that you will have seven different careers in your lifetime.

The fact of the matter is that you probably will have a number of different jobs over the course of your work life, and your college degree is an essential ingredient for a successful future (of course, you'll need to define "successful" for yourself—more on this at the end of Chapter 2). The series of jobs you hold should build your skills, abilities, and credentials, or as Carnevale (2011) put it:

People rarely leave jobs that require a college education because they have the best earnings, benefits and working conditions. There are many more brain surgeons who used to be cashiers than there are cashiers who used to be brain surgeons. A brain surgeon never starts as a brain surgeon, but would have likely had all types of jobs before entering college and medical school. Most jobs people hold in high school are in retail, food services, and other low-skill, low-wage jobs, and future brain surgeons are no exception. (para. 21)

Of course, you will occasionally hear the success story of someone who made it big without a college education. A few outliers will always pop up, but what do the general trends indicate? Carnevale (2011) reported that at the end of 2010, the unemployment rate for new college graduates (all majors, not just psychology majors) was 9.2%, while the unemployment rate for all U.S. workers was 9.8%. Looking at those two numbers together, it might appear that having a college degree is not much of an advantage compared with the general population, until you consider this—the unemployment rate for new high school graduates was 35%.

Unemployment rates are a function of the economy, and during the second decade of the 21st century the economy has been tough on job seekers. According to Newman (2010), our traditional assumptions about the relationship between education and work have been challenged not only by the American economic climate but also by our global economy. First, you cannot assume that a good education automatically leads to a good job and a satisfying lifestyle. College degrees are "a dime a dozen" in the workplace, given that America graduated 1.65 million baccalaureates during 2009–2010 (National Center for Education Statistics, 2011); an increasing number of desirable positions now require a graduate degree. Second, you cannot assume that working hard means your income will continue to increase. In some fields, average salaries have remained stagnant and even decline during a recession. Third, you cannot assume that devotion to your career will produce a comfortable retirement. Many jobs, including some that once required a baccalaureate, are being replaced by outsourcing to foreign countries or technology, or are simply eliminated and forced on other employees. Fourth, you cannot assume that each generation will be better off than its predecessor. View the news media and you will learn about our crushing national debt, burgeoning costs of Medicare, and the costly Social Security legacy later generations will inherit. In addition, student loan debt combined with a poor job market causes many graduates to move back home and to postpone marriage, children, and homeownership—traditional benchmarks of success and independence.

The Importance of Finishing What You Start: Do Become That Freshman Again

It seems the phrase "finishing what you start" has become a bit of a cliché in our culture, but it is nonetheless important that we encourage this goal. We believe there are direct and indirect benefits for you if you are able to complete your undergraduate training and earn your bachelor's degree (even if it turns out that psychology was not for you and you complete a different major). Even though each college student is different, many do share similarities—and we want you to think about how your accomplishment of degree completion could positively affect others in your life. For example, think about the message your earning a bachelor's degree would send if you are a first-generation college student in your family. Or think about how you might be an inspiration and role model to those in your life who might aspire to achieve what they saw you achieve, such as nieces and nephews, sons and daughters, your "significant other," and others close to you. When you struggle, learn, work hard, and persevere, you provide a route that people watching may choose to follow. Of course, there are situations where college students need to drop out or stop out for any number of reasons, but if the capability to finish is within your grasp, we encourage you with our strongest voice to finish what you start.

It's only fair to also let you know about the financial advantages you can experience by finishing college. The overall results, presented in Table 1.1, are fascinating.

So what is the value of finishing what you start? Well, over the course of a typical work life of 40 years, a high school degree recipient would net about $1.5 million, an associate's degree recipient would net $1.7 million, and a bachelor's degree (all degrees considered, not just psychology) recipient would net about $2.2 million. Thus, the value of finishing what you start would be between $500,000 and $600,000. If all the intrinsic reasons to finish your undergraduate degree presented previously were not persuasive enough, perhaps this new information might sweeten the deal and add another positive layer of encouragement.

We opened with the theme of transitions and starting over—that is, becoming a freshman again at many points in our personal and professional lives. The importance of successfully navigating transitions from one life stage to another (in this case, from college to career) is the overarching goal of this book, and we want to give you an advantage in entering into and succeeding within the world of work. To be fair (and as you already know), you have competition. For instance, looking at the most recent data, National Center for Education Statistics (2011) reported that there were 97,216 psychology bachelor's degree recipients in the United States. Although precise estimates are difficult to acquire, about 20% to 25% of those graduates will continue their education in a psychology graduate program or enter

Table 1.1   Estimates of Average Annual Earnings and Work-Life Earnings in 2009 for Full-Time, Year-Round Workers by Educational Attainment

Educational Attainment	Average Annual Earnings[1]	Work-Life Earnings Estimates[2]
Doctoral degree	$ 99,697	$ 3,252,000
Professional degree	$ 125,019	$ 3,648,000
Master's degree	$ 70,856	$ 3,252,000
Bachelor's degree	$ 58,613	$ 2,268,000
Associate's degree	$ 39,506	$ 1,727,000
Some college	$ 32,555	Not available
High school graduate	$ 31,283	$ 1,547,000
Not high school graduate	$ 21,007	$ 1,304,000

Note: that professional degrees include MD (physician), JD (lawyer), DDS (dentist), and DVM (veterinarian).
1. U.S. Census Bureau (2009), *Current Population Survey.*
2. Carnevale, Rose, and Cheah (2011).

some postgraduate education program (e.g., medical school, law school). So that gives you some idea of the annual volume of students you will be competing with for the best jobs. Employers will be able to "cherry-pick" the best and brightest students from this large field of possible employees. We want to help you be the cream that rises to the top—we want to be your "paperback mentors."

Time Out: Exercise—The Importance of College

As you will see throughout each chapter of this book, we'll urge you to stop, think, and reflect on big ideas from time to time. You've read about what employers want from college graduates and what psychology wants its graduates to achieve, but what about your own goals? Using this list of items from Malin and Timmreck (1979), take a moment to think about each item and then rate each on a scale of 0 (*not at all important to me*) to 100 (*extremely important to me*). As you are thinking about your ratings, think about why you selected the value you did. When complete, compare the scores on the ideas with one another. Do these scores actually reflect the relative value you place on each of the concepts listed?

Items	*Importance Rating (0–100)*
1. Preparation for a career, occupation, or profession	_____
2. Preparation to be a good citizen; knowledgeable about community and world affairs	_____
3. Preparation to get along in society today	_____
4. Increased understanding of myself and the world and increased ability to make good judgments	_____
5. Grasp of the subject matter, ideas, and method in my major field	_____
6. Increased ability to enjoy and care about myself and others	_____

Meet Your "Paperback Mentors": Our Blueprint for Workplace Preparedness

A mentor is a type of advisor, teacher, or coach; we will talk about workplace mentors in a later chapter. The purposes of our "mentorship," however, are to advise you about the activities we created to involve you with the material, to summarize the organization and content of this book, and to preview the chapters ahead—we want you to get the most from your efforts (and ours). You may study this book as part of a course or on your own. Feel free to read chapters out of sequence. We addressed a variety of topics, including some not usually found in career guides or "what-to-do-with-your-psychology-major" books.

This text is not a cookbook listing of simple, silver-bullet solutions to complex issues about college-to-workplace preparedness and transition. We do, however, offer a great deal of practical advice in the form of clearly stated recommendations or suggestions that are often woven into the fabric of our narrative. Sometimes you encounter topics rich in concepts and important to know even though they do not yield much immediate practical advice; that's the nature of theory and research. But we will not bury you in abstract ideas or overwhelm you with endless research studies. Because you are college students and in the social sciences, we assume you respect the value of empirical studies, theoretical concepts, analytical thinking, and experience. The chapters are anchored to a combination of data, concepts, and personal experiences, a great deal of which can be applied to your college setting. Topics such as "Avoid False Expectations: Onboarding and Your First 90 Days" (Chapter 10) and "Your Personal Life Changes After College" (Chapter 11) provide a preview of experiences to come but are also issues you should contemplate as you approach graduation and in your current jobs.

As psychology students, you also understand the importance of becoming actively involved with the material to enhance your learning, so here are the techniques we employ to facilitate your efforts. First, within each chapter you will periodically encounter sections labeled "Time Out: Exercise" or "Time Out: Reflective Questions," where we interrupt the narrative by asking you to apply the material to your situation. When the exercise requires considerable time to complete, we place it at the end of the chapter so it doesn't distract you from the material. Second, we close each chapter with a section we call "Getting Involved," which consists of three types of activities: journal starters, projects, and additional resources.

- For the **journal starters**, create a file on your computer or locate a lined notebook. The purpose of keeping a journal is to encourage you (a) to connect and *apply* the specific concepts and recommendations to your activities and, for many of you, to your job; (b) to *reflect* thoughtfully on how ideas we introduce have a bearing on your present activities and future plans; and (c) to *critically evaluate* the material we address. View the journal starters as an ongoing conversation with yourself. As you progress through chapters, periodically review your journal entries to gain insights and to note actions you have taken that promote your workplace readiness and actions you should take.
- The **projects** are specific opportunities for you to survey the literature, test hypotheses, and/or collect data regarding particular topics as part of an individual or group project. Perhaps you want to know more about the topic, question our conclusions, or investigate a related issue.
- The **additional resources** consist of selected websites or print documents meant to pique your curiosity for additional information. We include websites sparingly, because many have a tendency to change; besides, we know you are experts at seeking information from Internet resources.

We hope the in-chapter ("Time Out: Exercise" and "Time Out: Reflective Questions") and end-of-chapter ("Getting Involved") activities increase your desire to interact with the material; nothing, of course, substitutes for your intrinsic motivation to master and apply the material as you contemplate your transition to the workplace and other life transitions. Finally, we list the references cited in each chapter; we hope you find time to read one or two of those that spark an interest.

You should understand our rationale for presenting the material in this book, so here is our plan. We divide the book into four parts: "Get Ready for Your Transition to the Workplace," "Know Thyself—Better!," "Onboarding to Work," and "I Graduated and Got a Job: What's Next?"

Part I: Get Ready for Your Transition to the Workplace

The chapters in Part I promote workplace preparation by informing you of current occupational and economic situations, your career options with a baccalaureate degree, and opportunities you should pursue during college. In Chapter 1 (what you are reading now), we have painted with broad strokes a portrait of issues you will encounter in the changing landscape of the labor market where you will begin, once again, as a freshman. In our role as "paperback mentors" throughout this book, we describe the types of activities we embed in each chapter to encourage your active involvement with the material, and we conclude with a summary below of topics we believe can facilitate your transition.

Chapter 2 answers the critical question you hoped we would address when you opened this book: Yes! You can succeed in life with a bachelor's degree. You are introduced to career-exploration instruments, diverse career resources, and a long list of specific careers that use your psychology baccalaureate. We present studies that address career satisfaction with a bachelor's in psychology, cover basic concerns regarding graduate school, and conclude by exploring the meaning of success.

College offers numerous opportunities for promoting workplace readiness that augment your coursework, and employers will seek evidence that you actively pursued them. Chapter 3, "Make the Most of Your Opportunities—Now!," describes several major options. Because most employers seek applicants with work experience, your part-time jobs, internships, and departmental teaching and research assistant positions are essential opportunities to pursue. Your volunteer and extracurricular activities that help develop interpersonal and leadership skills are also valued. We strongly encourage coursework beyond the psychology major that develops work-related knowledge and skills.

Part II: Know Thyself—Better!

The four chapters that make up Part II exhort you to do just that—know who you are and who you are becoming even better than you do now. In Chapter 4, "What Is the Secret of Excellent Career Planning?," career and personal counselor Camille Helkowski encourages you to become aware of the people and events that have influenced your career beliefs. She stresses the importance of learning more about yourself and the world around you and the capacity each has for influencing your beliefs and choices. Finding a guide is an important source of support for this journey.

We continue the theme of knowing yourself in Chapter 5, "Your Journey Through Psychosocial Development Continues Long After Graduation." We introduce elements of different developmental theories and the insights you can gain from thinking about your own development in the context of these theories. We conclude by reviewing the results of a survey that asks young people what they seek in a job.

In Chapter 6, "Know the *Skills* You Need to Succeed (Course Content is No Longer the Focus)," we revisit a central theme in this book: the acquisition and transfer of skills. We discuss several surveys of skills graduates should possess in the contemporary workplace and how they connect to college. We review studies of specific psychology-related skills and their connection to work, as well as studies of broad skill sets such as communications and statistics/numerical skills. Finally, you will learn about colleges' covert curriculum of those skills and behaviors performed daily and how they apply to class and work.

You are now poised to learn the tools that will help you get a job. Chapter 7, "Jump-Start Your Job Search," was written by John Jameson, a former psychology major with several years of experience in corporate recruiting and career counseling. In this highly practical, hands-on chapter, you are introduced to essential tools and procedures for preparing a résumé, searching for a job, networking, and interviewing.

Part III: Onboarding to Work

Because "attitude is everything," we begin Chapter 8 ("Why Are Attitudes, Motivation, and Work Centrality Important?") by considering job satisfaction and negative attitudes. Next, we summarize and apply two theories of work motivation and subsequently examine results of a survey of young adults' attitudes toward the centrality of work in their lives.

In Chapter 9 ("Your First Real Job? It's Primarily about Communicating"), we speak to several basic concepts of communications and group work that you can readily apply to college and jobs. We conclude by summarizing an emotional intelligence model and explaining how it applies to your workplace success.

For recent graduates with little or no work experience, their first encounter in the workplace often produces culture shock because of a mismatch between their expectations and reality. In Chapter 10, "Avoid False Expectations: Onboarding and Your First 90 Days," we discuss the disparate differences in organizational culture between college and the general workplace, onboarding procedures used by several organizations, first-day strategies, performance feedback, office politics, and mentoring.

Part IV: I Graduated and Got a Job: What's Next?

Relationships change after college. Former psychology major, author, and educational researcher Abby (Wilner) Miller discusses the changing landscape in relationships with family and friends after graduation in Chapter 11, "Your Personal Life Changes After College." She also provides pointers for relationships with coworkers, time management, and dealing with feelings such as loneliness, anxiety, and depression.

In Chapter 12, "From Know Thyself to Manage Thyself," we review the common stressors that current college students may face and strategies to cope with stress in college and in the workplace. Practical advice and tips are offered about time management, finances, and finding a balance between your personal life and your professional life.

In Chapter 13, "Prime Yourself for More Transitions," we acknowledge that your transition from college to workplace is one of many major journeys of change you will likely pursue in life. We present multiple perspectives on transitioning, and these perspectives include models used in business consulting, another used in counseling settings, a phenomenological view, and a fourth perspective that addresses workplace entry issues.

Finally, we close with Chapter 14 ("What Lies Ahead?"), addressing a variety of issues, including straight talk about the psychology major (and why you should carefully consider that choice), preparing for a workplace where you may not be "doing" psychology directly, Millennials in the workplace, becoming a valued employee, and job-search strategies if you lose your job.

We return to the quotation that opened this chapter: "Forewarned; forearmed. To be prepared is half the victory." This book intends to strengthen your transition to the workplace by forewarning you of the knowledge, skills, experiences, and attitudes you should acquire in order to succeed during those critical years.

Closing Comments

As we indicated, the 21st century workplace is different from what your parents experienced and, perhaps, different even from what older brothers and sisters encountered. Because change is inevitable and may be the only constant, we firmly support Cervantes' sentiment about being forewarned and prepared. That preparation is aided when you know what employers want and what undergraduate programs deliver to psychology majors.

One of our major themes is to place greater emphasis on *skills* and less on the *content* of your psychology coursework. In fact, unless you are applying for a specific job for which only a psychology or social science major is qualified, a recruiter is unlikely to ask about particular psychology courses you completed (statistics and research methodology may be the exception). Recruiters know what a psychology major entails—that it provides a particular *perspective* on life different from that of biology and sociology. Most recruiters are not going to ask about the textbooks you used or your term paper topics; some may inquire about your GPA. Most likely, they will ask about specific skills you acquired and how you can apply them to the job for which you are interviewing.

Will you be able to translate coursework into transferable skills? This transition will become a challenge for you because traditional liberal arts disciplines focus explicitly on teaching content and only implicitly on articulating the skills you learn. Ultimately, you must assume ownership for your education and future, but this book will help you make informed decisions to pursue your goals. Finally, you must become *passionately* involved with your own transition to work, because, for most of you, it is a highly critical transition. Passiveness is not a marketable behavior, but passion is.

Getting Involved

Journal Starters

Try to respond to at least two journal starters for each chapter.

1. What are the most significant insights you gained from reading this chapter?

2. How well did you manage the transitions to the other levels of your education? Can you identify those behaviors or attitudes that helped you adjust to the next level of educational challenge?

3. Comment on the other transitions in your life, such as the death of a close relative, and how you handled the stresses associated with the events.

4. To what extent do you seek new situations that force you from your comfort zone?

5. What steps can you take to help make your next transition a positive event for you?

Projects

1. Create a "skills diary." Think about your in-class and out-of-class experiences in college to date. What skills do you think you are good at now? What leads you to this conclusion—that is, what experiences lead you to believe you are good at the skills you identified? What plan will you establish to remain good at what you are already good at and to improve in the areas you identified as needing

improvement? Don't forget to factor in outside-of-class activities—such as research assistantship, teaching assistantship, internship, service learning, study abroad, etc.—as methods of gaining skills. Since you won't have much control over how your remaining courses are structured, being planful with skills improvement may be more fruitful if you concentrate on outside-of-class opportunities rather than remaining coursework.

2. We maintain that most job recruiters will not ask you about specific courses, term paper topics, or grades. Survey the literature regarding questions interviewers ask and consult a career counselor for his or her opinion. What do you conclude? Can you transform this project into a report in one of your classes?

Additional Resources

URL	Brief Website Description
www.apa.org	Official website of the American Psychological Association
www.psychologicalscience.org	Official website of the Association for Psychological Science
http://www.quintcareers.com/college-to-career.html http://www.college aftermath.com/life-adventures-after-college/	Making the transition from college to career
http://www.p21.org/ http://www .careeronestop.org/ http://www .centerforpubliceducation.org/ Learn-About/21st-Century/ The-21st-century-job.html	Skills college graduates need for success

- American Psychological Association. (2007). *Getting in: A step-by-step plan for gaining admission to graduate school in psychology* (2nd ed.). Washington, DC: Author.
- Appleby, D. (2007). *The savvy psychology major.* Dubuque, IA: Kendall-Hunt.
- Kuther, T. L., & Morgan, R. D. (2007). *Careers in psychology: Opportunities in a changing world* (2nd ed.). Belmont, CA: Thomson Higher Education.
- Morgan, B. L., & Korschgen, A. J. (2009). *Majoring in psych? Career options for psychology undergraduates* (4th ed.). Needham Heights, MA: Allyn & Bacon.
- Schultheiss, D. E. P. (2008). *Psychology as a major: Is it right for me and what can I do with my degree?* Washington, DC: American Psychological Association.
- Wahlstrom, C., & Williams, B. K. (2004). *College to career: Your road to personal success.* Mason, OH: South-Western.

References

Bialik, C. (2010, September 4). Seven careers in a lifetime? Think twice, researchers say. *Wall Street Journal.* Retrieved from http://online.wsj.com/article/SB10001424052748704206 80457546816280587790.html

Cappelli, P. (2009, August 17). *Ill-prepared workers?* Retrieved from http://www.hreonline .com/HRE/printstory.jsp?storyId=242442555

Carnevale, A. (2011, January 14). College is still worth it. *Inside Higher Ed.* Retrieved from http://www.insidehighered.com/views/2011/01/14/carnevale_college_is_still_worth_ it_for_americans

Carnevale, A. P., Rose, S. J., & Cheah, B. (2011, August). *The college payoff: Education, occupations, lifetime earnings.* Georgetown University, Center on Education and the Workforce. Retrieved from http://www9.georgetown.edu/grad/gppi/hpi/cew/pdfs/ collegepayoff-complete.pdf

Malin, J. T., & Timmreck, C. (1979). Student goals and the undergraduate curriculum. *Teaching of Psychology, 6,* 136–139.

National Center for Education Statistics. (2011). *Digest of education statistics 2011.* Washington, DC: U.S. Department of Education. Retrieved from http://nces.ed.gov/ programs/digest/d11/tables/dt11_286.asp

Newman, R. (2010, March). Surviving the American makeover: How to stay afloat—and get ahead—when the old rules no longer apply. *U.S. News & World Report,* pp. 14–16.

U.S. Census Bureau. (2009). *Current population survey, annual social and economic (ASEC) supplement* (Publication PINC-03). Washington, DC: Author.

CHAPTER 2

Yes! You Can Succeed in Life With a Bachelor's Degree

You can't connect the dots looking forward; you can only connect them looking backward. So you have to trust that the dots will somehow connect in your future.

—Steve Jobs, cofounder of Apple Computer, Inc.

This chapter is all about you! We start by encouraging some serious self-reflection, including thinking about your own personality, your preferences, and what you want to do. We make suggestions that will allow you to explore some of these ideas while still an undergraduate, and we provide tips on finding specific and helpful advice about jobs in general and, in particular, jobs psychology graduates often pursue. To be fair with the data, we need to tell you about the job satisfaction and dissatisfaction levels of psychology majors, but please trust that if you are reading this book carefully and following our advice as much as you can (as well as the advice of your mentors and trusted advisors), we believe you can maximize your chances for satisfaction.

If you determine that your bachelor's degree is not enough education to achieve your goals, we'll briefly present some options, including certificates and specializations you can sometimes earn while still an undergraduate, and we'll provide a quick overview of the graduate school options in psychology. Finally, we return to our opening theme of self-reflection and ask you to think about what success means to you. To the extent possible, knowing what the final destination may look like can help in the routing and navigation to get there, but if you are unsure about the destination, we can provide helpful "travel tips" to assist you in your journey.

Career Exploration Instruments: Navigating Your Own Personality, Style, and Preferences

The question, "What do you want to be when you grow up?" often requires a complex answer. The amount of time, energy, and resources we contribute to the work portion of our lives is enormous. For some, who they are revolves around what they do for a living. Given that we each will probably have a 40-year work life, taking some time now, as an undergraduate, to explore who you are and what you want from your career seems like a good investment of time and energy. Of course, some of your values and attitudes may change during that time span, and certainly the world of work will reinvent itself many times over, but if you are well anchored in the knowledge of who *you* are and what *you* want, we believe this will help you navigate uncertain times.

One recurring theme throughout this book is making sure you utilize your local career center. This service unit sometimes goes by a different name on different campuses, but start with a search on your own college or university webpage—the career services center may be part of an alumni center on campus. The professionals who work in these centers will have the expertise to help you explore various aspects of the world of work, but they also may be able to assist you in completing some of the assessments described in this chapter. Although you can take some assessment instruments online (Kamenetz, 2010), such as Jung Career Indicator (www.humanmetrics.com/vocation/JCI.asp) and Career Explorer (www.careerexplorer.net/aptitude.asp), they require scoring and interpretation. Completing such inventories may be more meaningful to you when you have a trained professional aiding in their interpretation—just another reason to access the resources of your career center.

A sampling of some of the career assessments available (Satterfield, 1998) includes the California Psychological Inventory, the Temperament and Values Inventory, the Career Maturity Inventory, and DISCOVER. As you consider a strategy for seeking more information about your choices and options, these questions adapted from Carson and Dawis (2000) may help guide you through the process: (1) Have you identified possible occupational alternatives? (2) Are your skills, values, and interests aligned with your major and selected occupation? (3) Are you satisfied with your choices? (4) Have you limited yourself too much in your choices? (5) Are you being realistic about the accessibility of the career choices you are pursuing? You might be interested to know that career professionals and academics studying these topics have developed scales, assessments, and inventories to help understand the complexity of each of these issues. For instance, to help students identify possible occupational alternatives, inventories such as the Career Factors Inventory, the Career Decision Scale, the Career Thoughts Inventory, and My Vocational Situation are available (Carson & Dawis, 2000).

Your own self-study of your skills, values, and interests can lead to some valuable insights regarding not only your match and fit with your selected major but also your path toward the workforce and career selection and satisfaction. The areas of abilities, skills, values, and interests each have inventories and assessments dedicated to enhancing understanding. For example, some of the instruments available to help provide some insight into your *abilities* include the General Aptitude Test Battery, the Guide for Occupational Exploration, and the Armed Services Vocational Aptitude Battery (Carson & Dawis, 2000). Researchers study *values* in a number of different contexts, and connecting the study of values with those values leading to success in the workplace is a natural fit. Examples of assessments that measure values include the Minnesota Importance Questionnaire, the Survey of Interpersonal Values, the Temperament and Values Inventory, the Rokeach Value Survey, the Values Scale, the Career Orientation Placement and Evaluation Survey, and modules with large assessment batteries, such as DISCOVER and SIGI[3] (Carson & Dawis, 2000; McKay, 2010). *Interest* inventories have been available for some time, and these can be quite useful in providing students feedback about how their current interests match with successful individuals in the workforce who share the same interests. Examples of widely used interest inventories include the Strong Interest Inventory, the Kuder Occupational Interest Survey, the Campbell Interest and Skills Survey, and the Self-Directed Search (Carson & Dawis, 2000). (Self-Directed Search is discussed further in the box on p. 18.)

When it is time to explore career choices, instruments are available to assist in the process—for example, Career Decision-Making Difficulties Questionnaire, the Job Satisfaction Scale within the Career Attitudes and Strategies Inventory, and the Dissatisfaction with Career Scale within the Career Barriers Inventory-Revised. We tend to form stereotypes about certain fields of work (sometimes based on portrayals in the media), but it is important not to let stereotypes restrict your choices when exploring possibilities in the workforce. Researchers use scales such as My Vocational Situation and the Perceptions of Barriers measure to study and help students better understand the wide array of choices available and decisions to be made.

Being realistic about prospective career paths is also important; for example, only a finite number of jobs are available in the National Basketball Association or the National Football League, so students need to be realistic about how accessible a potential career path in those areas may be. Researchers and career professionals use subscales of existing measures (e.g., My Vocational Situation) to assist in these efforts. Subscales such as Learning Job Skills, Overcoming Obstacles, and Working Hard (all from the Career Barriers Inventory) can assist in identifying whether students are being realistic about pursuing a particular career path (Carson & Dawis, 2000).

The Self-Directed Search

In this feature, we explore the Self-Directed Search (SDS), a popular career planning tool developed by John L. Holland (1994). The SDS developed out of Holland's (1958, 1959) theories of vocational choice. According to Holland (1973), four working assumptions drive the theory:

1. In this culture, most persons can be categorized as one of six types—realistic, investigative, artistic, social, enterprising, or conventional.

2. There are six kinds of environments—realistic, investigative, artistic, social, enterprising, and conventional.

3. People search for environments that will let them exercise their skills and abilities, express their attitudes and values, and tackle agreeable problems and roles.

4. A person's behavior is determined by interaction between his or her personality and the characteristics of his or her environment.

The basic notion of this theory is that people are happier and more successful in jobs that match their interests, values, and skills. Scoring of the SDS is linked to occupational codes and titles. Thus, by determining your preferences for styles or types, the SDS gives you some indication of the jobs you might like and that would make the most of your skills and interests. The fundamental idea is that people and work environments can be classified according to Holland's six types; thus, if you know your own type and understand the types associated with particular careers, you can find a match.

Holland's (1994) SDS is a relatively straightforward inventory. An Internet version (http://www.self-directed-search.com) is available, and for $4.95 (at the time of this writing), you can take it on your computer and receive a personalized report with your results. Individuals answer questions about their aspirations, activities, competencies, occupations, and other self-estimates. These scores yield a three-letter summary code that designates the three personality types an individual most closely resembles. With this code, test takers use the Occupations Finder to discover those occupations that best match their personality types, interests, and skills. This comprehensive booklet lists more than 1,300 occupational possibilities—more than any other career interest inventory.

Although it is not possible for you to take the SDS here, we describe the six personality types and examples of corresponding careers in Table 2.1. If you are interested in taking the SDS, you might want to contact your campus counseling and testing center or career center. There may be a small fee for this service, but the insight and self-reflection gained from the SDS are worth it. Many times, psychology majors are identified with the summary code "SIA"—do a Google search on "Holland Code SIA" for some interesting results that may be relevant to your career pursuits as a psychology major.

Table 2.1   Types and Occupations of the Self-Directed Search

Realistic		Investigative	
Personality Type	**Occupations**	**Personality Type**	**Occupations**
▪ Have mechanical ability and athletic ability? ▪ Like to work outdoors? ▪ Like to work with machines and tools? ▪ Genuine, humble, modest, natural, practical, realistic?	▪ Aircraft controller ▪ Electrician ▪ Carpenter ▪ Auto mechanic ▪ Surveyor ▪ Rancher	▪ Have math and science abilities? ▪ Like to explore and understand things and events? ▪ Like to work alone and solve problems? ▪ Analytical, curious, intellectual, rational?	▪ Biologist ▪ Geologist ▪ Anthropologist ▪ Chemist ▪ Medical technologist ▪ Physicist

Artistic		Social	
Personality Type	**Occupations**	**Personality Type**	**Occupations**
▪ Have artistic skills and a good imagination? ▪ Like reading, music, or art? ▪ Enjoy creating original work? ▪ Expressive, original, idealistic, independent, open?	▪ Musician ▪ Writer ▪ Decorator ▪ Composer ▪ Stage director ▪ Sculptor	▪ Like to be around other people? ▪ Like to cooperate with other people? ▪ Like to help other people? ▪ Friendly, understanding, cooperative, sociable, warm?	▪ Teacher ▪ Counselor ▪ Speech therapist ▪ Clergy member ▪ Social worker ▪ Clinical psychologist

Enterprising		Conventional	
Personality Type	**Occupations**	**Personality Type**	**Occupations**
▪ Have leadership and public speaking ability? ▪ Like to influence other people? ▪ Like to assume responsibility? ▪ Ambitious, extroverted, adventurous, self-confident?	▪ Manager ▪ Salesperson ▪ Business executive ▪ Buyer ▪ Promoter ▪ Lawyer	▪ Have clerical and math abilities? ▪ Like to work indoors? ▪ Like organizing things and meeting clear standards? ▪ Efficient, practical, orderly, conscientious?	▪ Banker ▪ Financial analyst ▪ Tax expert ▪ Stenographer ▪ Production editor ▪ Cost estimator

(Continued)

(Continued)

The SDS presents some interesting options for persons thinking about a career. Although you haven't taken the SDS, you can look at the six different types and realize that perhaps one or two of them fit you well. The idea here is not to be afraid of some self-exploration; it is important for you to figure out what you would like to do for a career. College is a great time for career exploration, and if you put some work into it, you will reap the rewards.

Be True to Yourself: What Do You Want to Do?

If only this were as easy as reading a heading in a book. Being true to yourself requires that you first know yourself. When we say "know," we mean deep self-reflection by which you gain a solid comprehension of your own values, skills, and abilities—traits that researchers and career professionals can help you explore, as evidenced by all the assessments and inventories available. But, ultimately, you'll decide what's right for you and how well a job and career path fit your needs, wants, and desires. Throughout this book, we encourage you to take the time to reflect, whether with the journal starters and exercises found at the end of each chapter or by exploring external resources. We hope you will realize that this investment in you is worth the effort—being planful now, while in college, can help shape a path that maximizes your chances of success. Of course, you could "luck" into a great career without much thought, just as some individuals "luck" into a romantic relationship that lasts 50+ years. But do your best not to leave your future success and satisfaction to chance—be a proactive agent in advocating for your future.

Uncovering what you want to do in a job or career will take some exploration and effort. We highly recommend that you seek experiences outside of the traditional classroom, whether through participating in an internship, acting as a research assistant or teaching assistant, service learning, study abroad, clubs and activities, intramural sports, etc. To the greatest degree possible, your outside-of-class involvement should match your psychology major and your ultimate career goals. If you must have a job during your undergraduate career, try to work a job that is somehow connected to the industry or work environment you eventually want to be in. Of course, that is not always possible, but the more you can be planful and strategic, the greater insights you can gain while an undergraduate, as opposed to going from one job to another after graduation. Chapter 3 explores the many opportunities college provides for exploring your interests while preparing for the workplace.

Finding Resources About Jobs:
O*NET and Psychology-Specific Resources

O*NET, Occupational Information Network (http://online.onetcenter.org), is a comprehensive database of occupations, work attributes, and job characteristics. O*NET incorporates much of the information that was available from *Dictionary of Occupational Titles* (no longer published). Quite simply, O*NET is an amazing tool that anyone with Internet access can use. Covering more than 1,000 occupations, O*NET provides detailed information about each job, including knowledge, skills, and abilities needed; interests; general work activities; and a work context. It also provides links to salary information. All occupations are organized using O*NET-SOC (standard occupational classification) codes. This system is complex yet well designed and user friendly. You can examine not only the tasks involved in a given job but the knowledge required, skills necessary, abilities used, typical work activities, context of work, training expected, general interest of those in the job, work styles, work values, related occupations, and a link to wage information.

Within psychology, Rajecki (2007, 2008) and Appleby, Millspaugh, and Hammersley (2011) have provided advice and resources for utilizing O*NET resources, specifically geared toward psychology baccalaureates. For example, Rajecki (2007) provided a step-by-step guide to using O*NET and included examples, but he warned that some job lists often provided to new psychology graduates contain jobs for which other degrees also satisfy the educational prerequisites (Rajecki, 2008). We tend to take the broader view, as adopted by Appleby et al. (2011)—rather than limit a job listing to present only those items a psychology graduate is well suited for, we adhere to the approach of presenting a broad amount of information to the psychology major so he or she has a wide view of the potentialities. That is, sometimes in job lists, occupations are presented that do not require a bachelor's degree in psychology (such as bartender or cashier). Rajecki (2008) criticized that approach, but, again, we would rather provide you with the full view of the playing field, recognizing that some jobs listed do not require a bachelor's degree in psychology (Appleby et al., 2011). In that spirit, Table 2.2 presents the list of more than 170 occupations of interest to psychology majors—for specific links to more information about each of these careers, see Appleby et al. (2011) or utilize O*NET for further exploration.

Table 2.2   Career Titles of Potential Interest to Psychology Majors

Potential Careers With a Bachelor's Degree in Psychology	*Careers That Require a Degree Beyond the Bachelor's Degree in Psychology*
Activities director	Academic counselor
Admissions evaluator	Air Force psychologist
Advertising sales representative	Army psychologist

(Continued)

Table 2.2 (Continued)

Potential Careers With a Bachelor's Degree in Psychology	Careers That Require a Degree Beyond the Bachelor's Degree in Psychology
Alumni director	Art therapist
Animal trainer	Assessment professional/program evaluator
Applied statistician	Biogerontologist
Army mental health specialist	Biogerontologist
Benefits manager	Chief psychologist
Career/employment counselor	Child abuse counselor
Career information specialist	Child counselor
Caseworker	Child psychologist
Child development specialist	Clinical psychologist
Child welfare/placement caseworker	Clinical social worker
Chiropractor	Cognitive neuroscientist
Claims supervisor	Cognitive psychologist
Coach	College/university professor
Community organization worker	Community counselor
Community worker	Community psychologist
Computer programmer	Comparative psychologist
Conservation officer	Counseling psychologist
Consumer psychologist	Developmental psychologist
Correctional treatment specialist	Domestic violence counselor
Corrections officer	Educational psychologist
Criminal investigator (FBI and other)	Psychologist
Customer service representative supervisor	Exercise therapist
Database administrator	Experimental psychologist
Database design analyst	Family counselor/caseworker
Department manager	Forensic psychologist
Dietician	Gerontological counselor
Disability policy worker	Geropsychologist
Disability case manager	Guidance counselor
Elementary school teacher	Health psychologist
Employee health maintenance program specialist	Industrial/organizational psychologist
Employee relations specialist	Lawyer
Employment counselor	Licensed professional counselor
Employment interviewer	Marriage and family counselor
Engineering/human factors/ ergonomic	Marriage and family therapist
Financial aid counselor	Mathematical/quantitative psychologist
Fundraiser I	Media psychologist
Fundraiser II	Medical social worker
Group worker	Mental health counselor
Health care facility administrator	Military chaplin
High school teacher	Military counselor
Host/hostess	Military psychologist
	Minister, priest, rabbi, chaplain, etc.

Human resource advisor
Information specialist
Job analyst
Labor relations manager
Loan officer
Management analyst
Market research analyst
Mental health social worker
Mental retardation aide
News writer
Occupational analyst
Patient resources and reimbursement
    agent
Personnel recruiter
Police officer
Polygraph examiner
Preschool teacher
Probation/parole officer
Psychiatric aide/attendant
Psychiatric technician
Psychological stress evaluator
Public health director
Public relations representative
Purchasing agent
Real estate agent
Recreation leader
Recreation supervisor
Recreational therapist
Research assistant
Retail salesperson
Sales clerk
Social group worker
Social services aide
Substance abuse counselor
Systems analyst
Technical writer
Veterans contact representative
Veterans counselor
Victims' advocate
Vocational training teacher
Volunteer coordinator
Writer

Multicultural counselor
Music therapist
Navy clinical psychologist
Neurologist
Neuropathologist
Neuropsychologist
Neurosurgeon
Nurse
Occupational therapist
Optometrist
Pediatrician
Penologist
Personnel psychologist
Pharmacologist
Physiatrist
Physical therapist
Physician
Primary therapist
Psychiatric social worker
Psychiatrist
Psychological anthropologist
Psychometrician
Psychotherapist
Rehabilitation psychologist
School psychologist
School social worker
Social psychologist
Speech pathologist
Sport psychologist
Therapist for the blind
Veterinarian
Vocational rehabilitation counselor

Career Satisfaction (and Dissatisfaction) With the Psychology Degree

First, we'll present the broad overview data about college graduates in general and then eventually drill down to the data (available) for psychology graduates in particular. The National Association of Colleges and Employers (NACE, 2010) reported that, based on the 2010 graduating class, average starting salaries slipped 1.3% from the previous year, with the overall average at $48,661. An overall snapshot of job satisfaction is a bit more difficult to come by, but some work is available that looks at all employment sectors, not just new college graduates. When taken together, Smith (2007) reported the top and bottom professions with regard to both satisfaction and happiness, using well-established survey methodology. These overall data are presented in Table 2.3.

Salary data for new collegiate hires with a bachelor's degree in psychology are sometimes difficult to find, but probably the most reliable source for national data is NACE. When providing information about the Class of 2010, NACE (2010) reported that the average starting salary offer for psychology graduates was $32,358. But what about the satisfaction of psychology graduates?

Research data for this topic are available, and the studies tend to be (a) based on psychology alumni at a single institution or (b) based on a national sample of alumni from all majors, with the psychology majors selected and identified for comparative analysis. Rajecki and Borden (2009) studied psychology alumni from one Midwestern university and reported that "psychology alumni are likely to have higher qualifications than demanded by some of their first-year-out jobs" (p. 27). Although this leads to a positive trajectory for growth in future employment, it also means that psychology graduates may be initially frustrated or dissatisfied with those first employment opportunities because of the mismatched skill set, often occurring because psychology majors obtain jobs for which they might not need a bachelor's degree (Rajecki & Borden, 2009).

How might this mismatch between first post-baccalaureate jobs and psychology graduates' employability be ameliorated? Landrum, Hettich, and Wilner (2010) reported specific suggestions for colleges and universities based on an alumni sample from a Western university. Alumni detailed college-level activities that would help promote workforce readiness. For example, regarding the skill "work well with others," alumni suggested more group projects, more projects representative of the workplace, and enhanced group work. Regarding "motivate oneself to function at optimum levels of performance," alumni recommended using the class's organizational structure to enhance self-esteem and self-drive, to enter into a mentoring relationship with a professor, and to self-select a performance level to aspire to. Alumni who have successfully launched into the workforce can provide insights to current psychology majors that may help future graduates avoid the mismatch between first-year jobs and potential dissatisfaction.

What about the national data, including comparisons (when available) of different majors? As far back as 1990, Littlepage, Perry, and Hodge identified that although the work experiences of psychology graduates were similar to those of other liberal arts majors, "the work experiences of psychology majors were not as positive as the work experiences of business and science majors" (p. 50). Rajecki and Borden (2009)

Table 2.3 Top and Bottom Satisfaction and Happiness Ratings for American Workers

Satisfaction			Happiness
Clergy Physical therapists Firefighters Education administrators Painters, sculptors Teachers Authors Psychologists Special education teachers Operating engineers	**BEST**	Clergy Firefighters Transportation ticket and reservation agents Architects Special education teachers Actors and directors Science technicians Mechanics and repairers Industrial engineers Airline pilots and navigators	
Expediters Food preparers Cashiers Apparel clothing salespersons Freight, stock, materials handlers Hand packers and packagers Bartenders Laborers (except construction) Waiters/servers	**WORST**	Electronic repairers Pressing machine operators Maids and housemen Amusement and recreation attendants Welfare service aids Construction trades Construction laborers Molding and casting machine operators Garage and service station attendants	

reported a similar pattern of results when comparing majors and programs within an institution. In studying psychology alumni from seven institutions, Landrum and Elison-Bowers (2009) reported that alumni's self-reported salary levels were positively and significantly correlated with happiness and satisfaction with career choice and that older alumni reported that their undergraduate psychology courses could have been more helpful (as compared with younger alumni).

It may be that it takes some time for psychology alumni to realize the potential mismatch between job qualifications and opportunities. This trend for psychology majors to be more dissatisfied with their employment options compared with other majors was confirmed again by Light (2010), reporting on the outcomes of a national study that asked college graduates from 21 majors, "Overall, how satisfied are you with your current career path up until now?" Psychology graduates provided the lowest percentage of career satisfaction of the 21 majors studied, at 26% satisfied.

What does this mean for you as you are majoring in psychology and will eventually launch from college to career? First, that you are aware of this potential mismatch means you can more realistically align your expectations for that first job postgraduation. You will likely work your way up the ladder, and in the current economy, a mismatched job is preferable to no job at all. But just realize that over time that mismatch may lead to feelings of dissatisfaction about your undergraduate major. Second, do everything you can while an undergraduate to take the advice of the college professors, psychology alumni, and "paperback mentors" trying to help you. Harkening back to the title of this chapter, yes, you can succeed in life with a bachelor's degree in psychology, but it's going to take an investment of your time, talents, and energy to get the most bang for your buck—or what might formally be called "return on investment." The concern for satisfaction with the psychology major is a multifaceted issue that we will examine again in Chapter 14 ("What Lies Ahead?").

Time Out: Reflective Question

Why do you think psychologists are placed in the "best satisfaction" quadrant of Table 2.3 and not in the "best happiness" quadrant?

What if the Bachelor's Degree Alone Is Not Enough?

As you scan the field of employment opportunities, you might discover that the options available to you with your bachelor's degree in psychology may not allow you to do what you want to do. This realization is perfectly acceptable, and the earlier you arrive at it in your life, the more options you will afford yourself for fulfilling your goals. This is not the venue to provide a complete overview of the graduate admissions process or graduate education in psychology, but we'll provide a brief introduction.

It is important not to overlook education and training opportunities you might have while still an undergraduate. That is, at many institutions, you can earn a certification in a particular field or area of study that might make you more versatile and qualified in the job market. A certification is a carefully designed set of classes and experiences that allow you to gain some expertise in a topic, but these programs are typically smaller than minoring in a discipline and may be much more targeted and specialized. Also, certificate programs are typically more interdisciplinary, and minors usually are contained within one academic program or major. For example, at Boise State University, undergraduates can earn certificates in dispute resolution, family studies, drug and alcohol studies, public relations, cinema and digital media studies, and technical communication. These certificate programs are typically less work than a minor, but as you look at the list above, you can imagine how these specialized skill sets might make a psychology graduate more employable in a specific setting after graduation.

But what if during your undergraduate career, or perhaps after graduation, you decide you want more education, either toward graduate school in psychology or some other discipline? Here is a brief snapshot of graduate application statistics based on data from the 2008–2009 academic year (Mulvey, Michalski, & Wicherski, 2010):

- 1,273 U.S. doctoral programs reported receiving 84,691 graduate school applications (remember that one person may be applying to more than one program).
- There are 453 private doctoral programs and 820 public doctoral programs, and 46% of applicants apply to private doctoral programs.
- Just over 20% of applicants are accepted by doctoral programs, with the acceptance rate of private programs (30%) being twice the acceptance rate of public programs (15%).
- 275 master's degree programs reported receiving 11,187 graduate school applications.
- There are 97 private and 178 public master's degree programs, with a 51% acceptance rate.
- Regarding master's degree programs, the acceptance rate at public institutions was 46% and the acceptance rate at private institutions was 60%.

Numerous resources are available to help with the details of the graduate school application process, including the following:

- American Psychological Association. (2007). *Getting in: A step-by-step plan for gaining admission to graduate school in psychology* (2nd ed.). Washington, DC: Author.
- Keith-Spiegel, P., & Wiederman, M. W. (2000). *The complete guide to graduate school admission: Psychology, counseling, and related professions* (2nd ed.). Mahwah, NJ: Erlbaum.
- Kracen, A. C., & Wallace, I. J. (Eds.). (2008). *Applying to graduate school in psychology: Advice from successful students and prominent psychologists.* Washington, DC: American Psychological Association.
- Peters, R. L. (1997). *Getting what you came for: The smart student's guide to earning an M.A. or a Ph.D.* (Rev. ed.). New York, NY: Farrar, Straus, & Giroux.

Time Out: Exercise

Just as a quick exploration, complete the unvalidated graduate school potential test in Table 2.4 to get some quick ideas about whether graduate school is for you.

Once you are in graduate school, what does it take to be successful? Kuther (2003) reported that the top 15 characteristics that describe successful graduate students are (starting with the most important) working hard, getting along with others, writing ability, clinical and counseling skills, doing research, handling stress, discipline, good grades, high intelligence, empathy, establishing a relationship with a mentor, getting along with peers, broad knowledge of psychology, specialized knowledge in one or two areas of psychology, and reflecting program values. It is interesting to see the overlap between these characteristics and what employers want in general and, specifically, from psychology bachelor's degree recipients. The intent of this book is not to provide you with detailed advice about how to succeed in graduate school in psychology, but some of the resources available (e.g., Walfish & Hess, 2001) can provide you with more information about success in graduate school.

Table 2.4   An Unvalidated Graduate School Potential Test

Your answers to the following 22 yes–no questions will give you a good idea of your potential for success in graduate school, as determined by your current values and level of motivation. Answer each question honestly and truthfully. This is not a standardized or validated test, and its items are so transparent that anyone can fake them. Unless you are completely honest with yourself, the results will be of no value.

Circle one:

Yes   No   (1) Does the idea of living at near-poverty level for 2 to 7 years while studying most of the time repulse you?

Yes   No   (2) Do you enjoy writing term papers?

Yes   No   (3) Does the idea of making verbal presentations of academic material in front of a group bother you?

Yes   No   (4) Do you enjoy reading psychology books even if they are not assigned?

Yes   No   (5) Do you put off studying for tests or writing papers as long as possible?

Yes   No   (6) Do you often give up desirable social opportunities in order to study?

Yes   No   (7) Do you want to earn a high salary when you finish graduate school?

Yes   No   (8) Do you like to study?

Yes   No   (9) Do you have trouble concentrating on your studies for hours at a time?

Table 2.4   (Continued)

Yes	No	(10) Do you occasionally read recent issues of psychology journals?
Yes	No	(11) Do you dislike library research?
Yes	No	(12) Do you have a drive to enter the profession of psychology?
Yes	No	(13) Are there many other careers, besides being a psychologist, that you would like to pursue?
Yes	No	(14) Do you intend to work full-time at a career?
Yes	No	(15) Are you sick of school right now?
Yes	No	(16) Are your grades mostly As and Bs?
Yes	No	(17) Have any of your teachers ever suggested that you go to graduate school?
Yes	No	(18) Did you do well (i.e., receive an A or B) in statistics?
Yes	No	(19) Do you feel a PhD is desirable primarily because of the social status it gives to those who hold it?
Yes	No	(20) Do you like doing research?
Yes	No	(21) Do you dislike competing with other students?
Yes	No	(22) Can you carry out projects and study without direction from anyone else?

Scoring the test:

- Give yourself one point for each "yes" you marked for Items 2, 4, 6, 8, 10, 12, 14, 16, 17, 18, 20, and 22.
- Give yourself one point for each "no" you marked for Items 1, 3, 5, 7, 9, 11, 13, 15, 19, and 21.
- Total your points.
- Your score can range from 0 to 22. The higher your score, the greater your graduate school potential.

The test should also make you aware of some of the issues that are often relevant to the successful completion of graduate school.

Source: Adapted from Fretz and Stang (1988).

Ultimately, What Do You Mean by *Success?*

What does success *mean to you?* A recurring theme throughout this book will be the importance of self-reflection, and coming to an understanding of what success means to you will certainly be facilitated by serious and thoughtful reflection. So would success to you mean that you earn a particular salary per year? Would it mean that you help X number of individuals or are well known by many people on Facebook? Is success for you defined by your highest academic degree earned or by how others feel about your accomplishments? None of these suggestions is either right or wrong, better or worse. You will need to internalize and define what success means to you. And to make the process more complicated, your conceptualization of what success means to you today may not be the same 10, 20, or 30 years from now. People reinvent themselves all the time through transitions, whether that means changing jobs and relocating across the country, going back to school to pursue a previously neglected passion, or deciding to simplify your life and purposely choosing to own less stuff and to spend less time using technology.

If you were to examine the dictionary definition of *success*, you would probably find something along the lines of "a favorable outcome after attempting an endeavor." So our successes can be large or small, based on daily events or lifetime choices. You might achieve success in some aspects of life and not in others. You might be successful at work on some days but not on others. Self-reflection will help you explore what success means to you over the long haul.

Examining academic success as it relates to the psychology major, Meeker, Fox, and Whitley (1994) found that the best predictors of college success in the psychology major (defined as one's GPA in psychology courses) were high school GPA and measures of verbal ability (such as the verbal portion of the SAT) and college student performance in general education/core curriculum classes. But your judgment of success might not be related at all to GPA. Lunneborg and Wilson (1985) asked the question a bit differently. They asked psychology alumni, "Would you major in psychology again?" First, Lunneborg and Wilson reported that 69% of their respondents answered "yes" to this key question. In examining the outcomes of their research with alumni and what advice they could offer current students, they concluded:

> Retrospectively, our majors can be told that they will probably consider the most valuable aspects of the major to be their increased self-understanding, knowledge of people, and analytic/thinking skills. But they should also be aware that satisfaction with the major as career preparation and as preparation for graduate school are more strongly related to having acquired skills for doing research. They may continue to complain about statistics and laboratories, but at the same time they will greatly value the variety of skills these courses teach. (p. 20)

The advice we offer here sounds familiar to a theme from 25 years ago. In many ways, this is a "pay me now or pay me later" situation—meaning that, as an undergraduate, you can challenge yourself and take the difficult classes and be active outside the classroom now and become adept at key skills (pay me now), or you can "cruise" through college ("Cs get degrees") but then struggle later and display dissatisfaction, end up going back to school for more education, or switch jobs and careers until something fits (pay me later). In either case, to achieve the level of success we suspect you desire, which will it be—pay me now or pay me later? We think you can guess how we feel about this, but, ultimately, the choice *is* yours.

Closing Comments

If you can remember only one idea from this entire chapter, let it be this: You need to participate in some serious self-exploration of your future goals and desires so you can map out, as clearly as possible, the route to your personal success. Numerous resources typically available to students include career centers, websites that will guide these explorations, psychological instruments that may provide insight into trends or patterns within your preferences, and so on. Once the path is mapped, you can begin to plan the stops along the way or, for undergraduate students, the opportunities you can avail yourself to—opportunities outside the classroom, such as those described in the next chapter. The ultimate destination might be a specific career goal or realizing that more education is needed to reach the desired career outcome. In any event, finding a path to success is enhanced once students spend some time in serious self-reflection, defining their personalized vision of success.

Getting Involved

Journal Starters

1. What were the most significant insights or ideas you gained from reading this chapter?

2. Your self-reflection will likely identify occupations you do NOT want to pursue or situations you do not want to be in (e.g., working in a cubicle for a large corporation in a big city). Write about these occupations and situations, aware that knowing what you do not want may help you clarify what you do want.

3. Consult the long list of occupations in Table 2.2 and check the 10 or so occupations that most appeal to you. As a group, what do they have in common with one another, and how do they relate to the Holland types?

4. In a quiet spot, close your eyes and think about your imagined ideal day—walk through the steps using your imagination. You get up—what time is it? You get ready for work—what are you wearing? You go to work—can you walk there, bike there, drive there, take public transportation there? At your job, when do you see another person first—right away or a little later? Who is this person—is it your boss or a coworker? You get to your desk—is it in a private space or more like a cubicle? Throughout this exercise, think about your preferences for day-to-day job activities.

Projects

1. Thinking ahead to the general part of the country you wish to live and work in after graduation, do some Internet searches on the business and commerce opportunities in the area. In other words, do a little career homework. Is it a major metropolitan area where there will be numerous work opportunities for you? What about work opportunities for a significant other, if that applies? Is it a more rural area where the career opportunities may be more specialized to the region? Sometimes we build unrealistic expectations about the glamour of living in a particular location or pursuing a certain career—think about the environment in which you'd like to live when you are not working.

2. Some people keep a diary of their daily events (or these days, a blog), whereas others may keep a dream diary. Consider starting your own "careers/jobs" diary. When you hear about someone who has a fascinating job, jot down some notes about that job for possible reference later. Spend some time thinking about what that perfect job would look like for you. Do you know someone who has your perfect job? If so, contact that person and see if you can interview him or her. If not, then think about whether you will be able to invent this job after graduation. Can you fulfill an unmet need for a company? How will you make that convincing pitch after graduation?

3. This project is really an exercise adapted by Carole Kanchier in *USA Weekend Magazine*, issue dated April 12–14, 2002. The quiz examines your attitudes toward growth in a career. Answer the following yes/no questions, and then use the scoring key below to ascertain your level of positive, growth-oriented attitudes. Are you surprised by the results?

Now add your scores together. Kanchier (2002) suggests that the higher your score, the more you possess positive, growth-oriented attitudes and believe in the "new view" of career. She suggests that if you scored less than 7, you may want to reevaluate your attitudes concerning a career. For more information on working on yourself, see daretochange.com.

4. Locate Light's (2010) article on dissatisfied psychology majors and the sample on which the findings were based. To what extent could his conclusions be accounted for by other variables?

		Career Quiz
Yes	**No**	**Items**
Y	N	1. I welcome criticism as a way to grow.
Y	N	2. I do what I "should" rather than what I want.
Y	N	3. I periodically assess my career and life goals.
Y	N	4. I prefer activities I know to those I've never tried.
Y	N	5. I enjoy challenge and a sense of achievement.
Y	N	6. I'm too old to compete with younger job applicants.

Y	N	7. I expect good things to happen.
Y	N	8. I won't consider relocating for an attractive job.
Y	N	9. I accept responsibility for my successes and failures.
Y	N	10. I'll take a job I don't like for money or prestige.
Y	N	11. My job gives my life meaning and direction.
Y	N	12. I look forward to retirement so I can do what I want.
Y	N	13. I make my own decisions, even swim against the tide.
Y	N	14. Career success means having social standing and money.
Y	N	15. I'll take a lower-level job.
Y	N	16. If I'm laid off, I'll take the first offer in the same field.

Scoring: Give yourself 1 point for each "YES" for the odd-numbered items.

Give yourself 1 point for each "NO" for the even-numbered items.

Additional Resources

URL	Brief Website Description
www.daretochange.com	Dare to Change
www.humanmetrics.com/vocation/ JCI.asp	Jung Career Indicator
www.careerexplorer.net/aptitude.asp	Career Explorer

References

Appleby, D. C., Millspaugh, B. S., & Hammersley, M. J. (2011). *An online resource to enable undergraduate psychology majors to identify and investigate 172 psychology and psychology-related careers.* Office of Teaching Resources in Psychology. Retrieved from http://teachpsych.org/otrp/resources/appleby11.pdf

Carson, A. D., & Dawis, R. V. (2000). Determining the appropriateness of career choice assessment. In D. A. Luzzo (Ed.), *Career counseling of college students: An empirical guide to strategies that work* (pp. 95–120). Washington, DC: American Psychological Association.

Fretz, B. R., & Stang, D. J. (1988). *Preparing for graduate study in psychology: Not for seniors only!* Washington, DC: American Psychological Association.

Holland, J. L. (1958). A personality inventory employing occupational titles. *Journal of Applied Psychology, 42,* 336–342.

Holland, J. L. (1959). A theory of vocational choice. *Journal of Counseling Psychology, 6,* 35–45.

Holland, J. L. (1973). *Making vocational choices: A theory of careers.* Englewood Cliffs, NJ: Prentice Hall.

Holland, J. L. (1994). *Self-Directed Search® (SDS®) Form R* (4th ed.) [Instrument]. Odessa, FL: Psychological Assessment Resources.

Kamenetz, A. (2010). *DIY U: Edupunks, edupreneurs, and the coming transformation of higher education.* White River Junction, VT: Chelsea Green.

Kanchier, C. (2002, April 12–14). Does your attitude limit your options? *USA Weekend Magazine,* p. 9.

Kuther, T. L. (2003). *The psychology major's handbook.* Belmont, CA: Wadsworth/Thomson Learning.

Landrum, R. E., & Elison-Bowers, P. (2009). The post-baccalaureate perceptions of psychology alumni. *College Student Journal, 43,* 676–681.

Landrum, R. E., Hettich, P. I., & Wilner, A. (2010). Alumni perceptions of workforce readiness. *Teaching of Psychology, 37,* 97–106.

Light, J. (2010, October 11). Psych majors aren't happy with options. *Wall Street Journal.* Retrieved from http://online.wsj.com/article/SB10001424052748704011904575538561813341020.html

Littlepage, G., Perry, S., & Hodge, H. (1990). Career experiences of bachelor's degree recipients: Comparison of psychology and other majors. *Journal of Employment Counseling, 27,* 50–59.

Lunneborg, P. W., & Wilson, V. M. (1985). Would you major in psychology again? *Teaching of Psychology, 12,* 17–20.

McKay, D. R. (2010, December 18). *Career decisions: Self assessment.* Retrieved from http://www.bamaol.cc/Article/Career/4852.html

Meeker, F., Fox, D., & Whitley, B. E., Jr. (1994). Predictors of academic success in the undergraduate psychology major. *Teaching of Psychology, 21,* 238–241.

Mulvey, T. A., Michalski, D. S., & Wicherski, M. (2010, May). *2010 graduate study in psychology snapshot: Applications, acceptances, enrollments, and degrees awarded to master's- and doctoral-level students in U.S. and Canadian graduate departments of psychology: 2008–2009.* Washington, DC: Center for Workforce Studies, American Psychological Association.

National Association of Colleges and Employers. (2010, July 8). Average starting salary to new college grads slips 1.3 percent. Retrieved from http://www.naceweb.org/Press/Releases/Average_Starting_Salary_to_New_College_Grads_Slips_1_3_Percent.aspx

Rajecki, D. W. (2007). *A job list of one's own: Creating customized career information for psychology majors.* Office of Teaching Resources in Psychology. Retrieved from http://teachpsych.org/otrp/resources/rajecki09.pdf

Rajecki, D. W. (2008). Job lists for entry-level psychology baccalaureates: Occupational recommendations that mismatch qualifications. *Teaching of Psychology, 35,* 33–37.

Rajecki, D. W., & Borden, V. M. H. (2009). First-year employment outcomes of US psychology graduates revisited: Need for a degree, salary, and relatedness to the major. *Psychology Learning and Teaching, 8,* 23–29.

Satterfield, C. (1998). *What to do with a bachelor's degree in psychology.* Retrieved from http://psychology.okstate.edu/undergrad/booklet/bachbook.html

Smith, T. W. (2007). *Job satisfaction in the United States.* Chicago, IL: National Opinion Research Center, University of Chicago.

Walfish, S., & Hess, A. K. (Eds.). (2001). *Succeeding in graduate school: The career guide for psychology students.* Mahwah, NJ: Erlbaum.

CHAPTER 3

Make the Most of Your Opportunities—Now!

They who are ready to go are already invited.

—Henry David Thoreau (1817–1862), philosopher, naturalist

Preparing for career and life is not simply a matter of completing coursework (thinking). As important as courses are, getting ready also includes your active participation in diverse opportunities that exist on your campus. The purpose of this chapter is to summarize options that enhance your workplace readiness. Neither individually nor collectively do these options guarantee a successful transition, but each can contribute to your overall preparation for life after college. We present these options as "DOs to Pursue." If you are at the freshman or sophomore level, you can probably implement most of them; juniors still have time, and seniors will have to scramble—but it's not too late.

"DOs to Pursue" for Workplace Readiness

Critically Examine Your Part-Time Job

Students often view their part-time jobs primarily as a source of money and tend to discount aspects of their workplace that are potentially instructive. After all, you don't plan on being an administrative assistant, resident hall assistant, gas station manager, wait staff, or sales assistant for the rest of your life. You want a job that is bigger, challenging, and better paying. In the meantime, however, do not ignore the prospects your current job holds for developing individual, interpersonal, and technical skills; learning about what you like and dislike about work; and understanding your organization's operations, structure, and culture—dimensions you will need to master in your next full-time position. In any job, you have responsibilities, are accountable to a supervisor, must manage your time, and master specific tasks. Do not underestimate the importance of the "hard" skills (i.e., specific tasks you perform), the problem-solving and "soft" skills (i.e., communications), and how your work may transfer to advanced or new positions.

Time Out: Exercise

As an example of skills you need, complete the short exercise below by rating your proficiency on each item. Think about the jobs you held and currently hold, and think also about the kinds of work you want to do after you graduate. Now, rate your level of proficiency (be realistic!) for each item below using this scale: (a) excellent, (b) good, (c) fair, (d) poor.

To what extent do I . . .

possess self-discipline, including punctuality and dependability? _____

act responsibly and conscientiously in my job? _____

work well with others? _____

meet the needs of others, such as customers or clients? _____

set priorities and allocate time efficiently to meet deadlines? _____

identify, prioritize, and solve problems in my job? _____

make defensible and appropriate decisions? _____

possess the ability to work independently and without supervision? _____

manage several tasks at once, effectively? _____

adapt to changing circumstances in my work environment? _____

function effectively in stressful situations? _____

Count the number of responses in each of the four response categories, and enter the numbers below.

Excellent _____ Good _____ Fair _____ Poor _____

In what characteristics do you excel? Where do you need to improve? Specifically, what can you do to strengthen these qualities?

In a survey of university alumni, these items (in rank order) led the list of workplace-readiness characteristics employers expect new graduates to possess *when they enter* the workplace (Landrum, Hettich, & Wilner, 2010). Regardless of your feelings toward your current job, you may work in a setting where all or most of these behaviors are important to your supervisor. To the extent your job permits, actively use it to close the gap between your current skill level and the level future employers expect you to demonstrate. In future interviews, speak positively about what you learned and contributed regarding your current work and describe specific skills you gained. Your current job is not simply about making money to pay bills.

Work Through Work Study

Employment through work-study programs is available on most campuses, although jobs vary in challenge and skill-building potential. If you qualify, carefully consider the positions available and the responsibilities involved; the quality of your interview and previous experience may be important factors that determine the position you receive. Peer-tutoring positions are an excellent opportunity to master a body of knowledge while developing skills teaching the material to individuals or groups. We know former students whose tutoring experiences and knowledge of statistics, research methods, and introductory psychology were important components in obtaining a job or being accepted into graduate school. Also, seek work-study positions such as admissions representative or administrative assistant that place you in contact with a client population where you can strengthen communication and interpersonal skills. One of our favorite work-study positions is residence hall assistant. Resident assistants are trained in a variety of skill sets, including communications, conflict management, stress and time management, planning, programming, decision making, and related abilities. Compare this skill set to those listed in the above exercise, and note the many similarities.

Some campus jobs originate from outside contractors. As a sophomore, Erin worked in the school cafeteria cleaning tables, stacking dirty dishes, and performing similar menial tasks. Humbling as it was, Erin performed her job conscientiously and with a positive attitude. Her attitude and work ethic paid off at the beginning of her junior year when she was offered higher-level responsibilities and a pay raise. By her senior year, she was serving as the assistant cafeteria manager, and upon graduation, the food service company offered her the manager position at an area college cafeteria. It is doubtful that Erin began clearing tables and stacking dishes with plans to make food service management her first full-time position. Some part-time jobs may lead to higher responsibilities and rewards in the same organization.

If your experience with jobs is limited or nonexistent, be sure to gain work experience before you graduate. According to *Job Outlook 2012,* published by the National Association of Colleges and Employers (NACE, 2012), 73.7% of the employers surveyed prefer to hire candidates with *relevant* work experience, and another 17.5% prefer candidates with any type of work experience. Only 4.1% of the respondents indicated that work experience is not a factor when hiring a college graduate (and the remaining 4.6% were "Other" responses). Because employer preferences are independent of the current state of the job market (NACE, 2010) we cannot attribute employer preferences only to a poor economy or a "buyer's market" (i.e., where job applicants far exceed market demand). In short, you must show your next employer you have job experience (and abilities), preferably in work that is relevant to your future employer's needs. We know, however, that gaining relevant experience is often difficult.

One option to consider is working a temporary job—or "temping." Applying for work at a temp agency typically does not involve an in-depth hiring process, nor does the agency expect your long-term commitment. Temping provides an opportunity to work for several organizations, each with its own culture, work dynamics, and tasks. The tasks might not challenge you, but you can test your interests, interact with diverse individuals, and possibly develop new skills; you might think about this opportunity as a variable-term "internship" if you wish. We recall the student who sought temp jobs not only to earn money but also to learn business procedures, software, and computer skills she would have had to pay for in her college courses. In today's highly competitive job market, however, even temp workers may need proficiency in diverse technology skills to get the better jobs. Why not contact an advisor in your college's business or technology programs about a business technology course that might improve your chances for finding a job?

What about the potential conflict between work and coursework? Although some students flirt with academic risk by working and attending school full-time, at the opposite extreme are those who carry a light course load, do little outside of class, and fail to manage their time effectively. In his 10-year study of Harvard students, Light (2001) concluded, "There is no significant relationship between paid work and grades. Students who work a lot, a little, or not at all show similar patterns of grades" (p. 27). Three fourths of the students in Light's study claimed that work had a positive effect on their overall satisfaction with college, and the more hours an individual worked per week (to a point), the higher his or her satisfaction with the job as an integral part of college. Our experiences confirm that many full-time students who work part-time, or part-time students with full-time jobs, succeed in both commitments and are relatively satisfied with the combination of school and work.

Take Advantage of Your Psychology Department's Opportunities

Research Assistant

In an article by Clay (1998), Eugene Zechmeister, the director of the undergraduate program at Loyola University Chicago at the time, said: "I know this will sound sacrilegious, but skills are actually more important than course content" (p. 34). We agree with this statement. Courses lay the foundation for information and knowledge about psychology and provide a special perspective on people, but that information and knowledge will do little good without the skills needed to apply them. Teaching and research focus on the heart of the matter—we expand our knowledge about psychology through research, and this research is what gives us the subject matter we teach. For the discipline of psychology to succeed and thrive, we need a balance between teaching and research.

A research assistantship is an opportunity for undergraduate students to assist faculty members in a program of research. When you serve as a research assistant (RA), you will be involved in *doing* the research rather than just reading about it in a textbook or journal article. Serving as an RA has multiple advantages: (a) acquisition of skills and knowledge not easily gained in the classroom; (b) opportunity to work one-on-one with a faculty member; (c) opportunity to contribute to the advancements of the science of psychology; (d) exposure to general research techniques helpful for pursuing later graduate work; (e) opportunity to practice written and oral communication skills by preparing for and attending professional conferences and preparing and submitting manuscripts for publication; and (f) cultivation of a mentoring relationship with a faculty member that will be helpful for acquiring letters of recommendation (Landrum & Davis, 2010).

In a national survey, Landrum and Nelsen (2002) systematically studied the benefits of serving as an RA from the faculty member perspective. Out of a 40-item survey, faculty members ranked these benefits as most important: (a) an opportunity to enhance critical thinking skills, (b) preparation for graduate school, (c) gains enthusiasm for the research process, (d) participates in the data collection process, and (e) improved writing ability.

Teaching Assistant

Serving as a teaching assistant (TA) is usually much less involved and time-consuming than being an RA. Usually, a TA helps a faculty member for one academic term in the administration of a specific course, such as Introduction to Psychology or Statistical Methods. You might have a number of different responsibilities as a TA, depending on the instructor, the course, the history of your institution in utilizing TAs, etc. The teaching assistantship is an excellent way to build a mentoring relationship with a faculty member. Also, serving as a TA is a low-risk activity. Thus, if you really don't "bond" with that faculty member, there is no harm done (and you earned credits toward graduation). But the benefits can be substantial. Almost certainly, during the course of the semester, a situation will occur where you can step in and provide some real assistance to a faculty member teaching a course. These are the types of events faculty members will be thankful for and may write about in a letter of recommendation. Also, many of our students tell us that sitting in on the general psychology course is a great study strategy when they prepare for the GRE advanced test in psychology.

You should know, however, that not all schools offer the opportunity for students to serve as undergraduate TAs. If being a TA is not possible at your school, you may have to be creative in finding this opportunity—perhaps seeking out an instructor who "wants help" in administering his or her course and is willing to give you independent study or internship credit. If the formal opportunity does not exist, there are creative ways of gaining the beneficial experience anyway! If you are faced with a choice of serving as an RA or TA, try to do both. You will be busy, but you will gain valuable skills, abilities, and knowledge for your future. Finally, if you cannot obtain tutoring experience through your psychology department, consider volunteering for a social service agency that provides tutoring services.

Enroll in Internships

Everyone talks about internships. In a survey of 301 employers, sponsored by the Association of American Colleges and Universities (2008), respondents were asked which methods of assessing student learning are most helpful in evaluating a job applicant's potential to succeed at his or her company. Heading the list was a "supervised/evaluated internship/community-based project where students apply college learning in a real-world setting"; 83% of the employers regarded this form of assessment as fairly or very effective. Other forms and their perceived effectiveness include an advanced comprehensive senior project, such as a thesis, demonstrating depth of knowledge in the major and problem-solving, writing, and analytical reasoning skills (79%); essay tests evaluating problem-solving, writing, and analytical reasoning skills (60%); electronic portfolios of student's work, including accomplishments in key skill areas and faculty assessments (56%); and multiple-choice tests of general content knowledge (32%). Recall the NACE (2012) report of employers' preference for candidates with relevant job experience (73.7% of employers surveyed). Of the employers who prefer work experience, 55% view internships and co-op experiences as the way for applicants to acquire that experience (NACE, 2012).

The Collegiate Employment Research Institute (CERI, 2011) supports the role of internships in gaining employment. With a substantial portion of the labor force preparing to retire and be replaced by skilled employees, traditional starting jobs for new graduates are disappearing and being replaced by positions requiring abilities that were once expected of employees 7 or more years into the workforce. According to one report, "evidence suggests that the internship now replaces the starting job as the place where college students actually begin their journey into the workplace" (CERI, 2011, p. 1). The report does not specify the particular academic majors, fields, or abilities to which the statement applies, but we believe you should consider this finding seriously. CERI advises students to develop a good understanding of who they are and the type of work they seek and to spend considerable time researching the options thoughtfully. In short, your internship becomes a high-stakes decision that will probably influence your first job after graduation and possibly your career path, so plan it carefully. As the manager of internship programs for Fortune 500 companies in the pharmaceutical and financial industries, Keil advised:

> Research, research, research! . . . There are many opportunities beyond the clinical for psychology majors. Determine what field interests you . . . and target certain companies with an excellent reputation in your area. Next, contact these organizations and ask to speak with the professional in charge of their internships and find out how to apply. (Quoted in Hettich, 2012a, p. 8)

Whether you plan to attend graduate or professional school immediately after graduation or after a few years in a job, undergraduate internships are strongly recommended for the numerous benefits they can provide. Internships are building opportunities. They *build* your résumé, your business sense, your contacts, and your industry knowledge (Pollak, 2007). Table 3.1 was compiled from resources presented in Landrum and Davis (2010).

Table 3.1   Potential Benefits From Completing an Internship

Practical, on-the-job experience

Development of professional and personal confidence, responsibility, and maturity

Understanding of the realities of the work world and acquirement of human relations skills

Opportunity to examine a career choice closely and make professional contacts

Opportunity to test the ideas learned in the classroom out in the field

Opportunity to make contacts with potential employers

Enhancement of classroom experiences

Learning what careers *not* to pursue

Development of skills that are difficult to learn and practice in the classroom

College credit in some but not all circumstances

Possible earnings to help offset college expenses

In addition, internships enable you to develop confidence, responsibility, and maturity; they let you establish skills you can't acquire in the classroom, while letting you apply classroom knowledge in a field setting; and they let you test a possible career (Landrum & Davis, 2010). For example, when Al was a senior, he obtained an internship through an area crisis center staffed by several volunteers trained to respond to callers experiencing high levels of stress. All volunteers first completed a structured 26-hour training program where they learned and practiced several communications and interpersonal skills in various crisis scenarios requiring listening skills, empathy, appropriate responses, and skilled decision making regarding follow-up steps. Al subsequently completed a master's degree in public health, served as a caseworker for a county agency for 3 years, and later worked for a communications consulting firm. Years after receiving his BA degree, Al believed the skill sets he acquired at the crisis center were the single most valuable asset in all the positions he held.

An internship may be the first real job for some students. As the oldest child of a blended family, Linda cared for her four younger siblings while her mother and stepfather worked. She never held a part-time job, but she was mature, possessed a strong work ethic, and maintained a B+ average as a senior in an interdisciplinary business/psychology major. When the human resources director (a college alumna) of a local electronics manufacturing company contacted the Psychology Department chair for a student intern in human resources, Linda applied for and was awarded the position. She quickly became excited about her work, and her supervisor complimented her progress highly. A few weeks before the semester ended, Linda was hired by the company as a human resources generalist and remained there for several years. Linda did not have prior work experience, but her maturity, strong work ethic, eagerness, and solid grades were important compensatory qualities that earned her an opportunity that evolved into a full-time job.

If your internship ultimately dissuades you from entering a particular field, it may still be a valuable experience. Is it not preferable to learn through a semester-long internship that you do not want a particular career than to enter the field or a graduate program and gain that costly insight much later? For example, Keisha admired her mother's deep commitment to school social work, so she obtained an internship in a middle school setting to test her interest. Although she enjoyed the experience immensely, she did not want to become a school social worker. Instead, she found a rewarding position after graduation in a human resources department and later earned an MBA degree through her employer. Learning what you do not want to do can be as valuable as learning what you do want to do.

Internships vary in several ways. They can be credit or noncredit based, paid (sometimes as a small stipend) or unpaid, inspiring or mind-numbing, offered only through a department, anchored only in a university-wide course, or offered directly by an organization. Internships have become a source of controversy during periods of high unemployment. Some employers are criticized for offering unpaid internships because they save the company money it would otherwise have to pay employees, and students are often accused of taking jobs away from the unemployed. In addition, the work students perform is often below the standard of an entry-level job. Students desperate for experience may allow themselves to be exploited in such situations and possibly not receive a true learning experience. Log on to the NACE website listed in the additional resources at the end of this chapter to learn more about unpaid internships and the NACE standards for internships.

But do internships lead to jobs? That depends on the nature of the job, the economic climate, and other factors. According to NACE's *2011 Internship & Co-op Survey*, employers reported that an average of 39% of their Class of 2010 entry-level hires came from their internship programs. In addition, the responding organizations indicated that, on average, they were able to convert about 58% of their own interns into full-time employees (NACE, 2011). These high rates of conversion from internships to jobs are likely the result of many factors (e.g., relation between the specific job and the student's academic major—likely to be higher in certain technical and business-related disciplines than in liberal arts), and you should not assume that an internship you complete will lead to a job.

Whatever the variables operating in organizations that offer internships, the bottom line is that you should get out of the classroom and see the real-world working conditions of your occupations of interest, as well as giving yourself opportunities to network with professionals in your potential field of interest. Finding the opportunities and utilizing the resources available to you are critical for your success, both for the job search process and for your transitional launch from college to career.

As a psychology major in a field that reaches deeply into so many aspects of society and behavior, you may be interested in mental health, research, marketing, human resources, science, technology, public service, law enforcement, animal welfare, or numerous other areas. Whatever your interests, discuss them with your advisor and a career counselor; visit the alumni and student affairs offices if necessary. Be persistent. Do not give up. If there are no opportunities available through your school, then contact organizations in which you are interested, in person or through the Internet. Search wisely. Plan and ask many questions, and don't forget to ask faculty members about advice for gaining an internship opportunity. If the internship is sponsored through your school, expect to complete an application process that requires an interview, résumé, letters of reference, a transcript, and a statement of your skills. Become familiar with your school's expectations of you and its expectations of the internship site. Inquire about the kinds of tasks you will perform, if known. Most internships involve some dull assignments (e.g., filing, photocopying, data input), but you should be able to perform some tasks equivalent to an entry-level job for a new college graduate. In return for your work, you should receive training in certain tasks or procedures, regular supervision, and feedback (it may be infrequent and general). If you work part-time, you may be forced to choose between the benefits of a paying, perhaps dead-end job and the long-term benefit of a nonpaying, career-related internship, if you cannot do both.

If entry-level jobs require substantial skills and a solid internship experience, as the CERI (2011) report indicated, you might not be able to achieve those goals in one experience, and chances are you will have made some mistakes along the way. So plan your academic schedule for a second, more challenging, and more career-related internship; view it as a second "real-world" component of your academic program that instructs your career decision process and informs an employer or graduate school about your serious desire for practical experience. Finally, prepare thoroughly, as though you are studying for a major exam (which an internship is analogous to), and consult sources such as "CERI Thought Piece: Internships as High Stakes Events" (CERI, 2011) and other CERI reports. Your first satisfying full-time job may depend on it.

Two Digressions

Job Shadowing

Keisha's internship with a school social worker was credit based. It involved biweekly meetings with her academic supervisor (including discussions of her experiences, assigned readings relating to school social work, and a student journal) and biweekly meetings with her site supervisor in addition to Keisha's weekly hours. She was not permitted to observe therapy sessions, but she worked with staff and children in diverse ways appropriate to her ability level and ethical constraints. In addition, she shadowed her supervisor, an experienced school social worker, when the occasion permitted.

As its name implies, job shadowing involves following a person throughout a workday (or several days, in Keisha's situation) to observe the various tasks the individual performs, including meetings, communications, and other interactions when permitted. Job shadowing can be an effective way of learning basic elements of a specific position performed by a professional in a particular setting; as in research, generalizing to other situations is always a constraint. If you do not know a person whose work you want to shadow, contact your career center or alumni office for suggestions. Pollak (2007) offers some advice about job shadowing.

1. Do your homework. Research the position in advance to gain information that will make the day productive for you and efficient for the person you shadow; dress appropriately and act professionally.

2. Be clear in advance about what you want to observe, such as meetings, technical work, research, client interactions, or other events.

3. Listen carefully and use your peripheral vision (i.e., pay close attention to everything around you, including the physical aspects of the environment and atmosphere of communication and interaction).

4. Be prepared with specific questions, and take notes.

5. Reciprocate if you can, such as offering to take the person to lunch.

6. Follow up with a thank-you note that expresses your sincere appreciation and highlights a few key insights you gained.

Job shadowing is not a job; it does not pay, and it may last only a day. But the experience may shed light on a potential career, and it is better to have seen a shadow of a career—even briefly—than nothing at all.

Informational Interviewing

According to Gabhauer (2011; as cited in Hettich, 2012b), informational interviewing is a highly focused discussion with an individual for the primary purpose of acquiring knowledge about a particular job or occupation, the education and skills required to perform it, the setting in which the work occurs, and the tasks involved. It is *not* a job interview. Begin by obtaining information about a possible occupation or career that interests you by searching resources such as Appleby, Millspaugh, and Hammersley's (2011) *An Online Resource to Enable Undergraduate Psychology Majors to Identify and Investigate 172 Psychology and Psychology Related Careers*. This resource, along with other helpful career-related exercises, can be accessed through the Office of Teaching Resources in Psychology (http://teachpsych.org/otrp/index .php?category=Advising). This website also provides access to *Occupational Outlook Handbook, O*NET,* the *Dictionary of Occupational Titles,* and additional career-related links.

Next, create contacts for the occupations you seek to explore. For example, if you are interested in performing marketing research (using your statistics, research methodology, and environmental science coursework) contact your psychology faculty, business faculty, family, friends, and neighbors who may know someone who works in marketing. Check with your school's career services and alumni office, and ask your librarian for assistance in identifying companies involved in environmental services and products. Persist until you identify a source whom you can contact in person, by phone, through e-mail, or via Skype.

The third step is to conduct the informational interview. Gabhauer (2001; as cited in Hettich, 2012b) recommends you request an interview via e-mail or a LinkedIn message, with a three-paragraph statement containing an explanation of how you obtained that person's name, a concise summary of your background, and a request for an informational interview about that person's job and occupation. If you receive no response within a few business days, follow up with a phone call. Ask for only 20 to 30 minutes of the person's time, as many business calendars are based on half-hour units, but be grateful if you are offered more time.

If you secure permission for the informational interview, rehearse your questions in advance, dress and act professionally, and use your time efficiently. Your questions could inquire about the skills needed for the job, what the person likes most and least about his or her work, activities that make up a typical day, how the field is growing, and other occupations or settings where you can find individuals who perform this work. Also ask about the availability of internships, coursework you should complete, and contacts the person may have. Most of all, listen. After the interview, follow up with a thank-you card, give yourself feedback about the strengths and weaknesses of your activities, and plan to conduct additional informational interviews.

Aggressively investigate potential occupations now, while you are in college, so you can graduate oriented toward and better prepared for entering a particular occupation or career with at least some idea of a career you wish to enter. It's not just a job you are seeking after college; it's a career that will help you construct meaning in your professional and personal life.

To conclude, internships, job shadowing, and informational interviewing are strategies for obtaining insights about particular occupations. Internships are far more time- and labor-intensive than a day or two of job shadowing or a half-hour interview about a particular job, so do not regard them as substitutes for each other. Try to complete each. If your internship stimulates interest in a particular occupation, follow up with a second internship, if possible, that provides more challenge and career focus, and supplement your curiosity for additional information by creating occasions for job shadowing and informational interviews.

Time Out: Exercise

Identify two occupations that interest you. For each occupation, create a specific plan or list of steps you would most likely pursue to shadow a person in that occupation and to conduct an informational interview. What is stopping you from implementing those steps?

Volunteer: Learn From Giving and Receiving

The CERI (2011) report on internships as high-stakes events suggests that students can prepare for an internship and learn more about themselves by participating in a wide range of co-curricular activities, such as student organizations, community service, undergraduate research, study abroad, and similar pursuits. If you cannot obtain a quality internship—and some employers know they are scarce—then search for ongoing volunteer opportunities that provide skill building even in tasks that may not interest you. If you performed volunteer work in high school or for your church or community, you know it is easy to find (especially with underfunded not-for-profit agencies) and does not require a depth or range of skills; dependability and commitment are usually the key requirements. Yet volunteer work is an opportunity to develop empathy and demonstrate social and civic responsibility.

As a psychology major, you are exposed to a broad range of human conditions in diverse settings, but primarily from an academic perspective. Volunteering is an excellent occasion to apply textbook concepts to real-world settings while learning about yourself and helping others. Chances are your school provides service-learning courses or volunteer options through campus clubs and university department offices. Whether working for a homeless shelter, an international cause, with developmentally disabled children, in a political campaign, cutting brush in a local forest preserve, or promoting sustainable resources, such activities enable you to grow, give back to a community, spend time away from a sometimes deadening academic routine, discover your interests, build leadership skills, strengthen your résumé, make contacts (networking), or simply gain experience.

One of the authors attended a business networking event during the recent recession and asked a successful investment executive (a psychology minor in college) what students should do to improve workplace readiness. He advises students to become active, get involved in volunteer work, and show that they are on the go and *doing* things. Being active, not just the particular tasks performed, is what was important to him. As many companies are committed to volunteer work in their communities, do not underestimate the value your participation may have on your résumé. The NACE *Job Outlook 2012* reports that when employers have two equally qualified candidates, they consider other attributes, including (in rank order of ratings) academic major (for particular skill sets), extracurricular activities, a GPA of 3.0 or higher, volunteer work, and the school attended (NACE, 2012).

Seek volunteer work you really want to do, that you can perform on a regular basis over time (to establish a record of commitment and reliability), and where your continued involvement might lead to higher levels of responsibility. Do not be afraid to try something you are unsure about. For example, out of curiosity, Joseph attended a session at which a student, a formerly homeless woman, spoke of her experiences living in her car with two small children. Through an "angel" (a university trustee), the student was able to earn enough from a part-time job to provide the basics for her children, attend college, and volunteer at a homeless shelter. Joseph was ambivalent about working with homeless persons but was strongly affected by the woman's story and decided to volunteer. He learned about the economics of poverty and family dynamics that lead to homelessness (especially the notion that most people are only a few paychecks from a homeless shelter), worked different positions and schedules in the shelter, became familiar with its operations, and was "promoted" to assistant manager before graduation. During the college's senior convocation, Joseph spoke eloquently of his experiences and the insights he gained. Although his subsequent graduate degree in clinical psychology did not often bring him in contact with homeless people, he regards his work in the shelter as one of the most important parts of his education.

To conclude, view your volunteer work as an important strategy for improving workplace readiness for the experiences it provides, for the skills and insights to be gained, for the personal development it affords, and as a productive and rewarding way to become involved with your world.

Enroll in Workplace-Related Courses

If you truly enjoy your psychology major, you are probably tempted to take several elective courses beyond departmental requirements. But how many should you take? Arguably, any psychology course could fit well with certain bachelor's degree jobs. Psychology is about "helping people," but there are numerous and creative ways you can apply your degree. We support taking psychology courses beyond the requirements of your major. Organizational behavior, interpersonal communication/group dynamics, technical communication, social psychology, personality, and abnormal psychology are worthy options, as are others. Yet every additional psychology course you complete is a course you are not taking in another discipline. Even if graduate or professional school is in your future, admissions committees want to see breadth, not just depth, in their applicants. Consider a minor in any of the other liberal arts areas (especially in those that focus on critical thinking and writing) or in applied fields such as human resources, health sciences, or technology. Also consider a double major so you can enter the labor force with flexibility and depth in two academic areas, such as psychology and an applied field or psychology and another liberal arts major.

For example, one individual double-majored in English and psychology and subsequently entered a master's degree program in general psychology, with a concentration in neuropsychology. By the end of the program, she realized she did not want to continue in neuropsychology. After careful reflection on her interests and skills, she sought and obtained a position in a textbook-publishing company, where she was able to use her writing skills. After only 3 years, she reached the position of associate marketing manager in charge of the company's psychology and sociology texts, and she writes an introductory psychology e-newsletter for teachers (Hettich, 2011a).

There are many combinations of undergraduate majors as well as opportunities to apply a graduate degree. If you do not find the courses or program you want in your school catalog, check the offerings of area schools, such as community colleges, or discover if your school accepts online courses from other institutions.

The top skills employers seek are directly or indirectly related to the content or teaching methods used in your courses. They include (in order of importance, identified by between 80% and 51% of the employers) ability to work in a team, leadership, written communication skills, problem-solving skills, strong work ethic, analytical/quantitative skills, verbal communication skills, initiative, technical skills, detail-oriented, flexibility/adaptability, computer skills, interpersonal skills (relates well to others), and organizational ability (NACE, 2012). Notice how many skills are anchored in communications: team, written, verbal, and interpersonal. Yet employers complain that graduates enter the workplace deficient in such skills. Thus, students should complete additional courses in writing, perhaps technical or business writing (to communicate succinctly) and public speaking (to be organized and confident in front of clients or groups). A course in small-group communication can be very helpful for understanding the dynamics of interpersonal communication, a requirement for almost every job. Given the structure of most college courses, however, do not expect a perfect match between classroom assignments and "real-world" applications; still, these courses can be very valuable for mastering and applying underlying concepts.

Although the younger generation is often criticized for its attitudes and habits, new graduates are respected for their expertise and ease with communications technology. If you like technology, pursue your school's offerings and seek creative ways you can connect technology to psychology and work. Whether you graduate with a baccalaureate or master's degree, chances are good that you will work in a not-for-profit or corporate setting. Do you want to enter a business environment ignorant of basic business concepts such as economics, management, business ethics, and marketing? Consider a minor in business/commerce if you seek a career in a business setting. Such courses may not be required for your job, but basic knowledge of business concepts and operations reveals your genuine interest and perhaps gives you an edge over liberal arts graduates who lack such courses.

To summarize, you can boost your workplace readiness with your psychology major by choosing courses, academic minors, or a second major and by taking coursework that enhances the level of generic professional skills employers seek.

Time Out: Reflective Question

If your college suddenly required each student to have a double major, what would you choose? Explain how you would connect your double major to a particular career.

Join Extracurricular Activities

Extracurricular activities are no longer viewed primarily as a source of fun for students with time on their hands. These activities have always been a source of skill development, but employers are now weighting them in job applications. The NACE *Job Outlook 2012* reported that participation in extracurricular and volunteer activities is a factor employers consider when applicants are equally qualified; empirical evidence supports this claim. Rubin, Bommer, and Baldwin (2002) studied the extent to which students who were members of various campus organizations exhibited superior interpersonal skills compared with students who were nonmembers. The participants were 600 traditional-age, full-time advanced undergraduate business students (mostly majors). The measures collected included the number and type of extracurricular activities students reported and ratings on four dimensions of interpersonal skills (oral communication, decision making, teamwork, and initiative). The results revealed that members of clubs/organizations and fraternities/sororities (but not sports teams) demonstrated better interpersonal skills than did nonmembers. When measures on predictor variables such as intelligence, GPA, and affect were also included, a student's overall extracurricular activity was positively associated with each of the four dimensions of interpersonal skills. The authors believe their findings provide empirical evidence that recruiters ought to consider extracurricular activities as a useful component of hiring decisions. By the way, intramural and varsity sports can be very worthwhile extracurricular activities, but Rubin et al.'s study failed to show significant differences on the measures they used.

Extracurricular involvement can also influence your satisfaction with the psychology major. Strapp and Farr (2010) studied the relation between involvement in psychology-related activities, satisfaction, and academic achievement of 71 senior psychology majors. Potential involvement included two internships, experience as a TA or RA, and membership in two psychology clubs and Psi Chi. Satisfaction was measured by student ratings of nine aspects of the major, including course variety and availability, quality of instruction and advising, faculty accessibility and interactions, job market and overall preparation, and overall satisfaction. Achievement was operationally defined as the self-reported GPA. Results indicated that the more students were involved in departmental activities, the more satisfied they were with their psychology major. Different types of involvement were differentially related to levels of satisfaction. As a side note, satisfaction was not related to GPA, and students were least satisfied with their preparation for the job market.

In summary, Rubin et al. (2002) provided evidence that extracurricular involvement is positively associated with interpersonal skills such as oral communication, decision making, teamwork, and initiative; Strapp and Farr (2010) showed that involvement in psychology department activities can promote satisfaction with the major. Other good reasons for you to get involved with campus activities are to establish social relationships and support networks, to develop new interests and gain knowledge about them, and to develop leadership skills.

Leadership skills are prized by most organizations (NACE, 2012). You might not use leadership skills during your first couple of jobs, but leadership experience is important as you progress in your career. Consequently, when you join a campus organization, try to become involved by your sophomore or junior year, with a firm goal to serve in a leadership position during the next year. Consider becoming actively involved in at least two organizations, including your psychology club, Psi Chi, or Psi Beta chapter. Before you commit yourself to a specific activity, however, first attend a couple of meetings and try to ascertain what the organization accomplished during the previous year and its current plans, the quality of member interaction (especially with club officers), the extent members have input into decisions, and the organization's reputation on campus. Do not expect clear answers to these issues or for the group to function perfectly. The challenge of membership and leadership in a college organization is to deal with ambiguity constructively, achieve goals, and learn from mistakes. Some of the skills you can acquire as a member and subsequently use as leader include working cooperatively to achieve common goals; planning and conducting meetings; coordinating events; working with the organization's advisor, college staff, and vendors; interacting with individuals of diverse cultural, social, and academic backgrounds; performing public relations; and working under pressure while carrying a course load, holding a job (probably), and managing your personal life. In fact, the leader of a medium to large campus organization functions in some ways similar to a corporate midlevel manager (Hettich, 1998). Along the way, expect to make mistakes (they are less painful to correct as a student than as an employee) and to be criticized. But if you learn from your experiences, you will gain skills and insights that transfer to career and life situations.

Seek Career and/or Counseling Services

One of the most valuable resources on your campus is its counseling services, which may be located in one or more areas of the campus. Career planning and development is one of its major services, but too many students contact the career center only during the last academic term to learn interviewing, résumé writing, and job search skills. That misperception often produces frustration and discouragement when new grads subsequently find themselves weeks or months later in jobs they do not like, with no plans for the future and college loan payments due monthly. A wise strategy is to begin investigating career counseling services during your sophomore year and well before you are required to declare your major formally.

Career services will vary from school to school, depending on size, staffing, and your institution's approach to this service. In some colleges and universities, you may be offered just basic information such as group sessions and websites and then left alone to research your interests; other schools may offer more personalized and extensive services. Either way, you must be proactive in exploring your interests and career options. It's *your* life. College is your best opportunity for this critical part of your education, and your tuition has paid for the services. Chapter 4 ("What Is the Secret of Excellent Career Planning?") will help guide you along the way.

"There has been a growing concern in recent years about the large numbers of students coming to college counseling centers with serious psychological problems" (Gallagher, 2010, p. 1). This conclusion is based on data contained in *Highlights of the National Survey of Counseling Center Directors 2010,* and the concern is reported as a continuing problem by 90% of the counseling center directors surveyed. Whether the circumstance is depression, anxiety, panic attacks, suicidal ideation, alcohol or substance abuse, relationship issues, or sex and sexuality, many of these conditions can be successfully treated while you are in college.

If you experience any personal problems that interfere with the effective performance of your daily activities, please remember these points. First, you are not alone; many of your fellow students are in similar situations that must be recognized and treated. Second, you can receive treatment through your school's counseling center to control and even eliminate these conditions. Third, you *must* learn during college to develop strategies for coping with personal issues *now*, before you graduate. Whatever job, career, or graduate program you pursue, you will begin a new chapter in your life as a workplace freshman and will face a critical transition filled with uncertainties; challenges to your current attitudes, habits, skills, and expectations; new and sometimes overwhelming stresses; and far fewer supportive resources than currently available on your campus. Not only will your resources be fewer and less accessible (after work and on weekends), you will have to pay dearly for them ($75–$150 per hour, depending on where you live and the resources you use). Currently, your tuition covers the cost of professional counseling services.

Most important, *if you need help, seek help now.* Leibow (2010) contended that feeling shame is a major impediment to seeking help; shame leads to avoidance and the person's exaggeration of the problem.

> Everyone confronts psychological problems sometime during his life. Nobody is exempt. The only reason you feel ashamed about having psychological problems is because you imagine—wrongly—that no one else is having problems or, more likely, because you imagine—again wrongly—that no one else *like you* is having problems. People like you—strong, smart, successful people—don't have problems. Only weak, limited, inept people do. Wrong! Having psychological problems doesn't mean you're abnormal; it means you're normal. It might even mean you're *better* than normal. It might mean you're more sensitive, more self-aware, and harder on yourself than your friends who seem to be sailing smoothly through. (pp. 159–160)

If you need encouragement to contact the counseling center, talk with someone you trust, such as your advisor, a respected teacher, a family member, someone in a campus ministry, or a close friend. On more than one occasion, we as teachers or advisors have gladly served as the link between a troubled student and the first counseling session. Typically, the offices that provide personal counseling are off the beaten path on a college campus, and the individuals who staff them are trained to respect your privacy in all aspects of the counseling process. Be patient with the process, however. Many counseling centers are understaffed and insufficiently funded, so you may have to wait a few days (or longer) to meet with a counselor or have a second appointment. But the counselors are there to help you, and they will if you work with them. Some counseling centers sponsor workshops that focus on relationship issues, stress and time management, and similar topics of value to the mental health of all students.

Know How Your Psychology Major Contributes to Workplace Preparation

As you get to know your advisor, teachers, and department staff, try to become involved with psychology by participating in the kinds of activities Strapp and Farr (2010) described in their study. Your psychology major also works in ways that may not be apparent. Underlying the diverse course offerings of your department are principles that guide the curriculum and teaching decisions of your faculty. One set of principles is a series of performance benchmarks designed to help undergraduate psychology programs define their mission and goals and assess their effectiveness. One of the domains of the performance benchmarks is the assessment of five categories of student learning goals or outcomes: writing skills, speaking skills, research skills, collaborative skills, and information literacy and technology skills (Dunn,

McCarthy, Baker, Halonen, & Hill, 2007). Psychology departments differ in the extent to which these outcomes are embedded in your requirements and coursework. Each skill set, however, is valued to varying degrees by employers; Chapter 6 addresses this topic further. For now, it is important to know that assignments that require papers, oral presentations, group work, research, and information technology skills are important contributors to workplace readiness, because these are skills employers expect new hires to possess at high levels and to apply successfully.

You may never use the concepts, theories, or research that forms a particular course, but those assignments that reflect the five learning outcomes will be useful, whether or not your teachers explain their purpose in class or on the syllabus. Perhaps equally important is to establish a positive relationship with a teacher or advisor who can serve as a mentor as you progress toward those important decision points.

Study Abroad

Over the years, we have heard several students insist their academic term abroad was one of the most valuable experiences in their college education. An intense form of experiential learning by doing, study abroad enables you to interact with people from different cultures, operate independently yet often as part of a group, solve problems in ambiguous situations (e.g., navigating transportation systems and purchasing items used daily), develop new skills, and adapt to changing circumstances. We encourage you to contact your school's study-abroad office to learn more. Do not be quick to discount this experience because of costs. When you subtract the costs of an academic term on campus from the estimated cost of a term abroad, the difference could approach true costs.

One challenge you face, however, is to demonstrate subsequently to recruiters that your study abroad was not mere "academic tourism" but a skill-building experience. From a decade of research, Gardner (2008) identified four factors common to study-abroad experiences that are valued by at least 45% of the employer sample ($N = 450$) surveyed: interacting with people who hold different interests, values, or perspectives; understanding cultural differences in the workplace; adapting to situations of change; and gaining new knowledge from experiences. At least 30% of the employers valued the ability to work independently, undertake tasks that are unfamiliar or risky, apply information in new or broader contexts, identify new problems or solutions to problems, and work effectively with coworkers. In short, many employers will acknowledge that your study-abroad experience *can* influence the development of these nine skills, but you must clearly present the evidence. The extent to which your experiences help develop these skills depends on the quality of your efforts, how your program was designed and implemented, and your ability to translate your experiences into marketable skills. Consult Gardner for details about a process for evaluating study-abroad experiences.

Finally, recognize that America is part of an intricately connected global economy where many employers seek applicants with knowledge, cultural diversity, cultural competency or "cultural agility," and sensitivity that can be gained through study-abroad experiences.

Use All Your Campus Resources

In addition to the counseling services your school provides, other offices on campus can serve as resources for furthering your workplace readiness. At some institutions, the student affairs/student services departments sponsor workshops on topics such as group skills, interpersonal communications, conflict management, team building, time and stress management, business etiquette, money management, and similar generic workplace survival skills. When you check on the availability of these offerings, also ask about peer tutoring, residence hall assistant positions, immersion trips, and other experiential learning opportunities and events.

For example, Beth participated in various extracurricular activities and worked part-time her last 2 years of college. During her senior year, she served as president of the Student Governing Board and as a resident assistant in a women's residence hall. After graduation, she held a variety of jobs, eventually earned a PsyD, and headed a substance abuse certification program in a community college. When asked which of her undergraduate activities were most important for developing the problem-solving and interpersonal skills she needed in her subsequent positions, Beth quickly identified the experiences she acquired as a resident assistant and as Student Governing Board president. If you consider the many and diverse situations and responsibilities that characterize these two positions, it's easy to recognize how valuable they are for developing such skills (Hettich, 2011b).

Stop by your alumni affairs office and ask about an alumni/student mentoring program, networking, job shadowing, internships, and other options for meeting with alumni. The admissions office may be seeking students to volunteer for campus recruiting events. Also check the intramural and varsity athletic offices for possible occasions to work at sports events. As your college work-study office probably has connections with these and other departments, contact the staff about jobs available in these offices.

We may have missed some departments, but our point is to encourage you to search aggressively for ways to get involved in the life of your school. You may begin by volunteering for an event; you could continue with an offer of part-time work. Either way, identify how the activity is a chance to develop your interests and skills while simultaneously contributing to the overall life of your school.

Consider Military Options

One overlooked but powerful option for improving workplace readiness is service in the U.S. military. Army, Navy, and Air Force ROTC (Reserve Officer Training Corp) units have maintained a presence on college campuses for decades and continue to provide a large number of the U.S. military officer corps. Reserve and National Guard units are also options for skill and leadership development while earning benefits to reduce college costs. The following websites will lead you to specific information about the various branches of the military: www.usairforce.com, www.usarmy.com, www.uscg.mil/, www.marines.com, www.navy.mil/, www.nationalguard.com, and www.military.net.

We also encourage you to locate veterans or a veterans' club on your campus and seek the opinions of several men and women who served in the Armed Forces. Before you apply to the military, carefully weigh the benefits against the obligations. The opportunities to learn and serve our country in the military and the benefits it offers are powerful incentives. If at some point, however, you are required to withdraw from classes and are deployed to a war zone, you cannot decline your obligations; when you join, you sign a binding contract.

Closing Comments

We strongly believe that coursework must be supplemented by your active involvement in other instructive activities that prepare you to accept the invitation to a satisfying and productive role in the workforce. We identified numerous opportunities ("DOs to Pursue") that can strengthen your workplace readiness, and we provided empirical evidence along the way to support our recommendations. Now the ball is in your court: To what extent will you take advantage of these opportunities? What is your plan for translating this DO list into action?

Do not assume that high grades, good looks, a smashing personality, and the ability to function when you absolutely must will land you a good job, because there are countless recent and not-so-recent college grads with the same characteristics competing for the same jobs. You need a *record* of action and involvement, a history, a real résumé—something to show for yourself from the 4 to 6 years you may have spent in college.

Some career counselors recommend you create a personal "brand" for yourself. Just as you think of computers when you hear "Dell," smartphones when you see an ad for "Apple," and pizza when you hear "Domino's," you should be able to articulate an identifiable set of personal characteristics (e.g., problem solver, team player, determined, leader) to promote your brand. You build your brand from the totality of your experiences in college. What do you plan on doing during the remaining academic terms that will build your brand?

Getting Involved

Journal Starters

1. What were the most significant insights you acquired from reading this chapter?

2. Think back to your volunteer and extracurricular activities, current and past. What particular experiences, values, skills, or insights have you gained from them? Can these experiences be used to support your future goals?

3. The "DOs to Pursue" require that you commit yourself to being *actively involved*. What are the dimensions and motives in your personal life that can energize you to become involved? What are the internal and external factors that discourage you from further involvement?

Projects

1. Because this chapter is really a series of recommendations for improving workplace readiness, our remaining suggestion is that you translate this information into *action*. First, carefully reflect on each topic in terms of your interest, its potential long-range benefits, and feasibility of implementing it as a course of action. Second, rank each topic (1 = Do first, 2 = Do next, etc.) according to these criteria (the degree of your interest, benefits, feasibility), and note the resources (e.g., person, office) you would contact for information. Third, what do you specifically plan to do with this information to promote your workplace readiness? Make a list of specific steps you can take, and create a timeline for when you can begin them.

2. Nearly all the topics covered provided some empirical evidence to support their credibility. Choose a topic that interests you, and search for additional studies or reports to support or question the findings presented.

3. Compare your experiences in any two of these topics (e.g., part-time job, extracurricular activities) with those of your fellow students and the material presented. What can you add to what has been said? What are your concerns?

4. What additional activities could you add to our "DOs to Pursue" list? Explain why they would enhance workplace preparedness.

Additional Resources

URL	Brief Website Description
www.internmatch.com	Connects you to paid internships
www.naceweb.org/about/ membership/internship/	NACE internship standards for unpaid internships

- Vander Ven, T. (2011). *Getting wasted: Why college students drink too much and party so hard.* New York: New York University Press.

References

Appleby, D. C., Millspaugh, D. S., & Hammersley, M. J. (2011). *An online resource to enable undergraduate psychology majors to identify and investigate 172 psychology and psychology related careers.* Office of Teaching Resources in Psychology. Retrieved from http://teachpsych.org/otrp/resources/appleby11.pdf

Association of American Colleges and Universities. (2008). *How should colleges assess and improve student learning? Employers' views on the accountability challenge.* Retrieved from http://www.aacu.org/leap/documents/2008_Business_Leader_Poll.pdf

Clay, R. A. (1998, September). Is a psychology diploma worth the price of tuition? *APA Monitor*, p. 33.

Collegiate Employment Research Institute. (2011). *CERI thought piece: Internships as high stakes events.* Retrieved from www.ceri.msu.edu/wp-content/uploads/2010/01/High-Stakes-Internships.pdf

Dunn, D. S., McCarthy, M. A., Baker, S., Halonen, J. S., & Hill, G. W., IV (2007). Quality benchmarks in undergraduate psychology programs. *American Psychologist, 62*(7), 650–670.

Gabhauer, M. (2011). *Mastering the art of informational interviewing.* Retrieved from www.prezi.com/explore/search/?search=Mastering+the+art+of+informational+interviewing

Gallagher, R. G. (2010). *Highlights of the national survey of counseling center directors 2010.* Pittsburgh, PA: University of Pittsburgh.

Gardner, P. (2008). *Unpacking your study abroad experience: Critical reflection for workplace competencies* (CERI Research Brief 1-2008). East Lansing, MI: Collegiate Employment Research Institute. Retrieved from http://www.ceri.msu.edu./publications/pdf/brief1-2008final.pdf

Hettich, P. (1998). *Learning skills for college and career* (2nd ed.). Pacific Grove, CA: Brooks/Cole.

Hettich, P. (2011a). Connecting graduate degrees to the workplace. *Eye on Psi Chi. 15*(1), 10–11.

Hettich, P. (2011b). What would you say? What would you do? *Eye on Psi Chi, 15*(2), 10–11.

Hettich, P. (2012a). Internships! *Eye on Psi Chi, 16*(2), 8–9.

Hettich, P. (2012b). A three-step guide to exploring occupations with your baccalaureate degree. *Eye on Psi Chi, 16*(3).

Landrum, R. E., & Davis, S. F. (2010). *The psychology major: Career options and strategies for success* (4th ed.). Upper Saddle River, NJ: Pearson Education.

Landrum, R. E., Hettich, P. I., & Wilner, A. (2010). Alumni perceptions of workforce readiness. *Teaching of Psychology, 37*, 97–106.

Landrum, R. E., & Nelsen, L. R. (2002). The undergraduate research assistantship: An analysis of the benefits. *Teaching of Psychology, 29*, 15–19.

Leibow, D. M. (2010). *What to do when college is not the best time of your life.* New York, NY: Columbia University Press.

Light, R. J. (2001). *Making the most of college: Students speak their mind.* Cambridge, MA: Harvard University Press.

National Association of Colleges and Employers. (2010). *Job outlook 2010.* Bethlehem, PA: Author.

National Association of Colleges and Employers. (2011). Employers turned more than half of interns into full-time hires. Retrieved from http://naceweb.org/s04272011/intern_conversion/

National Association of Colleges and Employers. (2012). *Job outlook 2012.* Bethlehem, PA: Author.

Pollak, L. (2007). *Getting from college to career: 90 things to do before you join the real world.* New York, NY: HarperCollins.

Rubin, R. S., Bommer, W. H., & Baldwin, T. T. (2002). Using extracurricular activity as an indicator of interpersonal skill: Prudent evaluation or recruiting malpractice? *Human Resource Management, 41*, 441–454.

Strapp, C. M., & Farr, R. J. (2010). To get involved or not: The relation among extracurricular involvement, satisfaction, and academic achievement. *Teaching of Psychology, 37*, 50–54.

PART II

Know Thyself—Better!

What Is the Secret of Excellent Career Planning?

by Camille Helkowski, MEd, NCC, LCPC

Tell me, what is it you plan to do with your one wild and precious life?

—Mary Oliver (1992), poet

During my own undergraduate career as a social science major with concentrations in sociology and psychology, I certainly did not have an answer to Mary Oliver's big question. As a counselor in private practice and as the associate director of Loyola University Chicago's Career Development Center, I have come to understand that many individuals find their way to one of my offices because they don't have an answer either. In fact, one of the best-kept secrets about choosing your life's work is that concrete plans are most useful as a project management tool. For instance, if you are determining your goals for the week, or breaking a large project into manageable tasks, then specific plans are the path to your success. Planning is also the key to a lifetime where there is "nothing left undone." So writing a "bucket list" and deciding how you will begin to accomplish the things you most want to do in life is critical to making these dreams your reality.

On the other hand, holding on too tightly to specific, midrange plans (more than a semester, less than a decade) often impedes your curiosity, creativity, and receptivity to serendipitous possibilities. It is important to learn everything you can about yourself and the world as it is and might be—knowing all the while that the future will always be filled with the unforeseeable. In this light, it is helpful to review what you can know and what you cannot—in order to be prepared for the notion that a fulfilling career is the sum of countless small decisions made over the course of a lifetime.

What You Can Know

Who and What Has Influenced Your Career Beliefs?

People are often unaware of the individuals, events, and interactions that have shaped their self-concept and their beliefs about vocational possibilities. For instance, career choice can be driven by peers, teachers, extended family members, cultural icons, world events, the economy, technology, religion, gender, socioeconomic status, access to role models and information, geography, or the media. This is certainly not an exhaustive list; any or all of these factors may have had a role in the construction of your career belief system. It is critical to consider the ways these factors shape your thoughts about careers and the point in your life when you began to act on these ideas. Most of us would not want to be held to the dating or clothing decisions we made when we were in junior high; yet many students made their career decisions that early. These choices can be based largely on others' opinions-disguised-as-facts and rarely are backed by specific information about the world of work or about you. They can also be made in response to world events, market trends, or even the big new show on TV—all things that will change by the time you enter the workforce.

Of course, the strongest and perhaps most unacknowledged influence on career choice is your family. Although many things affect development of self-concept, perhaps none has the impact your immediate family does. Jacobsen (1999) suggested that families pass on their unfulfilled hopes and dreams to the next generation. The dreams may take the form of duty—a family member's unmet emotional need disguised as a moral imperative for you. Did you grow up hearing stories of your father, who was unable to finish med school and has saved since the day you were born so you could be a doctor? Your career path may be your destiny, in that fate or divine providence determines what the people in your family do. For example, when talking about jobs, you may have been told that three generations of women in the family have been teachers, so of course you will teach. Or genetics might be the tipping point for your occupational choice, in that you are a born salesman just like your uncle.

Often, others' dreams are communicated indirectly—the difference between what is said and what is implied. For instance, it is not at all unusual for parents to say that they want you to do whatever will make you happy. Although they are telling the truth, they typically have some specific ideas as to what constitutes happiness. While their ideas about work that will "make you happy" may be the same as yours, they will just as likely differ.

The Making of a Career Genogram

One way of identifying the impact of your family's dreams on your own career vision is to create your family genogram—a family tree of sorts that represents the career facts of at least three generations of your family (Malott & Magnuson, 2004). (See Figure 4.1 for a sample genogram and the "Projects" section of this chapter for directions on how to complete your own.) When your genogram is complete, you can begin to look for occupational patterns by asking a number of questions. For instance:

- What types of occupations are considered valuable in your family? Which are not?
- What are your family's beliefs about money and its importance to career choice?
- Did gender, race, class, illness, accident, or poverty have an impact on career choice for members of your family? Does it still?
- What are your family's standards for success? Who are considered the successful family members?
- What are your family's attitudes about leisure and retirement?
- Whom are you most like, according to your family? Why do they think so? Do you agree with these opinions?
- Whom do you most admire? Why? How could you be more like this individual?
- What other patterns do you notice?
- How have your family's career patterns affected your own career beliefs?
- What would you change if you could? Could you make the change for yourself, if not for your whole family?

Your genogram can provide you with a rather clear picture of whose career dreams you are carrying and why they have been handed down to you. It is critical that you decide whether you want to carry this legacy forward or not. As Jacobsen (1999) noted,

> If there is a constant in life, it is the evolution of dreams, handed down from one generation to the next. If you crack through the surface of every family's hand-me-down dreams, you will find a single, unifying dream at their core—the dream of a happy life. The art of finding it, however, is to remember that while the dream of happiness is passed on through families, *experience of happiness is sublimely individual.* You must build your own. This may seem frightening or impossible, but if you persevere, it will become necessary and inevitable. It won't be a dream anymore, it's the way **you** are. (p. 195; emphasis in original)

Knowing the Real You

So, who are you? It seems a simple enough question, yet most people have a tough time offering more than a cursory answer or some trite platitude that will satisfy the person asking and hopefully allow for a change of topic. With all the clamor about who you *should be* and what you *should want,* acknowledging and accepting who you are, embracing both your potentials and your limits, and choosing to live your

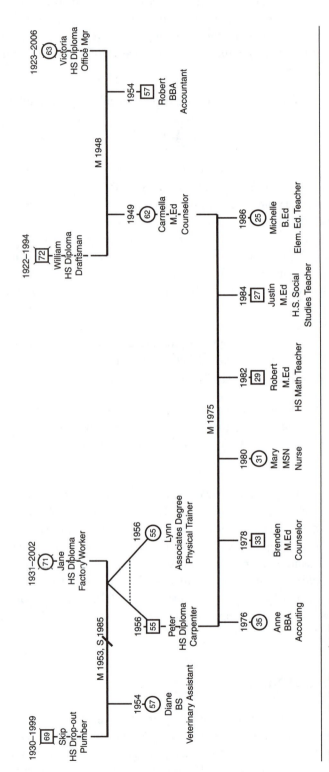

Figure 4.1 Sample Genogram

Notes: Numbers in circles and squares = age at the time the genogram was completed.
□ = man   O = woman   m = year married   s/ = year separated   x = deceased
Symbols adapted from Malott and Magnuson (2004).

one-and-only life authentically is both a confusing and demanding process. In *Let Your Life Speak: Listening for the Voice of Vocation,* Parker Palmer (2000) explains:

> From the beginning, our lives lay down clues to selfhood and vocation, though the clues may be hard to decode. But trying to interpret them is profoundly worthwhile . . . . [The clues] are helpful in counteracting the conventional concept of vocation, which insists that our lives must be driven by "oughts." As noble as that may sound, we do not find our callings by conforming ourselves to some abstract moral code. We find our callings by claiming authentic self-hood, by being who we are and by dwelling in the world. (p. 15)

There is no question that clarifying your identity—much like working a puzzle—happens in fits and starts, bits and pieces. As you determine the right place for each new piece, the secrets of the puzzle reveal themselves and it gets easier to fill in the blank spots.

Tools to Help You "Know Yourself"

A wide range of tools can offer pieces useful to solving the "Who am I?" puzzle. The box below contains an exercise called "Career Memories." (Because this exercise and the one shown on p. 64 require a substantial amount of time to complete, I encourage you to perform them after you have finished this chapter.) Sometimes, remembering the very first thing you wanted to be when you grew up and why you thought that was important to you provides clues to your first loves and first influences. Interpreted through the lens of time, these "firsts" can help you understand how you constructed your beliefs about yourself and your place in the world.

Career Memories

When I was very young, most of my childhood heroes wore capes, flew through the air, or picked up buildings with one arm. They were spectacular and got a lot of attention. But as I grew, my heroes changed, so that now I can honestly say that anyone who does anything to help a child is a hero to me.

—Fred Rogers (2003, p. 145)

Answer the following questions:

1. In the quote above, Fred Rogers explains potential changes in career outlook. What is your first career memory?

2. Why was this particular person or job attractive to you? What compelled you to believe that was who or what you wanted for yourself?

3. Are there threads of your first career memory in your life right now? In your career goals? In your leisure time?

Five Things That Rocked My World

List the five events that most changed your life:

1. _____

2. _____

3. _____

4. _____

5. _____

How did these things alter your world and impact your identity?

How did they/do they tie into your current career beliefs and career/life choices?

"Five Things That Rocked My World" is an exercise meant to help you get in touch with moments when your life shifted. Whereas these types of shifts can be positive or negative, they are almost always seismic in proportion. These shifts bring with them a sense of limits and of potential. These were moments that catapulted you to the brink of a new life—and you responded. In his speech to Stanford University's 2005 graduating class, Steve Jobs told four stories about his life—four times when his world was rocked—and how those four experiences made all the difference. He also said that he could not have understood those experiences in the same way when they were happening. It was only when he "connected the dots backwards" (Jobs, 2005) (you may recognize Steve Jobs's message from Chapter 2) that he realized how his life was directed by those events. How you handled those shifts in the moment and how you make sense of them now can offer you an enormous amount of information about who you are, what you love, and where you want to end up. The two exercises above can also be completed as journal starters.

There are many other career assessment instruments designed to help you access information about yourself. Check first with your campus career center to discover which self-assessment instruments are available to you through their services. Typically, career centers offer some combination of tools to help you clarify your values, skills, and interests. To get the most out of the results of these assessments, it is helpful, and sometimes required, to have them interpreted by a career counselor or coach. Career centers typically provide this interpretation individually or in group formats. If your campus offers a career planning course, consider registering for it. These courses usually offer several forms of self-assessment, as well as information on career research and the job search.

Knowing the Real World

The value of and necessity for occupational exploration is often lost on college students. We deem such exploration so important that we devoted Chapter 2 to this topic. In their freshman year, many psychology majors in any college or university believe they are going to be clinical psychologists. They believe this without knowing what clinical psychologists actually do every day. They believe this without knowing the standards they must meet to be accepted into a clinical psychology program. They believe this without knowing the cost to them—in years and dollars—for this level of education. They believe this without ever having spoken to a clinical psychologist. The other portion choose psychology as their major because they find people fascinating and want to understand humans in a deeper way. They love their classes because they are interesting and much of the material resonates with and expands their worldviews. Eventually, they ask themselves—and hopefully their professors and career center professionals—"What can I do with a psych major?" Often this question pops up in junior year, but some students don't really begin to integrate the things they have learned as psychology majors with their career choices until much closer to graduation.

As serendipity would have it, sometime during their last three semesters of college, many of those would-be clinical psychologists find themselves rethinking their occupational choice—or at least considering "taking a year off" before graduate school. In fact, graduate school is not a destination in and of itself but, rather, a vehicle to accomplish specific vocational goals. If you are not sure about your vocation, thoughts of graduate school are premature. An excellent way to spend the proverbial "gap year" (or more) is to get some practical experience and do some research. In short, you want to be crystal clear about your end goal before you put more time, energy, and money into more education.

Regardless of how you came to psychology, careful self-assessment and exploration of the field and related careers are critical activities. It is necessary to collect data from the National Association of Colleges and Employers, the Department of Labor, and other sources. It is necessary to learn the art of informational interviewing to talk to people who do work that is interesting to you. It is necessary to gather some experience through volunteer work, internships, and part-time and summer employment. It is necessary to read industry publications to understand the changes that have already taken place, as well as the ones anticipated for specific occupations.

While changes in the world of work are constant and you cannot always anticipate what will happen, you can uncover an enormous amount—information you need to know—to make knowledgeable career choices. Surprisingly, most of this information is easily accessible. Network with professors, university staff, friends, family, supervisors, and colleagues in all the places you have worked or volunteered. Read! Most universities have a career library and a range of Internet resources that have been purchased specifically for the purpose of career exploration. Using your self-assessment information as a template, integrate the occupational information you have acquired (review Chapter 2) and you will begin to discern the "goodness of fit" of various careers. It will be immediately obvious that some jobs are a fit with your identity, skills, and hopes for your life, while others simply don't fit your sense of self and/or the life you want to lead. Again, your career center can be instrumental in helping you develop a career exploration strategy.

Making Your Life List

The final task in compiling all the "*things you can know*" is the inclusion of your Life List (Hageman, 2005). Some people affectionately call it a "Bucket List." The reason to create a list like this as a college student is to ensure that you always have a *vision* for your whole life. Things that are important to you can fall by the wayside as you get swept up in the tasks of day-to-day living. Having a Life List reminds you to think broadly and act courageously in the service of creating a life you believe is worth living. Your list can be long or short, and, since it is your list, you can add or subtract items at will. Keep your items realistic—goals that are actually within your control to accomplish. For instance, I would like to be at Wrigley Field the day the Chicago Cubs win the World Series, but it is not on my list because I do not have the power to ensure the Cubs will ever get that far! You might include some items you have already accomplished—just to get warmed up. Then you want to start listing your goals and dreams. Some people find it helpful to write a few descriptive sentences about each item. This helps them remember why the item is important. Others choose to include a picture or some sort of visual representation of the items on their Life List. Anything that moves you to take on the task and make it meaningful is within bounds. So, after you finish reading the chapter, grab a piece of paper and a pen and start writing! (See Item 1 in the "Projects" section for a sample Life List.)

What You Can't Know Yet

The Impact of Personal and Global Change on Career Satisfaction

As you forge ahead on your career and life path, you will see a pattern emerge that can be fairly disconcerting. You begin to notice that every major decision you make requires information that is simply not available to you. Even if you are willing to explore and ask questions, even if you are willing to seek out the experts, there are just things you cannot prepare for because you don't know they are looming on the horizon. Some of these life events are very personal and very welcome: You are selected by the State Department for an internship in Croatia; you are offered a graduate assistantship you weren't expecting; you fall in love and now have another person to consider as you make your career and life choices; you win the lottery! Some personal situations are not particularly happy ones but must be factored into your career decisions nonetheless. For instance, you take an internship you believe will lead to full-time employment—and it does not; you injure yourself playing soccer, causing your athletic scholarship and your career dreams to disappear; your mother loses her job and can no longer help you with your tuition; the salary for the job you really want is not enough to cover your bills once you graduate.

Whether awe-inspiring or heartbreaking, personal events are often unpredictable and can change the course of your life. You have probably met college graduates who selected majors that correlated directly to particular careers only to discover that they could not tolerate the actual work—the education major who hates the classroom, the public relations major who despises writing press releases, or the pre-med major who dislikes attending to sick people. All the reading and shadowing in the world cannot always prepare someone for the day-in, day-out of a job. Sometimes, you just cannot know until you start working. Perhaps you ignored the warning signs because you wanted that career so much. Perhaps, not knowing what else you would do, you refused to let go of it. Regardless of your good intentions and advance planning, it is not unusual to find yourself at an unanticipated career crossroads.

Events completely outside of your immediate world can also bring you new perspective and a broader understanding of who you are and who you want to be in the world. Each generation has witnessed the birth of new occupations as well as the demise of jobs that suddenly became obsolete. Each generation can point to specific circumstances that changed the world in a substantive way and, in so doing, offered unanticipated direction to many people's career lives. For example, the Baby Boomers (b. 1946–1964) made career decisions in the midst of the Space Race, the Civil Rights Movement, Vietnam, Woodstock, the British music invasion, and the availability of the birth control pill and credit card. Generation X (b. 1965–1981) lived in a world where more women worked outside the home than ever before. Owning a personal computer, accessing the Internet, and using a cell phone became features of daily life. When people wanted an Apple, they weren't talking about fruit. AIDS became a household word, the Berlin Wall fell, and the *Challenger* crashed. The Millennials' (b. 1982–2003) view of the world, as well as their personal choices, were affected by 9/11, the Columbine shootings, the Gulf War, iPods/iPhones/iPads, helicopter parents, growing up as technology natives, the never-ending story of Harry Potter, and the "coffee" revolution. Certainly, world economic conditions have altered this generation's view of career longevity, property ownership, and the determinants of success (Scheef & Thielfoldt, 2011).

In the past few years, the economy has impacted every generation. In particular, it radically altered college graduates' aspirations and beliefs about the world of work. Most people were not in a position to predict the housing bust. And once it happened, even fewer people could have imagined the ramifications it would have on jobs across the economy.

Time Out: Reflective Question

Think about specific major events that have dominated the news during the past few months. To what extent could any of them *possibly* influence your decisions or actions in the next months or years?

Donald Super's "Life-Span, Life-Space Approach to Career Development"

Super was a preeminent career theorist who would not have been surprised by the ripple effect of our economic downturn on people's career decisions. A prolific researcher and writer, his work spanned more than 50 years and has had a global impact on the view that a "life-span, life-space approach to career development," as Super labeled this idea, is necessary. In fact, Super maintained that career choice as a *process* vs. an *event* was his single most important idea (Gysbers, Heppner, & Johnston, 2009). Super developed this perspective because he believed that self-concept (how you view yourself and your situation) is organic. It evolves and is impacted by your own personality development, the roles you play over the course of time, and the larger issues going on in your family, your community, the labor market, the economy, and the social and political climate (Scharf, 2006).

The Role of Chance in Your Career Development

Although many career theorists believe that chance inevitably plays a key role in everyone's career, this concept has been a focus for John Krumboltz and a premise for his theory of planned happenstance.

> Humans are born with differing characteristics and predispositions at a given time and place to parents not of their own choosing. They grow up in an environment where innumerable unpredictable events occur that provide opportunities for learning of both a positive and negative nature. Individuals can also generate events on their own [creating a possibility that would not have been there otherwise] and can capitalize on all kinds of events and resources to maximize their learning. (Mitchell, Levin, & Krumboltz, 1999, pp. 116–117)

Let's put this theory to the test. Consider any given Thursday in the life of a college student. You have a choice about how you will spend the evening. You have a paper to write. You would like to go out with your friends. There is also an alumni panel sponsored by the psychology department that you could attend for extra credit. By putting yourself in a particular situation (choosing the panel, for instance), you create an opportunity to meet someone who might help you with your career—an outcome that the other two options are not likely to produce. You attend the event and speak to a panelist afterward. Because you are prepared and impressive, she invites you to apply for an internship with her organization. You apply, and she puts in a good word. You become an intern there; they love you and offer you a full-time job after graduation.

The thing about taking a chance is exactly that—you just never know. You could have attended that panel and walked out without talking to anyone. You could have talked to people but had nothing come of it. The panelist's organization might not have been in the market for interns. You could have stayed home to write the paper or gone out with your friends, in effect taking the option for a chance positive encounter off the table. There are a hundred ways the night could have played out. Regardless, when you enter the room and make a decision to introduce yourself to someone, you leave yourself open to possible good outcomes.

Think about the last time happenstance played a role in the direction of your life. You were likely open-minded enough to at least consider moving in a different direction than the one you had planned. Mitchell et al. (1999) identified five skills you can employ to recognize, create, and make use of chance to generate career opportunities: *curiosity* about new possibilities, *persistence* in the face of obstacles, *flexibility* and open-mindedness to situations as they arise, *optimism* in being able to visualize what is possible, and a willingness to *take risks* in the face of uncertain outcomes.

Jack's Happenstance Story

If you are wondering whether people can really use chance to their advantage, consider Jack's story. Jack had just successfully completed his first year of medical school. He had performed very well but knew he didn't want to continue. He couldn't see himself leading a doctor's life. The trouble was that he could not say exactly what type of life he did want to lead. He took a leave of absence from his program and worked with a career counselor for the next 6 months to identify his interests, explore his options, and deal with his family's questions about his choice.

While he explored, he obtained a job at a high-end health club, which proved to be a great platform from which to conduct his career search. Jack was bright, extroverted, intuitive, and entrepreneurial. He learned quickly and read the environment extremely well. These talents were not lost on the members of the health club, and he soon became the staffer that people requested if there was a problem to be solved. The focus of his work with the career center was on identifying possible career paths—paths he was able to investigate through the network he had established with the health-club membership. Career counseling had revealed and helped him value his enterprising side. This led him to zero in on the members that worked in finance and real estate. He was invited to work sites and provided with contacts. Eventually, Jack was offered a position in commercial real estate, which he deemed an excellent fit and happily accepted.

A review of his story reveals that Jack utilized all the skills that Mitchell et al. (1999) believe are critical to making the most of chance. Leaving medical school was certainly a *risk,* and considering careers completely outside of health care required *curiosity* and *flexibility*. He was *persistent* in the face of his family's concerns and *optimistic* about his chance of success in a range of occupations. Jack's *curiosity, flexibility, persistence,* and *optimism* were also noted by the members of the health club who were willing to chat with him about their careers and industries and, in time, mentor him.

Time Out: Reflective Questions

Think of a time when you employed these skills and seized the moment. What were the choices to be made? What was the outcome for you? Would you do it again? What would you change? Take a moment to reflect on the skills you used and the skills you may need to develop to take a chance on yourself.

You Can Lead a Life, or You Can Follow One Around

In Daniel Pink's (2008) *The Adventures of Johnny Bunko: The Last Career Guide You'll Ever Need,* Johnny is a new college graduate who hates his job. Johnny is saved from a life of quiet desperation by Diana, an other-worldly career guide who provides him with six simple but profound rules to live and work by.

1. *"There is no plan."* Pink suggests that the most pragmatic approach to building a successful career is choosing work and a work environment that are interesting to you, regardless of a clear career path.

2. *"Think strengths, not weaknesses."* Successful people typically choose work that plays to their strengths.

3. Remember that *"it's not about you."* Your work should offer you the opportunity to focus your energy and talents on improving the lives of your clients and colleagues.

4. *"Persistence trumps talent."* Pink cautions that talent alone is rarely enough to get the job done. While talent can open up possibilities, only persistence can turn those possibilities into realities.

5. *"Make excellent mistakes."* An excellent mistake is defined as one from which the benefits of what you learned are greater than the cost of the error.

6. *"Leave an imprint."* Truly successful people utilize the first five rules in the service of something larger than themselves.

It would not be surprising if Johnny's adventures seemed familiar to you. Think about the Jungian concept of "hero" and you will recognize that Johnny is about to undertake an archetypal hero's journey. It is the journey of King Arthur, Don Quixote, *The Little Mermaid*'s Ariel, Luke Skywalker, the Karate Kid, Nemo, *The Lion King*'s Simba, *The Alchemist*'s Santiago, and a host of other fictional characters. Some would suggest that it is every man's and woman's journey and that taking it is critical to leading a real—meaning "authentic"—life. Career literature is replete with allusions to this journey. You choose a career *path;* you are at a career *crossroads;* you are on a career *voyage* or *expedition;* you take the *road less traveled.*

Moving Into the Great Unknown

Every hero's journey—every quest—has certain elements. It begins with a "call" to adventure or to a special duty that only the hero can accomplish. Jung positioned this call as the beginning of the struggle for psychological wholeness or individuation. Sometimes our hero longs to leave the safety of his or her comfortable, if ordinary, existence. Think Belle from Disney's *Beauty and the Beast*. Yet heroes are often resistant to and fearful of the unknown, and usually have to be reminded that "there is no plan."

What do you long for? What is the "call" you hear when you quiet the noise of everyday demands? What are you avoiding by staying "safe" but unfulfilled? Some college students began their journey when they selected a school that required them to live hundreds of miles from their homes. Some quests began with foreign study and experiencing "the other." And some journeys, like Johnny Bunko's, are set into motion when creating a life after college becomes the central task.

Heroes must discover their "virtues" or strengths as well as their flaws and decide what will best help them on their journey. The tasks demanded of the hero may require talents that he fears are more than he can manage. However, once he moves beyond his fears, he is free to explore and expand his strengths. In so doing, he begins to succeed. Johnny Bunko's mystical career advisor, Diana, cautions Johnny to "think strengths." So do many, many others, but perhaps no one as clearly as Robinson and Aronica (2009) in the best-selling book *The Element*. When you discover your "element," as defined by Robinson and Aronica, you find yourself at the place where the things you love to do and the things you are good at doing come together. "We all have distinctive talents and passions that can inspire us to achieve far more than we may imagine. Understanding this changes everything" (p. 8).

Robinson and Aronica (2009) tell story after story of successful people who achieved their success because they took the road less traveled. In fact, had these people followed more traditional paths laid out for them by family or school, they would have ignored their own capabilities and likely would not have found success at all.

The Importance of a Mentor

In most archetypal journeys, our heroine is reminded that she is not alone. A guide, often someone with mystical power, comes to the aid of the seeker. Johnny Bunko had Diana; Yoda was there for Luke Skywalker; Santiago had the Alchemist; Merlin was King Arthur's teacher; even Nemo had Dory as his companion. These guides—or mentors—help adventurers see a bigger world, one unbounded by their own egos. In other words, they create a vision of the world as it might be and, in so doing, remind the hero that "it's not about you."

While your mentors are likely not cultural icons, you most certainly have them available to you. However, if you are having some difficulty recognizing your mentors, the checklist below will help you identify them.

- Who are the people in your life who are willing to share their expertise?
- To whom do you turn when you need someone who will be completely honest?
- Who provides you with realistic assessments of yourself, others, and events?
- Who is best at reviewing situations rationally and analytically?
- To whom do you go when you need support?
- Who helps you identify and sort through your feelings and passions?
- Who always leaves you with something to think about?
- Who helps you set appropriate boundaries?
- Who is always willing to listen and serve as a sounding board?
- Who are the people willing to share themselves and their stories?

- To whom do you turn when you need permission to take risks?
- Who are your role models?
- Who inspires you?

This list of people who provide you with guidance and companionship as you proceed on your own hero's journey is invaluable.

> These are the people who can help you dream, aspire, and create a vision of the world and your place in it. They can help you manage the here and now, thrash out current problems and issues, and attend to the important as well as the urgent. (Hettich & Helkowski, 2005, p. 128)

As the journey continues, the heroine always faces serious setbacks. She is asked to do things that seem impossible. Dorothy must bring back the Wicked Witch of the West's broomstick; Luke Skywalker has to destroy the Death Star. Joseph Campbell, a renowned mythologist, referred to this phenomenon as the journey or road of many trials (Campbell, 1988). Failure is not an option for our heroine, and, although she does not know how she will achieve success, she keeps trying and discovers that "persistence trumps talent." The journey of trials is transformative, in that traditional ways of solving problems do not work here; thus, the heroine is forced to adopt a new and bigger perspective.

Along the way, she may "make excellent mistakes," allowing her to release old habits and defenses while envisioning new possibilities—and growing all the while. A journey of this magnitude is not meant to go smoothly. Mistakes are a natural result of trying something new and operating outside of your comfort zone. It is paradoxical that the only way to succeed is to be willing to fail and to risk failing again. But that seems to be the case for all human endeavors—especially those that occur during major life transitions, and establishing yourself after college certainly qualifies as that.

A cautionary note seems in order here. The concept of "excellent mistakes" implies risk in the face of actions and possible outcomes that are critically considered. While you are taking a chance, you believe the reward is ultimately attainable and worth the inherent difficulties. In other words, you have examined the trade-offs with your eyes wide open and are willing to make them.

Choosing to "leave an imprint" is the driving force behind happiness. Victor Frankl, the famed Austrian psychiatrist who survived years in a Nazi concentration camp, maintained that happiness was, in fact, the unintended byproduct of working for the greater good—something larger than oneself. Mihalyi Csikszentmihalyi (2003), one of positive psychology's most influential figures, emphasized this fact in his study of leadership. He determined that the one distinguishing trait that marked these men and women as visionary leaders was their intention not only to do "well" (run sound and profitable organizations) but also to do "good" (run ethical organizations that have a positive impact on the world).

Closing Comments

The good news about transition is that your *new* life simply becomes your life at some point. It may take you a while to realize that things are calmer, that you found what you were looking for in a career and, hopefully, in a life. It is not an event, as Super so clearly warned us; rather, it is a *process* with ebbs and flows. Sometime in your 20s, things get more settled and you drop the word *hopefully* from your statements about career and life goals, because many of them have evolved from dreams into realities. But, because it is a lifelong process, you will face shifts in your job, your industry, and/or your life that will require you to set out, once again, on a new path. The good news is that you have done it before and you can rely on the wisdom you gained during that post-college journey. Ideally, you will also have learned that the process is as important to your life and career satisfaction as the end results.

The title of this chapter promises a revelation—the answer to something that feels confusing and elusive. Like all important life secrets, the truth has always been right in front of you—hidden in plain sight. The secret to excellent career planning is that discovering yourself and understanding your world will lead you straight to yourself. Trust that and learn to enjoy the ride.

Getting Involved

Journal Starters

1. What has rocked your world? The exercise in Figure 4.3 asks you to name five events/situations that changed the course of your personal universe. After completing the exercise, list any additional significant events and consider their impact on your life.

2. Consider your "element" (the place where the things you love to do and the things you are good at doing come together). For instance, while living in France, chef Julia Child searched for something to keep her occupied while her husband was at work. She knew that she loved French food and decided to take a cooking class. In so doing, she found her element. What does your element look like, and what does this vision mean for your career journey?

3. Review your "plans" for your career. How have they served to enlarge your worldview and allowed you to take advantage of happenstance? How have they prohibited you from exploration and creating potentially positive chance events?

Projects

1. The items on one student's Life List are delineated below. Use this sample as a tool to jump-start your thinking; then make your own Life List and keep it easily assessable.

   a. Accomplished

   > Go to Mardi Gras
   >
   > Move away from home
   >
   > Live in Europe for a semester
   >
   > Kiss the Blarney Stone
   >
   > Work for a political campaign

   b. To Be Accomplished

   > Receive an advanced degree in history
   >
   > Find a teaching job and inspire my students
   >
   > Read all the books on *Time* magazine's "Top 100 Novels of All Time" list
   >
   > Visit all 50 states
   >
   > Raise a guide dog
   >
   > Fall in love, get married, and stay married
   >
   > Adopt a child
   >
   > Host a family Christmas

2. Create your own career genogram. Starting with your grandparents, list each family member's name, date of birth, highest education attained, occupation(s), major illnesses, date of marriage, and date of death. Once you have started your genogram, you may have to consult with other family members to gather all the facts. When your genogram is complete, use the questions in the chapter to explore your family's career patterns and values and the impact of these on your career constructs.

Additional Resources

URL	Brief Website Description
http://www.AllPsychologyCareers.com	Excellent listing of possible careers for psych majors; includes job listings as well as potential graduate schools
http://www.psychologycareercenter.org	Offers myriad information on a variety of psychology careers and industries, job listings, resources, articles, salary information, and more

- Osborn, D. S., Dikel, M. R., Sampson, J. P., Jr., & Harris-Bowlsbey, J. (2011). *The Internet: A tool for career planning* (3rd ed.). Broken Arrow, OK: National Career Development Association.

References

Campbell, J. (with B. Moyers). (1988). *The power of myth* (B. S. Flowers, Ed.). New York, NY: Doubleday.

Csikszentmihalyi, M. (2003). *Good business: Leadership, flow, and the making of meaning.* New York, NY: Viking.

Gysbers, N. C., Heppner, M. J., & Johnston, J. A. (2009). *Career counseling: Contexts, processes, and techniques.* Alexandria, VA: American Counseling Association.

Hageman, W. (2005, January 4). The life list. *Chicago Tribune,* Section 13, pp. 2–5.

Hettich, P. I., & Helkowski, C. (2005). *Connect college to career: A student's guide to work and life transitions.* Belmont, CA: Thomson/Wadsworth.

Jacobsen, M. H. (1999). *Hand-me-down dreams: How families influence our career paths and how we can reclaim them.* New York, NY: Three Rivers Press.

Jobs, S. (2005). *Stanford commencement address* [Video]. Retrieved from http://www.youtube.com/watch?v=UF8uR6Z6KLc

Malott, K. M., & Magnuson, S. (2004). Using genograms to facilitate undergraduate students' career development: A group model. *Career Development Quarterly, 53,* 178–186.

Mitchell, K. E., Levin, A. S., & Krumboltz, J. D. (1999). Planned happenstance: Constructing unexpected career opportunities. *Journal of Counseling and Development, 77,* 115–124.

Palmer, P. (2000). *Let your life speak: Listening for the voice of vocation.* San Francisco, CA: Jossey-Bass.

Pink, D. H. (2008). *The adventures of Johnny Bunko: The last career guide you'll ever need.* New York, NY: Riverhead Books.

Robinson, K., & Aronica, L. (2009). *The element: How finding your passion changes everything.* New York, NY: Penguin Books.

Rogers, F. (2003). *The world according to Mister Rogers: Important things to remember.* New York, NY: Family Communications.

Scharf, R. S. (2006). *Applying career development theory to counseling.* Belmont, CA: Thomson.

Scheef, D., & Thielfoldt, D. (2011). *Engaging a changing workforce: Study of four generations from The Learning Café.* Retrieved from http://www.thelearningcafe.net/2011/03/engaging-a-changing-workforce-study-of-four-generations/

CHAPTER 5

Your Journey Through Psychosocial Development Continues Long After Graduation

We have not passed that subtle line between childhood and adulthood until we move from the passive voice to the active voice—that is, until we have stopped saying "It got lost," and say "I lost it."

—Sydney J. Harris (1917–1986), newspaper journalist

We continue the journey of inner exploration in this chapter because when you graduate you are still a developmental work in progress. Your bachelor's degree does not signify the end of your intellectual, social, moral, and emotional development but, rather, one major milestone in a lifelong process of change. In short, you are still in the process of "becoming." For every graduate, there is a story of "becoming"—becoming a professional and becoming more mature in one's personal relationships, as you will see in Chapter 11, "Your Personal Life Changes After College."

As one example of becoming a professional, consider Angela. She graduated with a double major in psychology and business and accepted a job as a recruiter in a human resources/staffing firm (a typical job for a psychology/business major). One year into her new career, she felt her personal growth was being stunted and felt trapped in a small field of corporate America, reporting to people she did not always appreciate. Instead of remaining unhappy, she resigned (an option she was fortunate to have) and enrolled in additional business classes. After a year, she realized she needed something that nurtured her entrepreneurial spirit. Not only did Angela not abandon what she learned in her previous job, but she took the business knowledge, discipline, and communications skills she had learned there and ventured out on her own. She settled comfortably into an independent sales position for an investment firm. Angela never stopped growing and learning; she took her experience and built on it. Today, she is a confident, successful businesswoman who continues to advance in her career. Looking back, Angela's graduation from college was an important milestone, but so was her first job, where she learned a lot and subsequently left when she could learn no more; they were but two critical milestones in a continuing and successful journey in life (J. Keil, personal communication, September 20, 2011).

The extent to which you actively become the *agent* of your continuing change will guide your decisions, values, and actions for decades to follow. So who are you becoming? In this chapter, we explore some familiar and relatively new perspectives on psychosocial development from adolescence into adulthood. As we move from topic to topic, ask yourself, "How does this information inform my own process of becoming?"

Erikson's Fifth and Sixth Stages of Psychosocial Development

Erik Erikson (1982) identified eight stages of human development. At each stage, "changes within the individual and within the individual's social world combine to create a central conflict that defines the stage. The conflict must be addressed, though not necessarily resolved, within the given stages, says Erikson, before the individual can move to the next stage" (McAdams, 2009, p. 350).

In Erikson's fifth stage, adolescence and young adulthood, the conflict is between identity and role confusion. Identity is first confronted in adolescence because of physical and hormonal changes in the body, the introduction of formal operations in cognitive development, and societal expectations that occupational, ideological, and interpersonal dimensions of an individual's identity be explored and established (McAdams, 2009). The forces within and outside (family, community) the individual that promote identity development usually create tension. "The adolescent or adult should be neither victim nor master of his or her sociohistorical environment. Rather, the relationship between the self and society in the development of healthy identity is best characterized as one of dynamic tension" (p. 357).

An Identity Status Theory

The dynamic tension that powers the engine of identity development in its occupational, ideological, and interpersonal aspects is most obvious in an individual's choices in and progress through postsecondary education, if that option is accessible. Pursuing Erikson's belief that occupation and ideology (fundamental beliefs, especially as they relate to religion and politics) are at the core of identity, James Marcia and associates (as cited in McAdams, 2009) classified young persons on the basis of structured interviews into four identity statuses that represent particular developmental positions held by an individual: *identity achievement, moratorium, foreclosure,* and *identity diffusion.* The identity statuses are best understood through the interacting dimensions of *identity exploration* and *identity commitment.*

Identity Achievement: Exploring Identity and Commitment

Young adults who actively explore their career and values decisions *and* make commitments to a thoughtfully developed occupation and ideology have reached identity achievement, the most advanced of the statuses. Identity achievers internalize their goals, rely on their own abilities to meet challenges, make decisions in an autonomous and principled way, tend not to conform to peer pressure, base their moral decisions on abstract principles rather than popular convention, and are more academically inclined than persons in other statuses. In short, they know who they are and are viewed as mature individuals (McAdams, 2009).

Moratorium: Exploring Identity but Not Yet Committed

Young adults in moratorium status are currently exploring the questions of work and values but have not yet made commitments. They know they do not know who they are, but they are asking the necessary questions. Still, persons in moratorium share many characteristics with identity achievers, and Marcia views them as relatively mature individuals. Compared with those in foreclosure or identity diffusion, individuals in identity achievement and moratorium tend to create richer and more individuated conceptions of themselves, adopt an engaged and exploratory style in processing information, and employ mature defense mechanisms to cope with stress. Some young adults in moratorium, however, display *ambivalence* in their relationships with parents and other authority figures by creating a psychological distance from them and rejecting old values and forms of identification that reflect negative identities (McAdams, 2009). This ambivalence can lead to conflict in situations when new graduates are forced to relinquish their independence and move back home for economic reasons.

Foreclosure: Not Exploring Identity but Committed

Individuals in the foreclosure identity status are failing to meet the challenge of Erikson's fifth stage of psychosocial development because they have committed to a particular career and set of values without first exploring them. Perhaps they are yielding to the pressures of a parent who has specific career expectations—such as the freshman who confidently announced she was bound for law school because it fulfilled her family's expectations for a third generation of attorneys, yet had neither explored her interests in law nor performed even basic tasks in the family law office and was placed on academic probation after her first semester due to poor grades. Some graduate schools documented a rapid increase in applications for forensic psychology programs soon after television programs such as *CSI* appeared, in spite of the vast differences between the television series' portrayal of forensic operations and real-life situations.

Because foreclosures are conforming to outside authorities or models, they appear to be the "best behaved" of the four statuses. They tend to study hard, keep regular hours, seem happy, and express conventional values derived from family, church, or other authorities (McAdams, 2009). In short, the challenges of college may be quite manageable for foreclosures, given that many decisions about occupation, relationships, and life values have already been made without prior questioning. Some counselors maintain, however, that foreclosed students are ripe for a midlife crisis when events cause them to question earlier career decisions.

In some ways, colleges inadvertently promote the foreclosure status with recruitment procedures that implicitly reward high school applicants who uncritically express clear choices for a particular academic major and encounter advising procedures that do not promote wise exploration of that major's career options. The student who chooses to major in psychology to "help people" may question that decision when confronted by courses in statistics and research methodology, unless that student is also exposed to career options where quantitative coursework is essential. The new psychology major should ask: "Is coursework alone sufficient to help me properly explore my interest in helping people? What else should I be doing to reach identity achievement in its occupational and ideological dimensions?" Our answer: Begin by reviewing the options we described in Chapter 3.

Identity Diffusion: Neither Exploring Identity nor Committed

Identity diffusions, on the other hand, have neither searched for answers to questions about occupation and ideology (or are overwhelmed by the numerous options) nor made any commitments. Like those in the foreclosure status, they fail to resolve the challenge of identity development and instead are awash in role confusion. Often characterized as withdrawn, identity diffusions tend to feel out of place and isolated, distant from parents, and cautious in new relationships, and they "appear afloat in a sea of ambiguity" (McAdams, 2009, p. 360).

When the economy "goes south" and jobs are hard to find, pressures increase on young people to find their identity and a satisfying career—not only a career that satisfies their personal values and goals but also one that will speed the payment of their college loans and lead to financial independence. Consequently, it is crucial that you participate in the numerous opportunities college offers (see Chapter 3) and actively explore your career options (see Chapters 2 and 4).

Marcia's work has been criticized because the four identity statuses may not operate in a developmental sequence. Many studies that support the statuses appear to be more concerned with classification issues than with developmental issues. In addition, some researchers maintain that conscious exploration often does not occur in identity achievement (Cote, 2006). Still, the Marcia *framework* is helpful for understanding the journey toward identity for many young people.

In Erikson's sixth stage of young adulthood, the major developmental challenge is the achievement of intimacy over isolation. The relation between the fifth stage (adolescence and young adulthood) and the sixth is complex. Although Erikson believes a person must make substantial progress in establishing identity development before he or she can become truly intimate with another person, many people define their identity (Stage 5) through intimate relationships (Stage 6)—for example, "I am the loving partner of Chris."

Given the changes in contemporary society regarding relationships, sexuality, education, and mobility (discussed in the following section), the distinctiveness between these two stages may no longer hold. Complicating this developmental challenge is today's economy, where many young college graduates must delay the establishment of intimate relationships until they have acquired some degree of security in their careers and financial independence.

Time Out: Exercise

Before we explore another perspective on the person you are becoming, take a few minutes to digest and apply our summary of Erikson's and Marcia's concepts as they apply to your development.

1. What specific actions have you followed in the past 9 to 12 months that represent real steps toward exploring your career/vocational interests? How would you grade yourself in these efforts? What are your next steps?

2. The other aspect in Marcia's notion of identity development includes exploration of basic values regarding religious and political beliefs. What specific activities have you carried out during the same period that reflect your exploration in these areas? Grade yourself in this overall effort. What are your next steps?

3. What are the elements that define intimacy for you, and to what extent are you on the path to achieving intimacy in relationships? Do you view the process of achieving intimacy as a major path to identity or achieving identity as a major path to intimacy, or do they interact in some way?

Arnett's Emerging Adulthood

Marcia's research provides a framework for describing possible connections between exploration, commitment, and career choices, but it may not speak to the current social context in which many contemporary young people mature. Erikson's major contributions were in place before the 1970s. Prior to the 1980s, American society expected a young person to have completed his or her education, become financially independent through full-time work, established a family, and purchased a house, usually by his or her mid-20s.

The world has changed in numerous ways during the past 40 to 50 years, and some of these changes have influenced psychosocial development. Using the data from his qualitative studies of 300 young people ages 18 to 29 in San Francisco, Los Angeles, New Orleans, and rural Missouri, Jeffrey Arnett (2004) argued that the period between 18 and 25 in contemporary industrialized countries is neither adolescence nor adulthood (as in Erikson's view) but *emerging adulthood.*

The period of emerging adulthood has arisen due to demographic changes in industrialized countries, changes such as the accessibility of education for a larger number of people (especially women), a growing middle class able to afford higher education and higher standards of living, and delays in entering stable relationships.

In his earlier studies, Arnett identified five features of emerging adulthood that differentiate this stage from Erikson's framework (Arnett & Tanner, 2006). As you read about the features, try to reflect on the extent to which each contributes to your development.

Age of Identity Exploration

Emerging adulthood is the age of identity exploration in the sense that it is the period when people are most likely to be exploring various possibilities for their lives in a variety of areas, especially love and work, as a prelude to making the enduring choices that will set the foundations for their adult lives (Arnett & Tanner, 2006, p. 8).

In your parents' time, it was typical to complete high school or college in 4 years, get a job in an organization where they would likely remain (for 10, 20, or 30 years), get married, have children, and settle down for life. As you know, the times have changed, and students now have far more options to choose from. By age 25, about 70% of emerging adults have obtained at least some college or university education (Arnett, 2004). More than 45% of today's undergraduates are over 21, compared with 25% of undergraduates 30 years ago. In addition, the median time required to complete the baccalaureate has risen from 4 to 5 years; the proportion of students finishing in 6 years has risen from 15% to 23% (Fitzpatrick & Turner, 2006).

Although identity exploration characterizes the search of many emerging adults, Arnett (2004) maintains that there are many others in their late teens and early 20s who move during college from major to major and subsequently from job to job, often unsystematically, searching for what best fits their identity—in other words, they meander. "*Meandering* might be a more accurate word, or maybe *drifting* or even *floundering*. For many emerging adults working simply means finding a job, often a McJob, that will pay the bills until something better comes along" (Arnett, 2004, p. 150).

According to Levit (2009), the U.S. Department of Labor estimated that the typical American holds about nine jobs between the ages of 18 and 32. Other studies may show variations in the number of jobs held during this time span, but findings are not very dissimilar. In addition, "the median length of time workers stay on the job has shrunk by half since 1983—from 2.2 years to 1.1 years now" (p. 18). Further support of these results comes from Farber (2006), who analyzed changes in long-term employment and concluded that *churn* (a series of jobs lasting less than a year) is to be expected in an industrialized society where new employees, even those in their 30s, are searching for the right person–job fit.

In short, in their search for identity, emerging adults take a longer time to settle down and change jobs more often than did young people in previous decades.

When rewarding jobs are hard to find during economic crises, the search for self-identity is further exacerbated. These findings help explain the second characteristic of emerging adulthood, instability (Hettich, 2009).

Age of Instability

By instability, Arnett (2004) is referring to changing residences—for example, from home to residence hall to apartment and perhaps back home again, or from home to living independently, or from home to military or volunteer service. The rates at which people change residences are highest in the 20-to-29 age group, and they peak in the 20-to-24 range, with about 35% of that age group changing residences each year. Such moves are in part a response to identity exploration in work-related changes as well as relationship changes (e.g., cohabitation and/or marriage; Arnett & Tanner, 2006).

The Self-Focused Age

Emerging adults are self-focused to the extent that they leave the structures of home and have relatively few social obligations, duties, and commitments to others. Most have only themselves to worry about, but Arnett and Tanner (2006) maintain that this form of self-focus is not equivalent to self-centeredness. The self-focused age permits a person to concentrate on goals such as achieving self-sufficiency and career stability while simultaneously pursuing the fun and freedom of being an emerging adult before making commitments to a relationship (Arnett & Tanner, 2006).

The Age of Feeling in Between

Arnett (2004) chose the term *emerging adulthood* in part because many late teens and persons in their early 20s describe themselves with these words. Participants in Arnett's early study were asked: "Do you feel you have reached adulthood? Yes, no, or yes and no?" Of those between 18 and 25, about 40% responded "yes" and 5% "no." However, about 55% responded "in some ways, yes; in some ways, no." In comparison, more than 60% of those between 26 and 35 years old responded "yes," about 3% "no," and more than 35% "yes and no" to the same question. What are the criteria emerging adults use for defining adulthood? They do not define it with clearly marked transition events such as college graduation or getting married. Instead, they choose benchmarks that are gradually achieved: accepting responsibility for one's self, making independent decisions, and becoming financially independent (Arnett & Tanner, 2006).

These findings overlap to some degree with a survey of nearly 1,400 Americans 18+ years old who made up the 2002 General Social Survey conducted by the National Opinion Research Center. Participants were asked about the importance of attaining certain traditional benchmarks of reaching adulthood. The results revealed that "more than 95% of Americans consider the most important markers of adulthood to be completing school, establishing an independent household, and being employed full time—concrete steps associated with the ability to support a family" (Settersten & Ray, 2010, p. 22). In contrast, about half the sample regarded marriage and having children as necessary to be judged an adult. Nowadays, young people view marriage and parenthood primarily as life choices rather than requirements for adulthood (Settersten & Ray, 2010).

The Age of Possibilities

Two phenomena characterize 18 to 25 as the age of possibilities: great optimism and the opportunity to redirect their lives. Emerging adults have high expectations, optimism, and hope for the future because these beliefs and feelings have been strongly reinforced throughout their education by family, teachers, outside institutions, and themselves. Yet, for most emerging adults, these beliefs have not been tested by the realities of life and the workplace. "Before people settle into a long-term job, it is possible for them to believe they are going to find a job that is both well-paying and personally fulfilling, an expression of their identity rather than simply a way to make a living" (Arnett & Tanner, 2006, p. 13). Unfortunately, many college students develop and express unrealistically high expectations about their value in the workplace and are subsequently labeled by supervisors and coworkers as "entitled." Frustrations that result from unrealistically high expectations are exacerbated during periods of high unemployment, when college graduates must often settle for mundane jobs that do not require a college degree or become unemployed while still trying to repay loans.

Sometimes high expectations derive from parents, especially if there is a family tradition in a particular profession. The parents of Su Ling, an exchange student from Asia, had high expectations that she pursue a research career similar to her father's in the pharmaceutical field. Su Ling was fortunate to obtain two internships in a pharmaceutical company and was successful in them, but she felt something was missing. After careful thought and exploration of what she really wanted to do, Su Ling concluded she wanted a career with more direct human contact. She applied to and completed medical school. Given the similarities in rigor, reliance on research, and focus on health, it is unlikely her parents were disappointed in Su Ling's choice; Su Ling is very pleased with her career decision.

Emerging adulthood is also the age of possibilities for those who wish to transform their lives (especially if they experienced difficult family or living conditions) before making commitments to intimate relations and jobs that structure their adult life. "Regardless of their family background, all emerging adults carry their family influences with them when they leave home, which limits the extent to which they can change what they have become by the end of adolescence. Nevertheless, more than any other period of life, emerging adulthood presents the possibility of change" (Arnett & Tanner, 2006, p. 14). During this time, fulfillment of all hopes seems possible because the range of choices for how to live is greater than it has ever been before and will ever be again (Arnett & Tanner, 2006, p. 14).

What Are the Implications of Emerging Adulthood for Your Workplace Preparation?

We believe the characteristics of emerging adulthood provide a solid conceptual basis for the opportunities we recommended in Chapter 3. Part-time jobs, internships, workplace-related courses, extracurricular and volunteer activities, study abroad, military service, and using your college's counseling services can become important venues for self-exploration of personal values, career interests, and relationships. In addition, these opportunities enable you to establish short- and long-term goals, and extracurricular and volunteer activities may add fun to your life (self-focused age). Jobs, internships, leadership positions, and military service—as well as movement to different residences—may speed your progress to adulthood (feeling in between) when they strengthen your decision-making skills, enable you to accept more responsibilities, and provide income. Finally, several opportunities help you establish realistic expectations about the workplace and achieve possibilities you may never have dreamed of—for example, the fabulous internship that confirmed your interest and skills for graduate school; the semester abroad that strengthened your maturity and worldview; the career counseling, coursework, and leadership experiences that helped land an excellent full-time job; or the military service that tested your ability to endure incredible hardships.

What Are Additional Dimensions of Emerging Adulthood?

As research on emerging adulthood has advanced Arnett and his colleague Jennifer Tanner have identified additional features that argue for the distinctiveness of emerging adulthood, but in response to their critics, they have refined the meaning of distinctiveness. *Distinctive* means the characteristic is more likely to be found in emerging adulthood than in any other stage (i.e., not everyone possesses it), emerging adulthood exists in some cultures but not others (i.e., the stage is not universal), and most characteristics begin before emerging adulthood and continue afterward (i.e., they are not discrete; Tanner & Arnett, 2011).

Personality Organization

"With regard to personality, increased instability during emerging adulthood and increased stability thereafter distinguish certain aspects of personality development during these years" (Tanner & Arnett, 2011, p. 16). The research they summarize suggests that changes in emerging adults are generally in the direction of greater stability and self-constraint, more reflective and planful behavior, less emotional instability, more responsibility and caution, a stronger sense of agency and mastery over the environment, and an increase in their sense of self-achievement. All in all, this is potentially good news for emerging adults who are apprehensive about the general direction of their development! As one former student (and now business executive) disclosed to one of the authors of this text after reading about emerging adulthood, "I could write novels about the changes I've experienced between ages 25 to 32: everything from behavior, goals, personality, friendships, social life, and some extreme changes. It was an amazing time, maybe not the best of decisions sometimes, but I would never change a thing. But let me say, yikes! This is very real and relevant for me."

A Rise in Psychopathology Risk—and in Well-Being

Unfortunately, a distinctive feature of emerging adulthood is its high rate of psychopathology, including anxiety disorders (22% of the new cases), followed by (in descending order of prevalence) substance abuse, mood disorders, and impulse control disorders. Of those emerging adults who encountered a psychiatric disorder, 75% had at least one episode during childhood or adolescence. In contrast, about 70% of individuals deemed "low" in mental health problems during adolescence were classified the same in emerging adulthood. On the positive side, studies have revealed increases in perceived social support, satisfaction with life, self-efficacy, self-esteem, and resiliency, and decreases in loneliness, fatalism, derogation, anger, and depressive symptoms. The paradox of emerging adulthood as a period of simultaneous high hopes and increased psychopathology is attributed to findings indicating that most emerging adults experience rising well-being while an increasing minority confront psychopathology (Tanner & Arnett, 2011).

Respite From Physical Disease

Although the rates of serious physical disorders may be low in emerging adulthood, conditions that predict serious problems later in life are common. For example, obesity has become a problem of epidemic proportions for Americans, including emerging adults, and is a strong predictor of subsequent health problems. Some researchers believe that lack of physical activity is a major factor causing obesity in this age group. Although the use of tobacco has declined in America, about 25% of emerging adults use this addictive substance. Disease accounts for only 2% of deaths among persons between 15 and 34, whereas 70% of the deaths in persons aged 18 to 25 are due to motor vehicle accidents, homicide, HIV infection, and suicide (causes that account for only 8% of the deaths in the general population of the United States). Impulse and risk behaviors together with incomplete brain development are factors associated with preventable deaths in emerging adults (Tanner & Arnett, 2011).

Social Relationships and Educational Patterns

Emerging adulthood is also distinctive from other developmental stages in terms of the nature of social relationships and patterns of education. To understand these attributes of distinctiveness, Tanner created a framework she calls *recentering*. Recentering is a three-stage process that includes transition from adolescence to emerging adulthood (Stage 1), emerging adulthood proper (Stage 2), and transition out of emerging adulthood into young adulthood (Stage 3). Throughout these processes, the individual is challenged to accept increased responsibility for guiding himself or herself through this pivotal stage of life.

Stage 1 is a launching position in which the individual renegotiates his or her relationship with parents and weakens the bonds of dependency on them, as typified when an 18-year-old completes high school and leaves home for postsecondary education, a job, or military service. Cultural, religious, and social class differences may influence the nature of this transition. Family support during this stage is crucial and is predictive of a successful outcome of emerging adulthood.

In Stage 2, the emerging adult is peripherally tied to the identities and roles of adolescence but is also committed to trying out new identities (e.g., student, partner in a relationship, employee, volunteer, or soldier). In these roles, the individual is actively exploring roles and activities that may match his or her sense of identity to the extent that resources, opportunities, and time permit.

Emerging adulthood ends with Stage 3 of the recentering process, and young adulthood begins. "Identity exploration recedes at Stage 3, marking the beginning of identity consolidation occurring around commitments to careers, partners, children, community, and aging parents" (Tanner & Arnett, 2011, p. 24).

Recentering helps us understand the course of events during the early years of adulthood and provides a framework for predicting successful (or unsuccessful) adaptation to key events that shape an individual's life. Recentering promotes change from control by others to self-regulation, enables the individual to direct resources to choosing life goals, and can promote positive mental health (Tanner & Arnett, 2011).

Friendships

During this period, relationships with friends take on new meaning and may reach the peak of their functional significance. Not only are friends a valuable resource, but sometimes they can become more important than parents, on whom the individual is becoming less reliant. The number of friends remains fairly constant and the amount of time spent with them is high during this period; qualities such as loyalty, warmth, and sharing personal experiences remain important. Friends are often the preferred companions during this time, unless there is a romantic partner who serves that role. Emerging adulthood is the time when an individual's first serious romantic relationship occurs, when feelings of passion, intimacy, and social support are high. About 60% of emerging adults choose to cohabit with at least one partner before marriage, and about half these relationships culminate in marriage (Tanner & Arnett, 2011). In comparison with 1956, when the median age for marriage was 22 for men and 20 for women, in 2006, the median age was 28 for men and 24 for women (Arnett & Tanner, 2006). We examine friendships further with guest author Abby (Wilner) Miller in Chapter 11, "Your Personal Life Changes After College."

Education

Chances are you have been told since elementary school of the importance of earning a college degree (or higher) or you would not be reading this page. The attainment of a postsecondary education, whether in college or trade school, is a critical component in the transition from adolescence to adulthood, along with the establishment of healthy relationships. College can be viewed as your moratorium—some say an institutionalized moratorium—to figure out who you are, what you believe, who you want to become, and what career you seek to establish.

You seek to become one of the 30% of Americans between 25 and 29 years old who earn a bachelor's degree. You chose not to become one of the millions of vulnerable Americans who fail to attain a postsecondary education and a satisfying life income (Tanner & Arnett, 2011). Like a growing number of college graduates facing the changing world of work, you believe your bachelor's degree may not be sufficient in the long run to achieve your goals, but you may not want to commit to a graduate or professional program yet. Delaying that decision is wise until you know the specific career you wish to have. You are still on your journey of professional and psychosocial development, and there will be time along the way to make informed decisions regarding additional education.

In summary, the concept of emerging adulthood provides a contemporary perspective for young people to understand the developmental aspects of their journey to adulthood. The core of emerging adulthood is anchored in a set of characteristics that its adherents maintain distinguish ages 18 to 25 in contemporary industrialized societies from the developmental stages in the Erikson framework. Emerging adulthood is the age of exploration, instability, self-focus, feeling in between, and possibilities. Emerging adulthood is also a period of changes in personality organization, neurological and cognitive development, increased psychopathology for some but increased well-being for most, low rates of physical disease but high rates of preventable death, and changes in social relationships and education patterns. As emerging adulthood is a relatively new perspective on development, continued research is needed to clarify its concepts and answer the many questions the theory raises. It has generated research across a number of fields in psychology, including research on the role of emerging adulthood across cultures (Jensen, 2011).

Time Out: Reflective Questions

1. To what extent do you identify with the five characteristics of emerging adulthood and with the issues of personality and other changes?

2. What are some of the changes, if any, you have experienced with family, friends, and significant others during the past few years?

What Qualities Do You Seek in a Full-Time Job?

Does our discussion of Erikson, Marcia, and Arnett and Tanner appear relevant but a bit abstract? To the extent that their concepts inform your understanding of the person you are becoming and contribute to the formation of your identity, a next step in your journey may be to explore the qualities, values, and conditions you seek in the work you perform after graduation. You have invested considerable capital in the form of money, time, effort, and expectations (yours and your family's) to prepare for life after college, especially for a career that integrates your knowledge, skills, plans, and values; so what do you really want from the experience of your first job?

In a survey conducted by MonsterTRAK (Chao & Gardner, 2007), 9,000 young adults ages 18 to 25 were asked to rate 15 common job characteristics on their importance in a job search. Table 5.1 lists the characteristics in rank order of their importance.

Several points are worth noting about this data. As you scan the list, notice the values implied in the individual characteristics and their rankings. Chao and Gardner (2007) report that characteristics promoting long-term success (i.e., the first five) are rated higher than those reflecting a short-term emphasis (e.g., travel or prestigious company). The percentage of respondents who rated a particular characteristic as most important are as follows for the top six: interesting/engaging work, 88%; good benefits, 84%; secure job, 82%; promotion opportunities, 81%; learning opportunities, 77%; and location, 63%. Did you notice the percentage difference between learning opportunities (long-term factor) and location (more likely a short-term influence)? In the past, good benefits would not have received as high a ranking, but due to rising costs of health care and reductions in benefits implemented by many organizations, this aspect of employment has become a critical component of a satisfying job. Interesting work, chances for promotion, and opportunity to learn new skills are conditions that stimulate and reward high intrinsic motivation, whereas characteristics in the bottom portion of the table may be viewed as extrinsic

Table 5.1   Rank Order of 15 Job Characteristics Important to Young Adults' Job Search

Rank Order	Job Characteristic
1	Interesting work
2	Good benefits (e.g., health insurance)
3	Job security
4	Chances for promotion
5	Opportunity to learn new skills
6	Geographical location
7	Annual vacations of a week or more
8	High income
9	Flexibility in work hours
10	Regular hours—no nights/weekends
11	Being able to work independently
12	Limited job stress
13	Travel opportunities
14	Prestigious company
15	Limited overtime

Source: From Chao and Gardner (2007). Adapted with permission.

factors. High income was ranked in the middle in this survey, but students with high debt are likely to place income higher on the list.

The survey contained analyses across gender, ethnic affiliation, and academic major, but Chao and Gardner (2007) reported relatively consistent findings across these variables. You should also evaluate these characteristics within the context of the current economy. When the economy is down, companies often terminate employees and dissolve their positions (or outsource the work), reduce job benefits, limit promotions, and increase workloads; these are conditions that usually increase work hours (without overtime pay), alter work schedules, limit promotions, and increase job stress. Consequently, you should enter the workplace with realistic expectations: Be willing to be flexible in the tasks you perform, able to adapt to changing conditions, and willing to delay gratification of your most preferred job characteristics. It may be a few years and a few jobs before you perform interesting work that provides opportunities for promotion and learning new skills in an organization that offers good benefits and better security. During this time, you will probably reevaluate the importance of these characteristics and integrate the changes in your work values.

What effect does a poor economy have on emerging adults? When asked about coming of age in a post-recession world, Arnett (2011) offered the following observations:

1. Although young people are frustrated in a declining economy by not being able to find the kind of work they seek, they change jobs often in search of better opportunities and tend to be optimistic about the future.

2. The optimism of emerging adults, however, can lead to discouragement, anxiety, and depression if they experience unemployment year after year. If they can succeed in the struggle and find stable work, usually by the age of 30, the depression will likely lift.

3. When asked what resources emerging adults have for weathering a bad economy, Arnett replied,

They are very *resilient* physically and cognitively and emotionally. Yes, they're struggling, and they're struggling more than people in other age groups in some ways because of their higher unemployment rate, but they also have a lot to draw on in terms of their personal resources. (p. 34; emphasis added)

Why not take this quotation and tape it to your computer as a reminder during those tough days ahead that you are very capable of being resilient? As self-focused individuals, most emerging adults also have the advantage of having few if any responsibilities to individuals who may depend on them; many are able to move back home and live with family at least for a while.

4. Surviving a recession may become a wake-up call to emerging adults (and their parents) regarding the management of money. Overall, there appears to be an increase in savings and a reduction in spending and debt.

Time Out: Reflective Question

How do your perceptions and experiences with the national economy compare with Arnett's observations?

Closing Comments

View the completion of your baccalaureate in psychology as another milestone (but perhaps not your last) in your formal education *and* also as a point in your continuing psychosocial development. Concepts created by Erikson, expanded by Marcia, and extended to contemporary American society by Arnett and Tanner address conditions you may be experiencing and growth that will emerge in coming years. Yet recognize that entering the job market in a poor economy may also affect your trajectory of growth. Try to integrate the concepts you learned in this chapter into your continuing search for identity, especially as you plan the crucial steps of entering the workplace. Your early post-college experiences are likely to shape your future more than you know.

In earlier chapters, the material lent itself to providing specific recommendations. In this chapter, the information about psychosocial development may be less amenable to practical suggestions but is intrinsically valuable to understand. Our firm hope is that you study and reflect on the research presented here and evaluate and apply the concepts in the service of your ongoing development. Becoming an emerging adult is a period of apprehension, confusion, and concern even for the most confident and stable individual. Understanding the characteristics and experiences of other emerging adults can be comforting or disconcerting when we compare our thoughts, feelings, and situations with those of our peers as studied by developmental psychologists. If for no other reason, it is comforting to know an empirically derived literature exists for us to explore, test against the reality of our own experiences, and critically evaluate.

Getting Involved

Journal Starters

1. What are the most significant insights you gained from reading this chapter?

2. What insights gained from the previous chapter on career planning and development can you connect to your psychosocial development as they relate to (a) identity statuses and (b) emerging adulthood?

3. Review the rankings contained in Table 5.1. What are your five most important job characteristics? To what extent does each reflect primarily an occupational value or an ideological value?

Projects

1. Kloep and Hendry argue in Arnett, Kloep, Hendry, and Tanner (2011) that emerging adulthood should be viewed as a process, not a stage. Peruse this short book or similar discussions and prepare a report on the views of critiques of emerging adulthood. To what extent could the critics' arguments substantially change our discussion of emerging adulthood?

2. In the Chao and Gardner (2007) survey of job characteristics, high income was ranked eighth, but you may believe it should be higher. Locate other surveys about job characteristics and compare the rankings of the Top 5 to 10 most important qualities.

3. Arnett talks about resilience, a topic that has received considerable attention in recent years. Survey the literature on this topic in an area that interests you, such as health, the labor market, relationships, or the military's integration of this concept in the training of soldiers.

Additional Resource

URL	Brief Website Description
http://www.transad.pop.upenn.edu	The Network on Transitions to Adulthood examines the changing nature of early adulthood (ages 18–34) and the policies, programs, and institutions that support young people as they move into adulthood.

References

Arnett, J. J. (2004). *Emerging adulthood: The winding road from the late teens through the twenties.* New York, NY: Oxford University Press.

Arnett, J. J. (2011, March). Coming of age in a post-recession world. *Monitor on Psychology, 42*(3), 32–34.

Arnett, J. J., Kloep, M., Hendry, L. B., & Tanner, J. L. (2011). *Debating emerging adulthood: Stage or process?* New York, NY: Oxford University Press.

Arnett, J. J., & Tanner, J. L. (Eds.). (2006). *Emerging adults in America: Coming of age in the 21st century.* Washington, DC: American Psychological Association.

Chao, G. T., & Gardner, P. D. (2007, Winter). *Important characteristics of early career jobs: What do young adults want?* (White paper prepared for MonsterTRAK). East Lansing: Michigan State University Collegiate Employment Research Institute. Retrieved from http://www.ceri.msu.edu/publications/publications.html

Cote, J. E. (2006). Emerging adulthood as an institutionalized moratorium: Risks and benefits to identity formation. In J. J. Arnett & J. L. Tanner (Eds.), *Emerging adults in America: Coming of age in the 21st century* (pp. 85–116). Washington, DC: American Psychological Association.

Erikson, E. H. (1982). *The life cycle completed: A review.* New York, NY: W. W. Norton.

Farber, H. S. (2006, December). Is the company man an anachronism? Trends in long term employment in the U.S. between 1973 and 2005. *Network on Transitions to Adulthood Policy Brief, 38,* 1–2.

Fitzpatrick, M. D., & Turner, S. E. (2006, September). The changing college experience for young adults. *Network on Transitions to Adulthood Policy Brief, 34,* 1–3.

Hettich, P. I. (2009). College to workplace transitions: Becoming a freshman again. In T. M. Miller (Ed.), *Handbook of stressful transitions across the life span* (pp. 87–109). New York, NY: Springer.

Jensen, L. A. (Ed.). (2011). *Bridging cultural and developmental psychology: New syntheses in theory, research, and policy.* New York, NY: Oxford University Press.

Levit, A. (2009). *They don't teach corporate in college: A twenty-something's guide to the business world* (2nd ed.). Franklin Lakes, NJ: Career Press.

McAdams, D. P. (2009). *The person: An integrated introduction to personality psychology.* Orlando, FL: Harcourt College.

Settersten, R. A., Jr., & Ray, B. (2010). What's going on with young people today? The long and twisting path to adulthood. *The Future of Children, 20,* 19–41.

Tanner, J. L., & Arnett, J. J. (2011). Presenting "emerging adulthood": What makes it developmentally distinctive? In J. J. Arnett, M. Kloep, L. B. Hendry, & J. L. Tanner (Eds.), *Debating emerging adulthood: Stage or process?* (pp. 13–30). New York, NY: Oxford University Press.

CHAPTER 6

Know the Skills You Need to Succeed (Course Content is No Longer the Focus)

Whatever exists at all exists in some amount. To know it thoroughly involves knowing its quantity as well as its quality.

—Edward L. Thorndike (1918), educator

In providing advice to students about transferring skills—that is, the transition from college to career—Ellis (2009, p. 61) stated that "it all starts with skills." We believe he is absolutely correct. Ellis then described two types of skills: (1) work-content skills based on a specialized body of knowledge needed for work and (2) transferable skills, which consist of skills and abilities that are needed for workplace success but are not tied to any one particular discipline or content area. So your knowledge of human behavior and psychological research would be your work-content skills, and your problem-solving, critical thinking, and listening skills would be examples of transferable skills. As a preview, there are many organizations that study what employers desire from a college graduate with regard to skills and abilities. The National Association of Colleges and Employers (NACE, 2011) reported employers' ranking of the importance of skills and qualities (see the left side of Table 6.1). On the right side of Table 6.1 is a listing (not ranked) of "know-how" skills and abilities to learn in college (Coplin, 2003). Even though the phrases are not identical in all cases (and ignoring their ranking), you can begin to see the themes and the overlap from these two sources as to what is important for college graduates to be able to know and do as they enter the workforce.

Table 6.1   Example Comparison of Skills Listings

Ranked, Most Important First (NACE, 2011)	Unranked (Coplin, 2003)
Communication skills (verbal)	Establishing a work ethic
Strong work ethic	Developing physical skills (healthy behaviors)
Teamwork skills/works well with others	Communicating verbally
Analytical skills	Communicating in writing
Initiative skills	Working directly with people
Problem-solving skills	Influencing people
Communication skills (written)	Gathering information
Interpersonal skills (relates well to others)	Using quantitative tools
Computer-solving skills	Asking and answering the right questions
Flexibility/adaptability skills	Solving problems

In this chapter, we address the broad transferable skills first, and then we present the current thinking from psychology educators about skills and abilities needed to attain a good job with your bachelor's degree in psychology. Interestingly, Coplin (2003) offered "extra credit" advice about what new graduates can do to help stand out in a crowded field. His suggestions included (a) gaining software expertise beyond Word and Excel, (b) mastering in-depth knowledge of any field (such as psychology), (c) developing foreign language skills, (d) emphasizing artistic and music knowledge/skills, (e) stressing sports skills, and (f) pursuing pleasure activities. The well-rounded individual is a more valuable employee from Coplin's perspective.

What Are the Basic Skills Valued in the 21st Century Workplace?

There has been a long-standing interest in understanding the knowledge, skills, and abilities that lead to success for any employee in the workplace, not just new graduates making the transition from college to career. If we were to provide you with a comprehensive summary of all the research efforts underway to understand workplace skills and competencies, it could easily fill up its own book. Here we describe three snapshots of different approaches that organizations have taken to characterize and describe the knowledge and skills that graduates need for workplace success. In 2007, the Partnership for 21st Century Skills organization reported on voter opinions (i.e., the electorate) about the importance of skills; those skills, in rank order (starting with the highest), were reading comprehension, computer and technology skills, critical thinking and problem-solving skills, ethics and social responsibility, written communications, teamwork and collaboration, oral communications, lifelong learning and self-direction, mathematics (including algebra, geometry, and trigonometry), leadership, creativity and innovation, media literacy, global awareness, and science (including biology, chemistry, and physics). You can see the overlap here between this more current effort and previous efforts.

A different organizational structure from the skills needed by today's students was offered by the Association of American Colleges and Universities (2002) in suggesting that current college graduates need to be *intentional* learners who can adapt quickly, integrate knowledge, and engage in lifelong learning. Specific characteristics of intentional learners include being empowered (possessing a mastery of intellectual and useful skills), informed (about a knowledge base from the natural and social sciences, including inquiry methods), and responsible (for personal actions and civic values).

One last snapshot to contribute to this brief overview of skills conceptualizations is the view offered by the Lumina Foundation (2011) and its Degree Qualifications Profile (DPQ). The DPQ is a framework that articulates what college students should be able to know and do upon graduation. This is a broad formulation and not specific to any one degree program or disciplinary specialty. The DPQ consists of five fundamental areas of learning: (1) broad, integrative knowledge; (2) specialized knowledge; (3) intellectual skills; (4) applied learning; and (5) civic learning. The Lumina Foundation worked carefully to define each of these five areas and suggests that institutions can be depicted by a graphic "web" that demonstrates emphasis areas for each of the five dimensions; the web also considers the type of institution (public, private, etc.) and type of degree (associate's, bachelor's, etc.). Thus, the DPQ is an organizational approach to studying institutional achievement rather than individual student achievement.

Connecting College to Career

What do all these types of models and snapshots mean for college students and, more specifically, for psychology students? Thinking ahead and being planful about this upcoming stage of your career development might allow you to hone some of the desired workplace skills now, while still an undergraduate student. In fact, Ware (2001), using a typical listing of skills employers seek, asked enrolled students to generate examples of student products and experiences that would allow for skills development. Thus, you can consider the advice provided in Table 6.2 as peer-to-peer advice regarding what you can do—*now*—as an undergraduate to prepare for the pending transition from college to career.

As you can see from Ware (2001), you can make direct connections from your undergraduate experiences to those expectations in the workforce. As presented from the previous literature, however, there is more at stake than just the communication, cognitive, and social skills depicted in Table 6.2. Through a brief historical review and summary of current efforts, a more complex constellation of desired skills emerges. For example, Carnevale, Gainer, and Meltzer (1990) grouped

Table 6.2   Work-Related Transferable Skills With Student-Generated Examples

Skills Employers Seek	Student Products and Experiences
Communication Skills	
Writing	Wrote essays for scholarships while applying for colleges and graduate schools
	Prepared a research article and submitted it for publication
Speaking	Presented a speech to a group of students on a retreat
	Explained the strengths of our university to parents and prospective students
	Discussed research project in small groups, explained the project to our participants, and talked to professor about our findings
Cognitive Skills	
Coping with deadline pressure	Prepared manuscripts in advance of deadlines
	Completed reports on time when they were vital to patient treatment
	Refined an experiment to execute our study with a limited number of participants
Research	Wrote numerous manuscripts that required gathering information from a variety of sources
	Conducted a job search and made contacts with people, asking them about the nature of their work
Planning	Scheduled study time in preparation for several major tests
	Balanced homework, classes, extracurricular time, and time for myself
	Balanced when to study and when to write papers
Social Skills	
Human relations	Dealt with older patients, sick children, and families as a hospital volunteer
	Worked as a physical therapy aid to maximize quality of care and minimize waste of time
	Mediated between my roommates to ensure that tasks (e.g., paying bills) were completed
	Resolved differences between players and coaches
Negotiating/arbitrating/ organizing/managing/ coordinating	Organized a benefit concert
	Organized workers for a Habitat for Humanity project
	Coordinated dates, space, exhibitors, advertisers, and nurses for a health fair

Supervising	Monitored and directed the members of a team in my capacity as captain
	Ensured that personnel in training attended required clinics and completed research projects and manuscripts
	Monitored a research project and gave directions

16 skills identified by the American Society of Training and Development, which Hettich (1998, p. 56) offered as one method of highlighting the salient characteristics of the college-to-career transition:

- Learning to learn: the foundation skills on which all others are based
- Reading, writing, and computation: technical skills that employers consider basic for entry and advancement
- Oral communication and listening: skills that enable people to communicate in their jobs
- Problem solving and creative thinking: skills that enable employees to think and act flexibly
- Self-esteem, motivation/goal setting, and employability/career development: developmental skills that help people maintain their job and advance
- Interpersonal skills, teamwork, and negotiation: skills that enable people to work together in groups
- Organizational effectiveness and leadership: the "influencing" skills that help individuals navigate through the organization

From all the multiple models presented in this chapter, there is some convergence about what is expected from college graduates in the workplace. Now, let's narrow our focus. What does past and current research tell us about the specific expectations for psychology graduates?

Psychology-Specific Data About Desired Workplace Skills

Just as there is a historical trail of studies about the general expectations of college students and what they should be able to know and do upon graduation, specialized efforts in regard to psychology majors and undergraduate education have been underway for some time (Clough, 1993; Edwards & Smith, 1988; Hayes, 1997). Landrum and Harrold (2003) surveyed 87 employers of psychology graduates from three different states and asked for importance ratings on 88 different skills and abilities. The top 10 most important skills and abilities (beginning with the most important) were (1) listening skills; (2) ability to work with others as part of a work team; (3) getting along with others; (4)

desire and ability to learn; (5) willingness to learn new, important skills; (6) focus on customers/clients; (7) interpersonal relationship skills; (8) adaptability to changing situations; (9) ability to suggest solutions to problems; and (10) problem-solving skills. If such a study is representative of employer opinions, then there appears to have been a shift in emphasis from work-content skills to transferable skills.

Other research efforts focus specifically on undergraduate psychology majors as well. For instance, O'Hare and McGuinness (2004) surveyed undergraduate psychology majors, graduates, academic psychologists, and professional practitioners about skills developed by psychology majors and found that three themes or factors emerged from the 50 skills evaluated:

- *Thinking skills* (interpretation, evaluation, hypothesis generation and testing, critical thinking and analysis)
- *Self-management skills* (time management, self-discipline, organizational skills, public speaking)
- *Corporate management skills* (managing people and resources, adaptability, networking ability, empathy)

In many ways, these skills and categories do overlap with previous efforts on a more general scale. Kruger and Zechmeister (2001) developed a skills-experience inventory for psychology majors, in which current students self-reported their opportunities to develop academic skills. Kruger and Zechmeister asked students to rate their level of exposure to develop 90 different skills in these 10 general areas: written/oral communications, information gathering, groups/organizations/community, interpersonal/counseling/interviewing/mentoring, behavior management supervision/teaching, individual differences/special populations/cultural diversity, critical thinking/problem solving, research methodology/statistics, ethics/values, and technology/computer. This approach led to interesting observations. For example, when Kruger and Zechmeister asked freshman and senior psychology majors to rate exposure levels, senior exposure scores were significantly higher than freshman exposure scores on all but three scales: groups/organizations, behavior management, and individual differences. Thus, patterns of results can not only be informative to the student hoping to maximize opportunities over the course of an undergraduate career but also can help departments assess the resources and access to opportunities that student may or may not be receiving.

Time Out: Reflective Question

Choose one of the skills studies summarized above and one of the courses in which you are enrolled. Comparing the skills list to the assignments and requirements in your course, which particular skills from the list does your course explicitly or implicitly help you strengthen?

Broad Skill Sets and the Covert Curriculum

Written Communication Skills

"No matter what you major in, if you can't answer the phone, make a presentation, do a spreadsheet, or write a business letter, nobody needs you" (Combs, 2000, p. 14). In 2004, the National Commission on Writing (sponsored by the College Board) published the results of a survey of 64 human resource directors of major American corporations, and the following key results emerged:

- When considering salaried employees, writing is a "threshold skill" for both employment and promotion. Writing appears to be a ticket in or a ticket out. Half the respondents indicated that writing ability comes into play when hiring new professionals.
- "People who cannot write and communicate clearly will not be hired and are unlikely to last long enough to be considered for promotion" (p. 3).
- Writing responsibility spans two thirds of salaried employees in large American corporations.
- At least 80% of companies in the service and finance, insurance, and real estate sectors of the economy report that they assess writing ability during the hiring process.
- Half the corporations seriously consider one's writing skills when making decisions about promotion.

Practicing the type of writing required in the business world as an undergraduate provides an opportunity for a successful transition from college to career. Researchers for the National Commission on Writing (2004) indicated that e-mail and oral presentations are everywhere in today's business world, and more than half the survey respondents indicated that technical reports, formal reports, and memos and correspondence are very common forms of written communication. Accuracy and clarity are important but are more important in some business sectors than in others—the same pattern of results holds true for the visual appeal of written communications. Excellent writing skills are expected of everyone; thus, the lack of writing ability is more often a factor in termination decisions than in promotion decisions (those employees around long enough to be eligible for promotion are assumed to have the requisite writing skills).

What does this mean for you as an undergraduate? Embrace courses and opportunities that allow you the chance to hone your writing skills. This may seem counterintuitive to a least-resistance approach to college and course scheduling, but think of it as "pay me now or pay me later." That is, you can struggle, work hard, and improve your writing abilities in college where the worst result would be a low grade, or you can cruise in college and then struggle and work hard to improve your writing abilities while on the job. However, the stakes are higher postgraduation; not writing at the expected level could mean termination rather than a low grade. Russell (2011) offered multiple suggestions for improving your writing abilities (see Table 6.3).

Table 6.3 Writing Considerations

- Think about your audience and the appropriate format (e.g., e-mail, report, letter).
- Make your writing reader-friendly with section headings, paragraph subheadings, graphs, charts, and bullet points.
- Proofread your work or get someone else to review your work for accuracy, spelling, punctuation, and grammar.
- Be clear, avoiding jargon and acronyms.
- Be concise. Brevity is a skill.
- Be professional, especially in e-mails. Remember that anything you send can be forwarded.
- Employers often equate a person's writing ability with his or her intellectual ability, so project a professional image.
- Be comfortable with revisions. Everyone's first draft can be improved via revisions.
- Practice your writing and seek constructive feedback.
- Take classes to improve your technical and creative writing skills.
- Read your work out loud, verbatim, to catch mistakes.
- Cite references, and do not plagiarize others' work.
- It's not the reader's job to decipher the message; it's the writer's job to make the reader's job easier.

Time Out: Exercise

In your records, whether paper or electronic, retrieve the three term papers or major writing assignments you most recently handed in for a course. Now review your work compared with the suggestions in Table 6.3. Upon self-reflection, did your writing consistently adhere to the principles and suggestions offered? Why or why not?

E-mail communication is so prevalent in our business (and personal) world today that the topic deserves special consideration. Pollack (2007) offered excellent advice for e-mailing as a professional, suggesting the following:

- *Do not* use cute acronyms in professional e-mails (e.g., LOL, OMG).
- *Do* use proper capitalization and punctuation.
- *Do not* use emoticons in professional e-mails.
- *Do* limit yourself to one exclamation point (!) per professional e-mail.
- *Do not* leave the subject line blank.
- *Do not* mark every e-mail as "urgent."
- *Do* proofread every e-mail before clicking "send."
- *Do* add the e-mail address last; that way, if you accidentally click "send" while writing, the unaddressed message will go nowhere.
- *Do* avoid instant messaging with professional contacts.
- *Do not* forward dirty jokes.

Of course, the professional standards of any particular workplace will vary, but the above list is a good starting point in a new job situation. If the company's standard practice is to communicate via instant messages, then use your own judgment as to whether that mode of communication allows you to highlight your best efforts.

Statistics/Numerical Literacy Skills

If we were to ask college students which two academic areas they fear the most, two likely answers would be writing and math. Math anxiety may be an underlying factor for why your math skills are not as well developed as they could be and why you avoid courses that involve math (Ellis, 2009). However, most undergraduate programs in psychology include a substantial dose of mathematics, including one course (or more) in statistics. Oftentimes, unfounded assumptions provide the roots for math anxiety (Ellis, 2009), characterized by student beliefs such as (a) math calls for logic only, no imagination; (b) there is only one way to solve a math problem correctly; and (c) there is some secret (that I don't know) for doing well in math.

The reality is that you will depend on math skills, to some extent, for the rest of your life. Especially if you aspire to higher-paying, professional, white-collar jobs, math skills and abilities will be essential. Thus, you'll need to have the confidence to be able to analyze an Excel spreadsheet accurately and to recognize errors when they occur or trends when they appear. You can attain these skills, but it takes practice. When we have anxiety about a topic or situation, however, we typically avoid it. People with a fear of snakes do not just decide that the fear is gone and begin to embrace snakes with open arms—they have to work at it. So if you have math anxiety, you're going to have to work at it, because it will not likely go away on its own. Some of the best advice we can offer is for you to take more than the bare minimum of math courses required for your major. Remember, the stakes are relatively low in college (getting a bad grade) compared with the workplace (losing your job). College provides a safe place to land—a safety net, if you will. So if you confront your math anxiety by taking more math courses, we believe you'll be on track for future success. Make sure you optimally use the resources that may be available to you, such as math drop-in tutoring centers or math anxiety workshops organized by a counseling and testing center on campus.

But there is another reason to face your math and writing anxiety head-on. Your authors and other educators have a hunch (although we cannot cite any research studies to support this hunch) that gaining skills and abilities that are hard to learn and that others avoid could make you more marketable and employable. Think about it. If mass numbers of college students avoid becoming proficient at writing or math, then those who are proficient will have an advantage. There are hundreds of companies (Google it!) that advertise on the Internet for term paper assistance, ranging from sites that provide actual coaching to sites where you can buy term papers to sites where you can pay per page to have an original term paper written for you. So students who have not developed their writing skills and/or do not have confidence in their writing skills will sometimes plagiarize or pay others to do the work for them. Our assertion is that getting good at the skills that are a challenge to learn and that others avoid developing can make you more marketable.

Introducing the Covert Curriculum

When academics and students think about the curriculum, they are implicitly (by default) thinking about the overt curriculum—that is, the sequence of courses and experiences that, if satisfactorily completed, earns you a bachelor's degree at the conclusion of your undergraduate degree. Depending on your particular institution and even the type of calendar (e.g., semester, trimester, term), the overt curriculum is defined by the 120, 128, or 180 credits or units you must earn to graduate. As a general rule, the overt curriculum is divided into thirds: one third of your coursework is your general education requirements (core, foundations), another third fulfills your psychology degree requirements, and the final third consists of electives. Of course, your results may vary depending on your institution—these are just generalities. A fair amount of work is available on the psychology curriculum (Brewer et al., 1993), on trends in curricular offerings (Perlman & McCann, 1999, 2005), and on recommendations for future reform (Dunn et al., 2010).

Discouragingly, sometimes students (and even some faculty) think about the overt curriculum as "filling the buckets" toward graduation, and the phrase "getting it out of the way" is often used in reference to a core course. We believe this is an unfortunate characterization of coursework in the overt curriculum, because every course (including those outside of your major) provides opportunities to strengthen a particular skill or ability or increase knowledge that can be useful in your post-baccalaureate career. Our advice is, take advantage of the opportunities available to you and maximize your learning—sometimes the courses you believe you are "getting out of the way" can end up being the most valuable or most inspirational courses of your undergraduate career, such as the speech communication, writing, and math/statistics–oriented courses.

In contrast to the *overt curriculum,* Appleby (2001) and Hettich (1998) discussed the less obvious or *covert curriculum.* The covert curriculum comprises those "numerous, routine skill-related activities, behaviors, and attitudes that are transacted inside *and* outside of classrooms. Collectively, they reflect a student's overall work orientation and habits" (Hettich, 1998, p. 52). According to Appleby (2001),

> colleges and universities often call these "lifelong learning skills" because the covert curriculum refers not to the specific information that students acquire during their formal education (i.e., the contents of their education), but to how successfully they can continue to acquire information after their formal education has ended (i.e., the processes they developed as they acquired the contents of their education). (p. 28)

In other words, the covert curriculum addresses *how* to learn, as opposed to *what* to learn (Landrum & Davis, 2010).

The parallel ideas of an overt and covert curriculum are not unique to psychology. Wilson (2005) provided an entire directory of different types of curricula, and a common alternative name for the covert curriculum is the "hidden curriculum." Wilson depicted the hidden curriculum as the implied learning that occurs in school—that is, what is learned from the organization of a school or particular course, what we glean from role models, etc. The covert curriculum is about what students learn in the midst of studying the content matter of the course—a point that Wear and Skillicorn (2009) made in their research concerning psychiatry education. In their discussion of the covert curriculum in medical education, Puymbroeck, Austin, and McCormick (2010) noted that curriculum practices in higher education are often unstated, unexamined, and unacknowledged—that is, covert. In discussing the importance of the covert/hidden curriculum in medical education, Hafferty (1998, p. 403; as quoted in Puymbroeck et al., 2010) stated,

> Not all of what is taught during medical training is captured in course catalogs, class syllabi, lecture notes and handouts, or the mountains of documents compiled during accreditation reviews. Indeed, a great deal of what is taught—and most of what is learned—in medical school takes place not within formal course offerings but within medicine's "hidden curriculum."

Covert Curriculum Skills and Abilities

The skills presented below (with brief descriptions) (from Appleby, 2001; Hettich, 1998; Landrum & Davis, 2010) should be useful in the lifelong pursuit of knowledge at work and in your daily life. Remember that these learning opportunities might occur in general education classes, service learning situations, internships, or even volunteering in the community.

- *Read with comprehension and identify major points.* People employed in management positions are constantly in search of new ideas and methods to help them perform their jobs more successfully. They understand they must keep up with the current literature and innovations in their profession and obtain relevant information from other sources.
- *Speak and write in a clear, organized, and persuasive manner.* The ability to communicate in a clear, organized, and persuasive manner is one of the most crucial characteristics of successfully employed people. Failure to do so leaves others confused about what we have written or said (because we are unclear), convinced that we do not know what we are talking or writing about (because we are unorganized), and unlikely to do what we ask them to do (because we are not persuasive).
- *Write in a particular style.* Not only do you need to be able to write clearly; you need to be able to write in a particular style. Psychologists use the *Publication Manual of the American Psychological Association* (now in its sixth edition). Although future employers may not require writing in this particular style, the ability to follow the format guidelines of businesses

and clients and the ability to follow precise instructions are important. Attention to detail does matter to employers.

- *Listen attentively.* Successful employees listen carefully and attentively to their supervisors' instructions and team members' contributions, understand what these instructions mean (or ask for clarification to improve their understanding), and then carry out these instructions in an accurate and complete manner.

- *Take accurate notes.* Employees must often listen to others and accurately remember what they hear. This process can take place in a one-on-one situation or in groups. Unless the amount of information provided is small or the employee's memory is large, it is wise to take notes.

- *Master efficient memory strategies.* All jobs require employees to remember things (e.g., customers' names, meeting dates and times, locations of important information, etc.). Memory refers to the ability to select, store, and use information, and these skills are vital to effective and efficient workplace behavior. The results of a lack of memory skills are confusion, disorganization, and incompetence.

- *Develop critical thinking skills.* Employees must not only be able to remember vital information (i.e., *retention*) but also *comprehend* it so they can communicate it to others in an understandable manner. They must *apply* the information they comprehend to solve problems in the workplace. They must *analyze* large, complex problems or sources of information into smaller, more manageable units. They must locate, gather, and *synthesize* (i.e., combine) information from a variety of different sources into new and creative ideas. Finally, they must *evaluate* ideas and methods by applying appropriate criteria to determine their value or usefulness.

- *Submit assignments on time and in acceptable form.* Employers pay their employees to perform jobs accurately, completely, and in a timely manner. Employees are terminated if they cannot perform their jobs (i.e., their work is incorrect, incomplete, and/or late). In fact, to gather more details about how to keep your first job after college, see Project 1 at the end of this chapter.

- *Behave in a responsible, punctual, mature, and respectful manner.* Employees who fail to show up for work (or are often late) or whose behaviors are immature or disrespectful are seldom employed for long.

- *Manage stress and conflict successfully.* Employees are often exposed to stressful working conditions and must work with less-than-perfect fellow employees. Stress and conflict management are essential skills for successful employees.

- *Organize the physical environment to maximize efficiency.* Employees must be able to organize their physical environments so they can perform their jobs competently and efficiently. Poor organizational skills often result in appearing confused, making mistakes, and losing important information.

- *Observe and evaluate the attitudes and behaviors of role models.* Successful employees quickly learn the culture of their organization by observing their supervisors and other successful employees. Learning which behaviors to avoid and which to imitate is a crucial skill for an employee who wishes to remain with an organization, receive above-average salary increases, and earn promotions.

■ *Maintain an accurate planner or calendar.* Successful employees in today's fast-paced world must be capable of managing their time and controlling their complicated schedules. Behaving in a temporally clueless manner (e.g., forgetting meetings, neglecting appointments, and missing deadlines) is a signpost on the road to the unemployment office. Select an electronic calendaring system (e.g., Microsoft Outlook, Google Calendar, or Apple iCal), and learn this software to avoid embarrassing scheduling mistakes.

■ *Work as a productive member of a team.* Employers pay employees to perform complex tasks that almost always require some degree of teamwork—very few people work alone. The ability to work as a productive member of a successful team and to be seen as a "team player" requires a set of crucial skills and characteristics that must be acquired through practice. Teamwork is a key skill valued by employers.

■ *Interact successfully with a wide variety of people.* The working world is filled with people who differ in many ways. Successful employees are those who have developed the ability to interact in a congenial and productive manner with a wide variety of people (e.g., a supervisor who is older, a client of a different race, or a coworker with a different sexual orientation). Adaptability and sensitivity to sociocultural differences are key skills.

■ *Seek feedback about performance and use it to improve future performance.* Successful employees are interested in the quality of their performance, and they usually gain rewards such as promotions or raises when they improve. Unsuccessful employees remain at lower positions and pay levels or are terminated. Savvy employees understand that their performance must satisfy not only their own standards of quality but also the standards of their supervisor(s).

■ *Accept responsibility for your own behavior and attitudes.* Being able to act in a responsible manner is the cornerstone of personal growth and professional maturity in any occupation. College is the perfect time to learn how to take responsibility for your own actions (rather than blaming your failures on others) and to understand that the way you interpret external circumstances, not the circumstances themselves, determines how you will respond to them.

■ *Utilize technology wisely.* Future employees need to be technologically sophisticated to qualify for many jobs. Word processing, using spreadsheets, understanding databases, working with statistical programs, and doing library searches using bibliographic databases are important aspects of technological literacy.

As you can see, no one course could accomplish all those goals. However, by carefully examining this list, you might better understand why college teachers structure their courses the way they do. Over the course of your undergraduate education, the covert curriculum should provide multiple chances to develop and sharpen these skills and abilities.

Time Out: Reflective Question

Reflect on a part-time job or major activity in which you are involved outside of the classroom, and identify those covert curriculum skills that are most important. Which skills should you be developing that you are not?

Closing Comments

The clear emphasis of this chapter is identifying skills important to your future. Sometimes those skills may be obvious in the design of a class assignment or course, but other skills may be covert and turn out to be vitally important. Regardless of whether professors overtly do this for you or not, students need to be able to see the connections between course tasks and coursework and how these experiences connect to future challenges. By seeing the value of working in groups for a class assignment, for example, you may realize that in-class group work is actually preparation for many tasks in the future where working in teams, listening skills, and small-group leadership ability will be vital for success.

Be sure to pause and self-assess from time to time about your own competencies, and if you identify areas that need to be strengthened, seek out opportunities while still an undergraduate to gain practice and continue on the road to competency and perhaps expertise. Remember, such opportunities need not always be course based; many opportunities for growth exist outside of the classroom, such as serving as an officer in your local chapter of Psi Chi, volunteering in the community, serving as team manager for your intramural dodgeball team, helping a faculty member as a research or teaching assistant, and so on. Refer back to Chapter 3 for specific advice on making the most of your opportunities now.

Getting Involved

Journal Starters

1. Are there skills that you value that are not included in this chapter? Or are there more specific skills, such as writing for a particular genre or using a particular type of technology, that you would like to become more expert in? Explain why.

2. Why is expertise important in the workplace? How might the acquisition of skills help your short-term and long-term future?

3. How much time and practice does it take to acquire an expert skill set? You might be interested to know that in some areas of psychology, researchers have determined that it sometimes takes 10 years of practice to gain expertise—much the same as becoming an expert in chess. If you are able to identify key skills for your workplace and your professional future, how will you continue to learn and improve until you have attained expertise?

4. What are the most significant insights about skills that you have gained from reading this chapter?

Projects

1a. One of the major reasons your authors present to you these details about the covert curriculum is that we want you to be aware of these skills and abilities and to be planful about how you acquire and practice becoming adept in these areas. In a national survey of employers of new college graduates, Gardner (2007) was able to identify the most frequent reasons why new hires are disciplined on the job; furthermore, of those behaviors warranting disciplinary action, he identified which were the most frequent reasons for termination. See Table 6.4 for an overview of Gardner's results. Note that the reasons presented in bold are those most commonly cited for termination of new hires.

Take a moment and truly reflect on each of these 10 items. Now think about your current behaviors as a college student. How many of these items are you consistently guilty of today? If you persist in some of these areas, what impact do you think that might have on (a) your ability to get a job and (b) your ability to keep a job?

1b. Now think about how an instructor might structure his or her course. Will you have opportunities throughout the semester to practice avoidance of the behaviors in Table 6.4? How might your knowledge of this list impact your course selection, such as if two sections of a course were being offered but one included group work and the other did not? Or if one section was writing intensive and the other was not? What would be your best course

Table 6.4 *Factors Influencing the Disciplining and Termination of New Hires*

Frequency (starting with most frequent)	*Reasons for Discipline*
1	**Lack of work ethic/commitment**
2	**Unethical behavior**
3	**Failure to follow instructions**
4	Ineffective in teams
5	Failure to take initiative
6	**Missing assignments/deadlines**
7	Unable to communicate effectively—verbally
8	**Inappropriate use of technology**
9	**Being late for work**
10	Unable to communicate effectively—writing

Note: The items in bold are reasons for new hires to be terminated.

route if you are thinking ahead about your transition from college to career?

1c. In Table 6.5, across from each of the reasons for discipline, write your concrete strategies for avoiding these behaviors and characteristics while in college. Be specific and planful—what can you do to avoid increasing your probability for disciplinary action and termination?

Table 6.5   Avoidance Strategy Plan to Help Prevent Disciplinary Action and Termination

Reasons for Discipline	Specific Avoidance Strategies (What will I do so I can avoid these behaviors and characteristics?)
Lack of work ethic/commitment	
Unethical behavior	
Failure to follow instructions	
Ineffective in teams	
Failure to take initiative	
Missing assignments/deadlines	
Unable to communicate effectively—verbally	
Inappropriate use of technology	
Being late for work	
Unable to communicate effectively—writing	

Source: Gardner (2007).
Note: The items in bold are reasons for new hires to be terminated.

References

Appleby, D. C. (2001, Spring). The covert curriculum: The lifelong learning skills you can learn in college. *Eye on Psi Chi, 5*(3), 28–31, 34.

Association of American Colleges and Universities. (2002). *Greater expectations: A new vision for learning as a nation goes to college*. Washington, DC: Author.

Brewer, C. L., Hopkins, J. R., Kimble, G. A., Matlin, M. W., McCann, L. I., McNeil, O. V., . . . Saundra. (1993). Curriculum. In T. V. McGovern (Ed.), *Handbook for enhancing undergraduate education in psychology* (pp. 161–182). Washington, DC: American Psychological Association.

Carnevale, A. P., Gainer, L. J., & Meltzer, A. S. (1990). *Workplace basics: The essential skills employers want*. San Francisco, CA: Jossey-Bass.

Clough, J. (1993). Which knowledge and skills should psychology graduates have? Balancing the needs of the individual, employers, the science and the profession. *Australian Psychologist, 28*, 42–44.

Combs, P. (2000). *Major in success: Make college easier, fire up your dreams, and get a very cool job* (3rd ed.). Berkeley, CA: Ten Speed Press.

Coplin, B. (2003). *10 things employers want you to learn in college: The know-how you need to succeed.* Berkeley, CA: Ten Speed Press.

Dunn, D. S., Brewer, C. L., Cautin, R. L., Gurung, R. A. R., Keith, K. D., McGregor, L. N., . . . Voight, M. J. (2010). The undergraduate psychology curriculum: Call for a core. In D. F. Halpern (Ed.), *Undergraduate education in psychology: A blueprint for the future of the discipline* (pp. 47–61). Washington, DC: American Psychological Association.

Edwards, J., & Smith, K. (1988). What skills and knowledge do potential employers value in baccalaureate psychologists? In P. J. Woods (Ed.), *Is psychology for them?* (pp. 102–111). Washington, DC: American Psychological Association.

Ellis, D. (2009). *From master student to master employee: Annotated instructor's edition* (2nd ed.). St. Charles, IL: College Survival/Houghton Mifflin.

Gardner, P. (2007). *Moving up or moving out? Factors that influence the promoting or firing of new college hires* (CERI Research Brief 1-2007). East Lansing: Michigan State University Collegiate Employment Research Institute.

Hayes, N. (1997, July). The distinctive skills of a psychology graduate. *APA Monitor,* p. 33.

Hettich, P. (1998). *Learning skills for college and career* (2nd ed.). Pacific Grove, CA: Brooks/Cole.

Kruger, D. J., & Zechmeister, E. B. (2001). A skills-experience inventory for the undergraduate psychology major. *Teaching of Psychology, 28,* 249–253.

Landrum, R. E., & Davis, S. F. (2010). *The psychology major: Career options and strategies for success* (4th ed.). Upper Saddle River, NJ: Prentice Hall/Pearson.

Landrum, R. E., & Harrold, R. (2003). What employers want from psychology graduates. *Teaching of Psychology, 30,* 131–133.

Lumina Foundation. (2011, January). *The Degree Qualifications Profile.* Retrieved from http://www.luminafoundation.org/publications/The_Degree_Qualifications_Profile.pdf

National Association of Colleges and Employers. (2011, October 26). Job outlook: The candidate skills/qualities employers want. In *Job outlook 2012.* Retrieved from http://www.naceweb.org/s10262011/candidate_skills_employer_qualities/

National Commission on Writing. (2004, September). *Writing: A ticket to work . . . or a ticket out; A survey of business leaders.* New York, NY: College Entrance Examination Board. Retrieved from http://www.collegeboard.com/prod_downloads/writingcom/writing-ticket-to-work.pdf

O'Hare, L., & McGuinness, C. (2004). Skills and attributes developed by psychology undergraduates: Ratings by undergraduates, postgraduates, academic psychologists and professional practitioners. *Psychology Learning and Teaching, 4,* 35–42.

Partnership for 21st Century Skills. (2007). *Beyond the three Rs: Voter attitudes toward 21st century skills.* Tucson, AZ: Author.

Perlman, B., & McCann, L. I. (1999). The structure of the psychology undergraduate curriculum. *Teaching of Psychology, 26,* 171–176.

Perlman, B., & McCann, L. I. (2005). Undergraduate research experiences in psychology: A national study of courses and curricula. *Teaching of Psychology, 32,* 5–14.

Pollack, L. (2007). *Getting from college to career: 90 things to do before you join the real world.* New York, NY: HarperCollins.

Puymbroeck, M. V., Austin, D. R., & McCormick, B. P. (2010). Beyond curriculum reform: Therapeutic recreation's hidden curriculum. *Therapeutic Recreation Journal, 44,* 213–222.

Russell, J. E. A. (2011, May 22). Are writing skills necessary anymore? *Washington Post.* Retrieved from http://www.washingtonpost.com/business/capitalbusiness/career-coach-are-writing-skills-necessary-anymore/2011/05/18/AFJLUF9G_story.html

Ware, M. E. (2001). Pursuing a career with a bachelor's degree in psychology. In S. Walfish & A. K. Hess (Eds.), *Succeeding in graduate school: The career guide for psychology students* (pp. 11–30). Mahwah, NJ: Erlbaum.

Wear, D., & Skillicorn, J. (2009). Hidden in plain sight: The formal, informal, and hidden curricula of a psychiatry clerkship. *Academic Medicine, 84,* 451–458.

Wilson, L. O. (2005). Curriculum: Different types. Retrieved from http://www.uwsp.edu/education/lwilson/curric/curtyp.htm

CHAPTER 7

Jump-Start Your Job Search

by John Jameson, BA in industrial/organization psychology

Do what you say you're going to do—what you say to others, and what you say to yourself. Offer value. Cultivate relationships. Do it even when you don't need anything in return.

—Jeffrey Gitomer (2011), author and founder of TrainOne

You are on your way to joining the full-time workforce and delighting in the opportunity to become a young professional. Since earning a bachelor's degree in industrial and organizational psychology, I have applied the skills and knowledge acquired in psychology coursework to empower job seekers, conduct research, and manage programs. By investing time now to develop your job-search skills, you can leverage (a business term meaning to exert influence on or control) a psychology education in future career pursuits and in the workplace. Up to this point, you have explored work preparation strategies accessible in college and career planning concepts, and you have learned the importance of looking inward to use self-knowledge to your advantage. In this chapter, you are introduced to an assortment of techniques and information, including job-search strategies you will need to succeed in an interview, which I call a job-search tool kit. By the way, *the information and suggestions contained below can also be used productively when you search for part-time jobs during your remaining time in college.*

Time Out: Reflective Questions

Topics presented in previous chapters will help answer the questions below. Think about the jobs and potential career paths you are considering as you answer them.

1. What do I need to know about the jobs and careers I am pursuing?

2. What are my most reliable sources of information?

3. Who can I ask for help and advice?

Compared with past decades, employees now have less tenure with each employer, and as the nature of work evolves in the 21st century, it is possible you will search for a job every few years. The cycle of self-evaluation—creating a résumé and cover letter, networking, applying for jobs, interviewing, and managing follow-up—will occur again and again (Levitt & Harwood, 2010). Therefore, the importance of continuously cultivating professional relationships and honoring commitments in an increasingly transparent and connected society is integral to a job seeker's success. Further, consistently managing relationships and looking for ways to help others along the way makes it easier to ask for help when you are in need of advice or job-search assistance. By obtaining this information now, you can use the job-search tool kit and your foundational skills in subsequent searches. In the next section, we explore the first component in your tool kit, a winning résumé.

Résumés

The purpose of a résumé is to represent your abilities and experiences in a manner that makes the reader want to know more. Prior to writing your résumé, thoroughly review your education, skills, and accomplishments. If you feel nervous because you have little or no work experience, include other experiences that may be attractive to prospective employers—for example, academic honors, participation in community groups, sports, and recognitions received. Among the skills employers search for on résumés are ability to work on a team, leadership, and communication skills (National Association of Colleges and Employers [NACE], 2011). To what extent did you develop such skills when you were serving in volunteer activities, youth groups, or as captain of your sports team? The format used to describe these activities is similar to summarizing work experiences. Consider the example from a student résumé on the following page.

Employers prefer résumés that are clear, uncomplicated, and quick and easy to read. If you cannot clearly explain each experience reflected on your résumé in detail during an interview, it does not belong on your résumé (Levitt & Harwood, 2010). You can help yourself and the reader by highlighting the skills you believe the employer seeks. Let's take a closer look at the contents of an effective résumé.

LEADERSHIP EXPERIENCE

West Chatham Panthers—Chicago, IL 06/2011–11/2011

Assistant Coach

- Taught a little league team baseball fundamentals and the importance of sportsmanship

- Organized team practices and developed rapid response system to communicate game delays and cancellations which increased team support and attendance at games

Introductory Statements

Hiring authorities are persons whose opinions positively or negatively influence the employer's hiring decisions. Their titles may include *recruiter, human resources manager,* or *department manager.* Frequently, they are able to determine within seconds of viewing your résumé if your qualifications justify a follow-up phone interview. Located at the top of your résumé should be a concise statement of your objective or a summary crafted to the job you are seeking. After reading that statement, a hiring authority should understand why you are applying for a particular job and why you are a good fit.

Psychology baccalaureates can be employed in a variety of positions and industries; therefore, include analytic, interpersonal, and problem-solving skills that are relevant to many jobs so your résumé is tailored to different positions. Also, highlight those transferable skills you possess that an employer is seeking (they are usually found in the section of the job description that addresses responsibilities and preferred/required qualifications), as well as other skills if your previous experiences justify them. For example, if you apply to a nonprofit position and the job description requires customer service experience, highlight your experience to the extent it is justified. Capturing the hiring authority's attention with a tailored objective is a good first step to developing a winning résumé.

Résumé Formats

The most common résumé formats are chronological and functional. To create a *chronological* résumé, list the jobs in reverse chronological order with the most recent experience first, highlighting the accomplishments and transferable experiences in each bullet point. Dates are important because employers like to see patterns (e.g., of involvement in activities and groups) over a period of time.

If you have limited work experience, a *functional* format may be more appropriate because it emphasizes competencies and transferable skills (i.e., functions you performed). A benefit to using the functional résumé is that relevant work experiences are listed near the top even if they occurred early in your work history. Consider the following example: You are interested in working at a social service agency as a counselor serving disabled children. During past summer breaks, you volunteered with the local youth ministry organization and at a summer camp. Despite the fact that you have held four jobs since those volunteer activities, you can highlight the transferable skills you gained from your volunteer work near the top of your résumé using a functional format. Also, grouping several complementary skills together will increase their overall collective value. For instance, include statistical analysis, problem solving, and research methods together to add credibility to your application of psychology skills for a job that involves research. List the most relevant skills at the top of the functional résumé.

A combination chronological and functional résumé can reflect both transferable skills and chronological order. It is used primarily when you possess the main competencies needed for success in your desired job that are supported by an impressive progressive track record of experience with reputable employers (Sukiennik, Bendat, & Raufman, 2010).

Finally, creating concise *bulleted* statements on either type of résumé to capture your experiences can be difficult, so search for jobs online with the same or similar titles of your previous jobs and consult the position descriptions.

Time Out: Exercise

Review the chronological and functional formats on the following page and explain which format is more suitable for the jobs to which you are applying.

Emphasizing Results With Keywords and Phrases

In addition to describing the responsibilities you held with previous employers, show that your work had a positive impact (assuming that it did) on the group or organization associated with your experience. Showing details about results of your work enables the hiring authority to understand why you were tasked with particular job responsibilities.

Time Out: Reflective Questions

Think back to your previous work and activities, and answer the following questions where appropriate:

1. In what ways did your work impact the organization's profitability?

2. How many customers, orders, or projects did you service daily/weekly?

3. How many hours did you volunteer? What were the results of your work?

Example 1: Functional Rèsumè

Notice the skills have their own defined space

SKILLS SUMMARY

<u>Counseling</u> — Four years of *youth development* with an emphasis on active listening and behavioral self-management through identification of goals and values

<u>Administration</u> — Broad organizational and *administrative* abilities, including typing correspondence, compiling reports, and filing

<u>Leadership</u> — Served as a role model and led by example through volunteer and counseling roles with focus on *confidence building* and, *social development*

EMPLOYMENT HISTORY

Youth Group Volunteer – **Pinedale YMWA** – Pinedale, IL	02/2009 – Present
Camp Counselor (volunteer) – **Camp Thompson** – Pinedale, IL	05/2007 – Present
Research Intern – **Pinedale High School** – Pinedale, IL	06/2008 – 09/2006

Example 2: Chronological Rèsumè

Notice the skills are nested in the work experiences

WORK EXPERIENCE

Youth Group Volunteer – **Pinedale YMWA** – Pinedale, IL   02/2009 – Present
- Coordinated and led study groups, field trips, and scheduled guest speakers
- Created a positive experience for youth participants through active listening and developing creative group activities. Assisted in the *development of social values.*

Camp Counselor (volunteer) – **Camp Thompson** – Pinedale, IL   02/2007 – Present
- *Recreation program* development and *administration*
- Enabled youth to *develop confidence* and *coping strategies* by demonstrating *counseling abilities*
- Provided follow-up information to parents and guardians and addressed concerns

Research Intern – **Pinedale High School** – Pinedale, IL   06/2006 – 09/2006
- Supported a professor in a *research* study to understand the impact of different light on the photosynthesis of plants
- Sorted, proofread, and filed surveys; analyzed initial survey results and keyed survey information database; developed attention to detail and organizational skills

The examples above illustrate the presentation of an applicant's skills and employer experience in chronological and functional formats

Such questions help you think about the results of your work. Quantify the tasks you performed with numbers, where feasible, because it provides hiring authorities with a better understanding of the influence of your work and adds greater detail. Use dollar amounts and percentages, if possible. The key phrases below can be used multiple times and will assist in writing results-focused statements.

Resulting in . . .

Increasing . . .

Ensuring . . .

Enabling . . .

UNDESIRED: Worked hard to complete additional projects and help more clients

DESIRED: Worked overtime to complete an additional two projects daily, which enabled volunteers to meet the needs of 20 additional clients

Did you notice how use of *enabled* and *20 additional clients* described your results and provided a strong, clear picture through details? Quantifying job responsibilities and results-focused statements exemplifies the effect of your work and paints a clear picture for the reader.

Hanna, Radtke, and Suggett (2009) maintain that these "telegraphic phrases" (action verbs) strengthen the presentation of your experiences; they add sizzle and leave the distinct impression that you have been active. The accurate use of telegraphic phrases will describe with power the action you took in a particular job responsibility or activity. You must be honest, however, with the verbs you use.

Let's examine another contrasting pair of statements:

UNDESIRED: Talked to new employees to make sure they had a positive hiring experience and began working effectively

DESIRED: *Counseled* new employees to ensure they had a positive hiring experience, *resulting in* more immediate employee productivity

Notice how injecting action verbs and results in the desired statement provides a clearer picture and lets the reader know that your work had a positive impact on the organization. Additionally, you can create bullets using such terms each time you update your résumé. The following list of action verbs will get you started:

achieved, built, calculated, decreased, established, fostered, guided, initiated, launched, monitored, organized, proposed, restructured, strengthened, simplified, transformed

For additional examples, search the Internet for résumé action verbs or reference www.thesaurus.com. If you have limited job experience and the use of action verbs does not seem appropriate, create descriptive bullets by providing specific details. Examine the following examples for a librarian position.

> **DESIRED:** Accurately shelved an average of 300 books per shift, *demonstrating* attention to detail

> **DESIRED:** Answered about 25 patron questions per shift *to ensure* resources were utilized

The subtle but fundamental differences described above will set your résumé apart from those of other applicants. For further assistance with your résumé writing, visit www.resume.com.

Cover Letters

Cover letters are another essential component of the job-search tool kit because they serve several purposes. Cover letters (a) introduce the writer and the résumé, (b) indicate knowledge of and interest in the employer and position, (c) promote your experiences and transferable skills, and (d) invite an interview. "A well-constructed cover letter gets the hiring authority excited to view the résumé" (J. McGinty, personal communication, June 4, 2011). Like an excellent résumé, excellent cover letters should be tailored to the jobs you apply for, but the cover letter should also bridge the gap between the employer's needs (listed on the job description) and your résumé. A sure way to ruin your chances for an interview is to omit essential information. Rather than restate the experience listed on your résumé, provide specific examples of your past experience and the skills relevant to the position. Proofread your cover letter more than once, and ask a friend or family member to review it to ensure it is free of spelling, grammar, and punctuation errors and incomplete sentences. Study the following examples taken from the body of a cover letter.

> **UNDESIRED:** As an academic advisor at Jones State University (JSU) my primary responsibilities included meeting and servicing student needs, administering student paperwork, and working with team members to complete various projects in a timely manner.

> **DESIRED:** The ability to establish trust with students is essential in academic counseling and is a skill you are seeking in a new hire. I have developed this skill, along with a passion for helping others, through my experiences at Jones University and my previous experiences. As an advisor at JSU, I achieved a 100% student graduation rate by establishing trusting relationships that enabled me to effectively service student needs that supported their success.

The format of a cover letter can vary, but it must contain an introductory paragraph that explains why you are applying for the job, a paragraph that highlights your transferable skills, and a closing paragraph to invite feedback about the next steps.

Introductory Paragraph

Address the letter to a specific person using his or her full title. If you do not have a name, send your cover letter and résumé to Human Resources or a hiring authority. If you have been referred by someone you know, the introductory paragraph is the place to mention your referral. Next, state the position for which you are applying and indicate where you learned about the opportunity (e.g., Internet or university career center). Be clear to the reader about why you are writing.

Body Paragraph

Describe why you are a good or ideal fit for the position by honestly communicating past experiences that parallel the employer's needs. Provide one or two behavioral examples that complement the employer's needs. For instance, if the employer is seeking exceptional verbal communication ability, provide a behavioral example of your exceptional communication abilities, such as your successful sales experience in a past job or a well-received talk you gave in class. Also, what can you say about the organization and yourself to match your candidacy and stand above other applicants? Do you have similar values? What are your noteworthy accomplishments?

Closing Paragraph

Restate your interest in the job and your appreciation of the employer's consideration of your application. Also, request an interview at the employer's convenience, and share when and how you plan to follow up with an e-mail or phone call.

Crafting a well-thought-out cover letter is less daunting if you take the time to organize and outline your thoughts and each section before getting started. You might begin with a master list or template of information about yourself and then customize each cover letter to meet the specific needs of each job application. From a list of potential employers you have researched, select an employer and position you want to apply for. Give thought to what you want to communicate to the employer, and complete each of the sections above. If you want to view and subsequently create your own letter page, go to Item 2 in the "Projects" section at the end of this chapter.

How to Search for a Job

In addition to preparing résumés and cover letters, your job-search tool kit should contain multiple *sources* for learning about interview opportunities that enable you to shift gears if one approach does not yield positive results. You must also become aware of circumstances that help you identify jobs and subsequently take steps that maximize your prospects. The visible job market consists of sources that are easily accessible and viewable, such as the Internet, newspapers, and your career services office—sources you normally associate with finding information. The invisible job market is made up of opportunities that are not published but can be uncovered through networking and word of mouth. Many organizations conduct campus interviews, job fairs, career days, and industry nights where you can meet one-on-one with employers (Yena, 2011). You can also obtain job leads through family and friends; directories of employers; the Chamber of Commerce; career-development books, clubs, and professional organizations; university alumni associations; placement agencies; university career days/fairs; and job fairs.

Expect to spend time, money, and energy in the early planning stages, and remember that persistence, continuous activity, and a clear understanding of your goals are vital. The Internet also provides an abundance of career resources, webinars, podcasts, virtual career fairs, and professional and social networking sites. Networking sites such as LinkedIn and Twitter can be used to facilitate relationships, generate a professional image and brand, and manage a contact list. Tips and tutorials about networking sites and social media are available through YouTube and Google.

Many job seekers spend a significant amount of time applying to jobs online, an approach that should be viewed as only part of a larger strategy. Listed below are some popular online job boards:

American Psychological Association—http://jobs.psyccareers.com/jobs/

Psychology Jobs.com—http://www.psychologyjobs.com/

All Psychology Jobs.com—http://allpsychologyjobs.com/resources

LinkedIn—http://www.linkedin.com/

Indeed—http://www.indeed.com/

Simply Hired—http://www.simplyhired.com/

USAJOBS—http://www.usajobs.gov/

Job Search Goals

Having clear but flexible job search goals is essential. Ask yourself questions such as these: Specifically, what are my goals for the type of job I seek? The type of organization I want to work for? The place (e.g., region or city) where I will live? My deadline for finding a job? What are my priorities for these goals? If I cannot meet my stated goals, in what ways can I be flexible and adaptable?

Achieving your goals will increase your confidence and momentum as you make progress in your search. Why not write your specific goals and post them next to your computer or on your refrigerator? In fact, writing your goals can increase your chances of achieving them by 80% (Levitt & Harwood, 2010). Goals are also more achievable if they are specific, measurable, attainable, realistic, and timely—the S.M.A.R.T approach to goal setting (Kaye, 1997)—and you are more likely to achieve your final goal if you set a series of smaller realistic goals (Hanna et al., 2009). Remember, however, that when the job market is depressed, you must be flexible, adaptable, and willing to lower your sights, at least for the short-term future, if your job opportunities are limited and your need for income is urgent.

Job Search Plan

While you search for a job, it is important to create a weekly schedule and establish a routine for every day of your search. You must be proactive about this because procrastination is the job seeker's worst enemy. Those of you who are currently seeking a job should complete Item 1 (weekly plan) in the "Projects" section at the end of this chapter. Consider teaming up with a partner and discussing what the first week of your job search will entail. Organize and track your job application progress because it helps you recall where, when, and how you applied for specific jobs. Equally important is documenting the names, titles, dates, and locations of people you met. The sample table below illustrates how you can stay organized, measure your progress, understand what you are doing well, and identify areas you need to improve. Why not create a spreadsheet on your computer in the following format?

Date	Job Title	Company	Website	Login	Password	Referral	Result
3/11/11	Counselor	Brown College	www .brown .edu	Ksmith	Smith	Tim Robin, professor	Pending
3/17/11	HR Representative	Simmons	www .simmons .com	Kimsmith	Smith23	N/A	Rejection letter

In addition, be sure to form a positive, "can-do" attitude about your job search plan, because attitude influences interview performance, confidence, and even health, particularly during transitional times. Think of yourself as a successful person, and construct your activities to promote positive outcomes for each job search task. Employers hire people who project positive energy and enthusiasm. We know that a positive attitude will be difficult to sustain if you receive rejection after rejection, so it is important to have a support system. Successful job seekers can receive support from an *accountability partner,* someone who will support you emotionally and make sure you are completing your job search objectives. Your partner can be a friend, significant other, family or church member, or another person you trust. By sharing your weekly job search goals and activities with another person, you hold yourself accountable for your activities. Serving as an accountability partner requires time and effort, so choose one carefully, express your gratitude for that person's help, and communicate what you expect of yourself and your partner. Mentors can serve as accountability partners, but ensure they have the time available and genuine willingness to help you. Similarly, teaming up with another job seeker to share successes and obstacles can also be an effective practice. By remaining positive and enlisting a partner to lean on for support and feedback, you are being proactive in your search.

Selecting *references* is another important step for preparing your job search. Prospective employers typically check references prior to extending a job offer to ensure you have the experience and are, in fact, the person they met during the interviewing process. Choose trustworthy people in well-accepted positions—such as teachers, academic advisors, and supervisors—who know well your attitudes, abilities, and past experiences. Determine if they are comfortable acting as referees, describe the kinds of positions you are seeking, and provide them an updated résumé with a statement of goals. Contact each person prior to your search and provide specific information about the position(s) if possible, because the names of references are frequently requested during an interview. Finally, if a hiring authority discovers during a reference check or an interview that you falsified information on your résumé, you will be dropped from further consideration. Honesty remains the best policy.

In summary, it is essential to create a job search plan that includes several sources for locating jobs so that if one source fails, you can consult others. Your plan should also include specific search goals, an accountability partner, and individuals who know your accomplishments well enough to support you as references.

Time Out: Reflective Questions

What steps could you take to separate yourself from competing graduates in your search for job sources?

1. What impact have positive and negative thoughts had on your successes and failures in the past, and what could you do to sustain a positive attitude during a job search?

2. If you were searching for a job now, who would you ask to be an accountability partner in your search?

Networking

Your background in psychology and the skills you are acquiring can afford a competitive edge for using the next component of the job-search tool kit: networking. Networking is a communications technique that involves forming connections with other individuals and developing contacts through which career planning activities and potential job openings can be shared (Ellis, 2009). View it also as a form of qualitative research. Networking is not as formal a relationship as mentoring (see Chapter 10). Instead, individuals find mutual support in meeting their goals and helping others meet their goals to determine if there is value in continuing the relationship. You may have networked already without knowing.

Some students feel pressured from parents, counselors, or teachers and become nervous when it is time to network actively. However, when you view this form of connecting for what it really is—the sharing of knowledge and resources for mutual benefit—much of the pressure disappears. Your career will be a journey, and the relationships established and maintained over time will probably lead to greater satisfaction.

In a survey of 103 business executives, 85% of participants reported that establishing a professional network directly increased their overall career satisfaction (Jameson, 2010). The study suggests that connecting with others is an investment in one's future career success. Below are tips and resources for becoming an effective networker. Whether you are seeking a job or new friends, networking is a general skill that can be used by anyone to accomplish various goals. Are you looking for a new job? A mentor? A significant other?

Time Out: Reflective Questions

The first step in networking (not exclusive to job searching) is to understand your reason—mission or objective—for engaging in this process. You can create your personal mission statement by asking yourself the following questions:

1. For what reasons do I want to network?

2. What attitudes, feelings, and impressions do I want to communicate in conversations with others?

3. What knowledge do I bring to a networking relationship?

Mobray (2009) observed that the longer it takes to learn what you want to be known for, the more you lack sufficient knowledge of yourself, affirming our emphasis throughout this book on the importance of seeking higher levels of self-awareness. So how can you build a network?

Building a Network

Networking can be conducted anywhere and anytime with your intention to accomplish particular goals. You can network at a gym, in a restaurant, on an airplane, or even at a bus stop—anywhere the environment is friendly for conversation. Before thinking about other specific places, make a list of the people you know and determine whether or not they could be connected to your mission statement. The process of developing a network of professional acquaintances will probably pay off when you need to begin a job search. Ellis (2009) recommended the following actions to facilitate a search:

- Make direct contact with a person who can hire you.
- Make such contacts even when the job you want is not yet open or even conceived.

- Cultivate a list of contacts, join professional associations, and meet people in your field.
- Use information interviews to research companies and meet people who support your career success.
- Approach a former employer with your updated résumé. Talk about the kinds of positions you can apply for *now* with your recent degree.
- Join a support group for people who are looking for work.
- Write thank-you notes after an interview.
- Present yourself impeccably—everything from error-free résumés to well-polished shoes.

How to Network for Job Search Events

Networking at events is analogous to taking tests: Over time, you develop skills for focusing on important details while attending to the "big picture." Events are held for every occasion, and a great place to start is with your university and alumni groups. Similarly, some local community organizations and church groups also host networking events. When you evaluate which groups to join or events to attend, remember to keep your job search and networking goals in mind: your purpose for attending, the type of person you are seeking (i.e., field, level of experience, and skills), and the need for further information (i.e., about the company or career).

The level of confidence you project will often influence your success at such events. If you feel anxious upon entering a room full of people, remember the words of Machiavelli: "Everyone sees what you appear to be, few really know what you are." Projecting confidence with a firm handshake, direct eye contact, a wise choice of clothes, and a warm smile are easy first steps to make a positive first impression. Besides attending to these nonverbal elements of communicating, state your name and something about yourself, such as your current job or academic major.

Whether we like it or not and whether or not it is fair, individuals applying for entry-level positions are judged highly on appearance and grooming; it is better to err on the side of formality, with the default choice being a dark suit (Pollack, 2007). Other grooming tips include the following: (a) It's better to be overdressed than underdressed; (b) basic black works (and do not forget the iron); (c) wear clothes that fit; (d) accessorize cautiously (go light on scents and fragrances); and (e) think carefully about outerwear such as coats, scarves, etc. Universal answers may not fit all situations, but these are good basic tips to start with. Be sure to consult with those in your network about expectations for appropriate dress at particular companies or for specific entry-level positions. What is standard in one industry or workplace does not necessarily hold true for other industries, or even for different workplaces within the same industry. By the way, be sure to silence all your electronic devices (Pollak, 2007), including the vibrate mode on your phone, and do not send or receive text messages (Rose, 2010).

Remember a new contact's name, because it is instrumental in building rapport; calling someone by name demonstrates that you are listening and attending to the person you are speaking with. In *How to Win Friends and Influence People,* Dale Carnegie (1981) observed that a person's name is to them the most important sound in any language. You may recall learning in an introductory psychology course that if you want to remember a person's name, use it in conversation, repeat it to yourself, and try to associate it with the person's appearance or a specific physical feature. Has someone ever addressed you by the wrong name? How did it make you feel?

Establishing commonalities helps build rapport, so make it a point to find something in common with everyone you meet; similar interests can serve as a foundation on which to build a relationship. Networking events are a great way to meet like-minded individuals who may be in a position to help you accomplish your goals, and vice versa.

Time Out: Reflective Questions

Managing your network will require effort, so try to remember the people and relationships associated with your job and career goals. After you meet a new contact, answer these questions:

1. Does this person have the resources to help me reach my job search goals?

2. Do I have the knowledge or resources to further this person's goals (if relevant)?

3. Is this person someone I would want to stay in touch with?

Internet Networking

Just as there are job search networks, so also are there popular websites for networking on the Internet, such as the following:

http://www.linkedin.com/

http://www.socialpsychology.org/

http://twitter.com/

http://www.xing.com/

http://www.facebook.com/

https://profiles.google.com/

LinkedIn and Facebook offer smaller communities within their websites in the form of groups. These "subcommunities" offer platforms for psychology graduates and professionals to connect. Joining groups creates opportunities to meet professionals in fields you may be interested in getting into. You can uncover job opportunities, join in conversations, and connect with mentors and hiring authorities within each group. For example, below are the names of several psychology-focused LinkedIn groups:

The Psychology Network—10,000+ members

Psychologists, Psychotherapists, and Counselors—9,000+ members

Psi Chi, International Honor Society in Psychology—100,000+ members

LinkedIn HR—400,000+ members

Job Openings, Job Leads, and Job Connections!—400,000+ members

By now, the importance of using the Internet as a job search tool is obvious. Ferazzi and Raz (2005) suggested that your career success is determined as much by how well others know your work as by the quality of your work; therefore, becoming visible through technology during a job search and during career discovery is an excellent way to uncover opportunities. With a professional head shot (typically a glossy, 8x10, black-and-white photograph of you), contacts, recommendations, and a complete profile, you create a professional image in the minds of others even before meeting them in person. If you are unfamiliar with Internet networking, take a first step and put yourself out there, but do so thoughtfully and carefully. Similar to face-to-face networking, the more exposure you have on Internet networking, the more comfortable and confident you will be using the Internet as a job search tool. Gitomer (2011) suggested that social media is an opportunity, a new frontier, a space in cyberspace that gives you an individual place to play, build awareness, brand yourself, and is a source from which you can potentially profit.

To gain momentum with an online presence, search online for people you already know. How are they using the Internet to connect with others? Your family, friends, mentors, advisors, teachers, and coworkers (former and present) are your most valuable advocates and should be the first identified. Do you know how and where they are using social media? If not, ask them. Taking these steps will help you begin developing momentum in your networking and job search strategies, and with application of the tools provided, you will come to realize they are all connected to your goals.

There is no one answer for learning how to establish meaningful and lasting relationships through networking. Finding commonalities with others, clearly communicating intentions, possessing an excellent reputation, and understanding the needs of others are networking bedrocks to build on. Above all, put forth the extra effort needed to stay in touch with people who can support your progress and with whom you enjoy communicating.

Networking is a two-way street. Remember, it is merely the action taken to identify others with similar interests and passions that can support individual endeavors. Professional contacts can lead you in the direction of greater career and life satisfaction if you let them. To avid networkers, understanding another's needs and developing mutually beneficial relationships becomes second nature. Furthermore, with time and experience, connecting people who can benefit from knowing one another becomes a way of life. You can do the same!

A Digression: Remember That "Big Brother Is Watching You"

George Orwell's *1984* describes a hypothetical society in which the state uses various devices to monitor the activities and conversations of all citizens; the book is well known in part for the line, "Big Brother is watching you." Most people would agree that we do not live in such a society yet, but many citizens are concerned about the increased intrusion of technology in our private lives. As organizations take various risks whenever they hire new employees, many employers utilize online searches to make better judgments about a candidate's character. A 2009 global research study that surveyed 275 human resources professionals found that more than 75% of employers actively research candidates online. Further, of the 75% of employers researching candidates online, more than 70% of U.S.-based recruiters have decided NOT to hire a candidate based on what they found (Cross-Tab, 2010).

Employers monitor prospective hires' Internet activities, and job seekers must therefore take the initiative to review and manage online content. Collectively, your profiles, pictures, and other Internet activities (including website visits and e-mails) leave a trail called your "digital footprint." This trail allows interested parties (usually prospective employers and marketers) to access your personal information. In addition to popular sites such as Facebook, LinkedIn, and Twitter, employers are also searching pictures and content from sites such as Skype, Flickr, StumbleUpon, and Pinterest.

You may justifiably believe that such searches are an intrusion into your privacy, but they represent the reality of many organizations' recruiting practices. Consequently, you should take the following steps to manage your digital footprint proactively:

1. Review each of your online profiles, pictures, and recent e-mails. Ask yourself, "Would I share this information (or pictures) at a family reunion? Would I share this information with the parents of a significant other?"

2. Proactively shape the results of your name query by setting up your LinkedIn and Twitter accounts in the following formats: linkedin.com/in/firstnamelastname or twitter.com/firstnamelastname (rather than, for example, twitter.com/partygoer01). This configuration increases the likelihood that profiles will show up in search results.

Beware: Don't rely on privacy settings for your social media profiles to separate your personal life and the professional image you intend on projecting to employers. It is safe to assume that anything posted on the Internet could leak to an unintended receiver of the information. Friends, family, and classmates also have the ability to influence your digital footprint if your name is included in the published information, so ask others if they have posted anything that includes your name.

In a recent student survey, nearly all respondents indicated having a presence on social networks (NACE, 2011). However, the report indicated that most students do not use social media as part of their job search and, further, are resistant to employers using social networks in the recruiting process. The decision to utilize social media to secure employment is an important one, but, whatever you decide, your digital footprint must be managed.

Time Out Exercise: Discover Your Digital Footprint

Visit your most reliable search engine (Google, Yahoo, etc.), and type your first and last name in the search bar. Next, type your name again, but this time, include the name of your high school and/or college. Repeat this exercise yet a third time and add names of any organizations, teams, or keywords that might be associated with your name online. If you have a common name, such as Chris Smith, it may take numerous keywords to find you. Periodically completing this exercise enables you to monitor your footprint and begin to think as a recruiter does: "What are the risks in hiring this person?"

Interviewing

A job interview is a conversation where each party determines if the other side fulfills his or her needs relevant to work. The topics addressed include conducting company research, preparing questions for the interviewer, and rehearsing answers. Your mastery of these issues will increase your skills, confidence, and comfort—the key factors of winning interviews.

How to Research Prospective Employers

Effective time management is critical prior to an interview. Ten to twenty percent of preparation should be spent researching the company's website and communicating with its employees (current and former), if feasible. A critical element of a good match during the interview process is demonstrating that the prospective employer will be a good or excellent fit. If you obtain an interview on short notice, at the very least determine who the organization's customers are, or in other words, source of income. Employers hire staff based on the individual's personality fit as well as technical competencies; therefore, it is critical to demonstrate that your values are similar to those of the organization.

Time Out: Exercise

Completing the Organizational Research Grid in Item 4 of the "Projects" section right now would require too much time away from our material, but page over to that project and study the types of categories included. To what extent would the information you collect help you (a) gain a sense of the organization's culture and (b) develop thoughtful questions to ask the interviewer? What other information would you like to gather that is not contained on the grid?

Behavioral/Situational Interview Questions

The best indicator of future performance is past performance; employers want to hear how you have handled situations in the past that are similar to those you may encounter in the job for which you are interviewing. For example, for a counseling position, the employer may expect you to describe occasions when you dealt with a challenging client that required you to demonstrate patience and problem solving. What were the obstacles in this particular situation? What was the result of your ability to persevere despite obstacles? Employers want to know not only what you can do for them but also how you manage adversity and challenging situations. To answer such questions, use the SOAR technique: situation, obstacle, action, result.

Interview question: Describe a situation in which you dealt with a challenging client who required you to demonstrate patience and problem solving.

Situation: You describe those circumstances, events, and necessary details that required you to be patient and resolve a problem with a client/customer you found difficult to work with. Also, what organization were you working for when this occurred and when? Who was involved?

Obstacle: Why was the situation challenging to you? What obstacles did you encounter in this particular circumstance?

Action: What actions did you take? What was your decision based on? (e.g., "I responded by . . .")

Result: What was the result of your efforts? (e.g., "As a result I/we achieved . . .") What did you learn?

For the hypothetical situation below, an undesired answer is presented and then followed by the desired situation. In each, see if you can identify the situation, obstacle, action, and result.

Interviewer: Can you tell me about a difficult decision you had to make?

UNDESIRED: As an assistant coach of the Chatham Tigers, I had a lot of tough decisions to make. In my second season, one of our stars missed a few practices prior to the playoffs and I made the decision to punish her, but we still won anyway. It was a tough decision, but it was also the right one.

DESIRED: In my second season as assistant coach of the Chatham Tigers, I had the opportunity to step into the coaching role when the coach had an unexpected family emergency shortly before the first playoff game. We were matched up against the No. 1 team, and our star player missed the final practice prior to playoffs—though with an acceptable reason. Even though it was little league, we had a strict attendance policy for practice. The decision was a difficult one because it was my first decision and I would either compromise the integrity of the rules set forth or put the Tigers at a disadvantage by not letting our superstar play, but I did have some flexibility to compromise. I notified our all-star that she would not start in the field but was able to bat. Everyone accepted the decision, and the Tigers won the first round of the playoffs. I was able to uphold team rules and minimize the potential impact of her inability to play by closely evaluating circumstances and the implications of my decision.

Can you discern how these two descriptions differ in terms of the specific details presented in the situation? The description of the obstacles? The specific decisions and actions implemented? The results of your efforts?

Time Out: Exercise

Using S.O.A.R., answer the same question based on one of your experiences.

Situation:

Obstacle:

Action:

Results:

Other Interview Pointers

Proper interviewing attire varies based on company culture and industry norms, but it is good to get into the habit of dressing conservative, tasteful, and business professional. Clothing should be pressed and stain free, and it is wise to remove piercings. A job interview is not the proper time to show your future employer your unique style.

In many colleges and universities, the business department or counseling center periodically conducts etiquette dinners that instruct students how to dress, eat, and communicate appropriately at business luncheons and dinners. Take advantage of any opportunity to acquire the knowledge and skills afforded by such events. For example, would you order an alcoholic beverage during an interview luncheon if your interviewers did not order one? (We know of a job applicant who did and was dropped from the applicant pool.) By the way, how would you explain those partially hidden tattoos? There are numerous customs and aspects of etiquette you should master to deal with such situations. Enjoying a delicious meal in an attractive restaurant is an opportune time to let down your guard (and your hair) and expose your vulnerabilities.

One of the questions you can receive from an interviewer is, "What is one of your major strengths and one of your major weaknesses?" Such questions are likely to catch you off guard, but you should be ready to answer them clearly and concisely. Employers want to know that you are aware of your faults and that you have a plan, or took action on a plan, to reduce or eliminate those flaws. It is important to be honest, but avoid describing a weakness that is one of the qualifications contained in the position description or you will likely be excluded from further consideration. Do you want your next supervisor to know you feel compelled to check for text messages during a meeting? Below is an example of an undesired and desired answer to a disclosure that the applicant doesn't remember names well—perhaps not a serious flaw in some jobs, but it could be in others.

UNDESIRED: I don't remember names very well, but they are always polite when I ask them to repeat their names, like they did when I ran focus groups. I always tell them I'll try harder, and I am trying harder to remember and people seem to understand that it's hard to remember three or four names at once.

DESIRED: One of my weaknesses has been my inability to remember a series of names. I recognized it was an issue at my last job when I failed to remember the names of the focus group participants. It was important that I did remember their names because we needed their qualitative data and we wanted each person to feel valued. My psychology teacher recommended a memory retention program developed by his colleague in an educational research lab, and I have been practicing the suggestions it contains. I have improved significantly, but my goal is to remember the names of six people at once, which is about the size of a focus group

Time Out: Exercise

Are you especially strong or weak in any of the basic skills and qualities employers seek? Could you describe situations that illustrate how you have used them to the benefit of your previous employer(s)? Using the behavioral answer format to explain your competency in such skills will put you on the path to receiving a job offer! Apply the S.O.A.R technique to

- verbal and written communications,
- teamwork,
- showing initiative, and
- solving problems.

Choose the skill: _____

Situation:

Obstacle:

Action:

Result:

Prepare Questions for the Interviewer

A job interview should be a two-way communication process. When you ask questions, you demonstrate genuine interest in the position and gather information to make an informed decision if an offer for employment is extended. Your questions help you determine if the position will be a good fit by gathering information about management styles, position responsibilities, mutual expectations, and the company and team cultures. Ask questions that help you decide if the manager and coworkers exhibit qualities of persons with whom you want to work. For instance, if you tend to work best when you are given autonomy, ask, "To what extent would you describe your management style as hands-on or hands-off?" or "How much decision-making authority does someone have in this role?" The people with whom you work and your boss can make or break your job. Other questions you may wish to ask, time permitting, include, "Why is this position available?" "What traits do high performers in your organization share?" "How would you describe the culture of the organization?" "What challenges does your team face?"

Following Up After Interviews

Within 24 hours of the interview, send a thank-you e-mail and mail a handwritten thank-you card to each person you interviewed with. A handwritten note adds a personal touch to your candidacy, reiterates your genuine interest in the opportunity, and is a rapport-building tactic that attaches you and your candidacy to an object (i.e., the thank-you note). In both your e-mail and handwritten note, acknowledge the interviewer's time and highlight high points in the conversation for his or her consideration. Every communication between you and a hiring authority is evaluated; therefore, the content of your follow-up e-mail and handwritten note must contain flawless grammar and punctuation. In a survey of 45 human resources executives, 75% of respondents stated that a handwritten thank you had a positive impact on their impression of a candidate if their initial impression in the interview was positive (Jameson, 2011).

Successful interviewing takes practice, and the sooner you realize that it is primarily a two-sided conversation and requires investment from both parties to determine if needs and goals can be met on both sides, the easier it will become to ask the right questions and succeed in interviews. Employers are looking for a reason to hire you; give them more than one.

Closing Comments

Your job search is a process that will repeat itself over the course of your career; becoming a professional requires a keen knowledge of self and the ability to communicate that knowledge and utilize available resources. After completing the projects below, visit your career center and ask a counselor to review your résumé and cover letter. Résumés are a work in progress. Remember that everyone has opinions and preferences, so listen to advice and seek more than one opinion before making drastic changes to yours. Successful résumés contain action verbs, quantifiable experience, consistent formatting, and are tailored to specific opportunities. Cover letters explain your interest in the position and why you fit. Support explanations with an example of skills and experiences that fulfill the position's requirements. In addition to contacting the career center, ask your networking contacts to review your résumé(s) and cover letter(s). The process of developing a network and linking it to job search goals becomes much easier when existing resources and relationships are utilized. Additionally, seek support from family and friends to help you persevere and stay positive despite obstacles. Collectively, the processes of building contacts and searching for a job are a form of exploration that generates new experiences that facilitate your personal and professional growth. Enjoy the journey. Get ready, get set, and go get a job!

Getting Involved

Journal Starters

1. What are the most significant insights you gained about yourself and the job search from reading this chapter?

2. Each section of this chapter presented you with a series of questions to reflect on. Revisit the sections and answer at least some of the questions, keeping in mind that the purpose is to increase your self-awareness and promote idea generation.

3. After reflecting on these questions, respond to at least three of the following questions of your choice.

   a. How do you feel about selling yourself on a job interview? Are there particular questions you feel confident or nervous about?

   b. Which section of this chapter did you find most useful? Why?

   c. If you are currently searching for a job, what steps will you take in the next 2 weeks to build momentum in your search?

   d. What additional job search resources could you use to supplement the content presented in this chapter?

   e. If you are feeling nervous about your journey to find a rewarding career, who will support you along the way?

Projects

1. Create a weekly plan of goals for your job search.

Week of _____				TARGETED		ACTUAL		Weekly Totals
	Mon	**Tues**	**Weds**	**Thurs**	**Fri**	**Sat**	**Sun**	
# of applications submitted								
# of networking contacts made								
Time spent researching companies								
# of events (school or professional)								
# of job interviews								
Daily totals								
Comments/ Notes								

2. Create a cover letter. Begin with the *salutation*. A salutation is a greeting used by the sender so the recipient knows who the communication is intended for. The use of "Dear" is common in professional correspondences such as cover letters. For example, "Dear Hiring Authority" is an appropriate salutation if you do not know the recipient's name.

_____

Introductory paragraph—State your purpose in writing. How did you become interested in the position and organization?

_____
_____
_____
_____
_____

Body paragraph—Describe your qualifications.

_____

_____

_____

_____

Closing paragraph—Indicate your intention to follow up, and refer to your enclosed résumé.

_____

_____

_____

Closing

_____

[Written signature]

[Typed name]

[E-mail address]

[Phone number]

3. Networking map. Create a networking map; this is a good first step for identifying potential opportunities through people you already know. Take a large sheet of blank paper, write your name in the middle, and circle it. Branching out in each direction, write the names of groups or associations you may have (churches, teams, groups, family, etc.). Next, draw branches out from each group and list people whom you have close relationships with and who may possess resources to advance your networking efforts. Form groups of five or grab a partner and share your ideas. Listed below is a sample to get you started.

4. Conduct research on an organization of your choice and fill in the blanks below.

ORGANIZATIONAL RESEARCH GRID	
Source/contact name:	Research date:
Company name: Company headquarters:	Size assets/# of employees: CEO/president:
Core service lines: _____ _____	
Recent press: _____ _____	
Company mission: _____ _____	
Organizational values: _____ _____	
History: _____ _____	

5. Communicate your value to employers—take a few moments to reflect on your past experiences and develop answers for each of the following questions.

What accomplishments am I most proud of?

1. _____
    _____

2. _____
    _____

In what situations has my work made the most impact on a team?

1. _____
    _____

2. _____
_____
_____

What is an obstacle or adversity I overcame at a job or in a group setting?

Situation: _____
_____

Obstacle: _____
_____

Action: _____
_____

Result: _____
_____

What are my major strengths? _____
_____

What is a major weakness of mine, and what have I done to improve it? _____
_____

Additional Resources

URL	Brief Website Description
http://www.connectinginsights.net/	This site contains an interactive networking self-assessment and feedback tool.
http://jobsearch.about.com/	This site contains tips for job searching, interviewing, résumés, cover letters, networking, references, and a wealth of additional information related to searching for jobs.
http://www.glassdoor.com/index.htm	This site provides company information and reviews, job-specific salary data, and interview questions. Job seekers also use the site to describe their employment and interviewing experiences.
http://www.shrm.org/TemplatesTools/ Samples/InterviewQuestions/Pages/ default.aspx	This site provides hundreds of sample interview questions grouped into 32 categories by industry, job function, job level, and interview question type.
http://www.bc.edu/offices/careers/ skills/resumes/verbs.html	This site provides a list of 200+ résumé action verbs.

References

Carnegie, D. (1981). *How to win friends and influence people.* New York, NY: Simon & Schuster.

Cross-Tab. (2010, January). *Online reputation in a connected world* (Public report prepared for Microsoft). Retrieved from http://www.job-hunt.org/guides/DPD_Online-Reputation-Research_overview.pdf

Ellis, D. (2009). *From master student to master employee: Annotated instructor's edition* (2nd ed.). St. Charles, IL: College Survival/Houghton Mifflin.

Ferazzi, K., & Raz, T. (2005). *Never eat alone.* New York, NY: Doubleday.

Gitomer, J. (2011). *Social boom.* Upper Saddle River, NJ: Pearson Education.

Hanna, S., Radtke, D., & Suggett, R. (2009). *Career by design: Communicating your way to success* (4th ed.). Upper Saddle River, NJ: Pearson Prentice Hall.

Jameson, J. (2010). *Uncovering the career impact of networking.* Unpublished raw survey data.

Jameson, J. (2011). *Interviewing skills.* Unpublished raw survey data.

Kaye, B. (1997). *Up is not the only way.* Palo Alto, CA: Davies-Black.

Levitt, J. G., & Harwood, L. (2010). *Your career: How to make it happen* (7th ed.). Mason, OH: Cengage Learning.

Mobray, K. (2009). *The 10Ks of personal branding.* Bloomington, IN: iUniverse.

National Association of Colleges and Employers. (2011). *Class of 2012 student survey report.* Bethlehem, PA: Author.

Pollack, L. (2007). *Getting from college to career: 90 things to do before you join the real world.* New York, NY: HarperCollins.

Rose, J. (2010, May 28). Study: College grads unprepared for workplace. NPR. Retrieved from http://www.npr.org/templates/story/story.php?storyId=127230009

Sukiennik, D., Bendat, W., & Raufman, L. (2010). *The career fitness program: Exercising your options* (9th ed.). Upper Saddle River, NJ: Pearson Prentice Hall.

Yena, D. J. (2011). *Career directions: The path to your ideal career* (5th ed.). New York, NY: McGraw-Hill.

PART III

Onboarding to Work

Why Are Attitudes, Motivation, and Work Centrality Important?

The greatest discovery of my generation is that human beings can alter their lives by altering their attitude of mind. . . . If you can change your mind, you can change your life.

—William James (1842–1910), philosopher

One of the founders of American psychology speaks here to our current generation. How important is attitude? "Attitude is everything," we are told by the instructor in a sales training seminar; the counselor in a conflict-resolution session; the coach of a superbly conditioned, highly synchronous sports team; the drill sergeant in basic training; and in countless other venues. Your attitudes toward work and the workplace are critical. Attitude can spell the difference between a second interview and a rejection, or between feeling overconfident after getting hired for a job and succeeding in it (two different situations). Attitude is usually the difference between learning to get along with a supervisor several years your senior who thinks all new college grads feel "entitled" and quitting in frustration. Attitude enables you to remain in a poor-paying, boring job when there are no alternatives, to develop a work ethic you never had in college, and to go the extra mile to reach that promotion. Your attitudes are expressions of your values. In this chapter, we introduce you to essential topics regarding workplace attitudes and motivation, and their connection to work.

Attitudes

An attitude is generally defined as a relatively stable belief, feeling, or behavioral tendency directed to particular ideas, individuals, events, or objects in the environment. The three components of an attitude (beliefs, feelings, and behaviors) interact in complex ways as they apply to our jobs and the settings in which we work. For example, suppose you accepted a somewhat-low-paying job in a not-for-profit organization because you *believe* strongly in its mission. Soon after you begin, however, you notice (and your coworkers agree) that your supervisor seems to be somewhat authoritarian, insensitive to employee issues, and seldom acknowledges tasks you perform well; you *feel* frustrated about this. You would like to express your feelings (*behavioral tendency*) to the supervisor but fear you may lose your job. Our work attitudes can be a powerful influence both during and after work. In this instance, your attitude about your job and supervisor are likely to have an impact on your personal life, relationships, long-term goals, and certainly your job satisfaction.

Job Satisfaction

To shed light on the nature of job satisfaction, we take a snapshot of three perspectives: value theory, the social information processing model, and the dispositional model.

The *value theory* of job satisfaction maintains that almost any aspect or dimension of the job can become a source of satisfaction provided it is something the employee values. The more an individual experiences a particular value that he or she deems important, the higher the level of satisfaction (Greenberg, 2010)—but be prepared to work hard and attentively over a period of time to discern those values. In the example above, if the behavior of the supervisor persists, you may feel forced to evaluate which aspects are most important to you: your organization's mission, for which you have a passion; your desire to be treated as a mature adult; or your salary. Many college students develop ideals they seek to practice in their post-college jobs (e.g., working with disadvantaged individuals, being part of a Fortune 500 company, living in a particular location, or joining the Peace Corps) only to discover, once on the job, that there are major discrepancies between their expectations and the realities. Because values are an essential ingredient of work, we urged you in Chapter 3 to critically analyze the components of your part-time jobs, complete internships to gain experience, enroll in workplace-related courses, and become involved in volunteer and extracurricular activities. These are not silver-bullet suggestions, but when you actively examine how such activities can add to your experience and shape your values, you may find your level of satisfaction with that brand-new job to be more nuanced because of past experiences.

Greenberg (2010) also summarized the *social information processing* model of job satisfaction, developed by Salancik and Pfeffer. They stated that your workplace attitudes and behaviors are strongly influenced by the information you receive from others and by the cues you detect in the work environment. In the example above, it may be wise to suspend judgment of your supervisor's behaviors, as well as coworker comments, until you have been in the organization long enough to make independent judgments of the supervisor and the "big-picture" contexts in which your tasks are performed. First impressions may be lasting but not always accurate. Perhaps your supervisor's behavior models an authoritarian upper-management leadership style that treats employees as second-class citizens, or perhaps your supervisor is under unusually high stress due to job and family pressures. If the former is true, you may never be content with your work there and would be advised to consider other organizations with similar missions. Remember, however, to avoid job-hopping. You don't want a prospective employer wondering during an interview if your true reasons for leaving a job are due to a lack of goals, negative attitudes toward work, inability to get along with others, inability to deal with authority, or just being "difficult" (J. Keil, personal communication, September 12, 2011).

Judge's *dispositional model* views job satisfaction as a relatively stable attribute that is consistent in its expression over time. That is, a person who likes his or her job in one situation tends to like it in other situations, even if the job is different (Greenberg, 2010). If your true passion is the organization's mission, you may experience job satisfaction in an authoritarian as well as a person-oriented company. If your primary values lie in personal challenge and rewards for excellent performance, you may achieve job satisfaction in a company with vastly different missions, whether a Fortune 500 company or a well-managed, not-for-profit, community-service environment.

Negative Attitudes

When you are dissatisfied with one of your courses, what are you tempted to do? Withdraw your participation in class discussion, submit inferior-quality assignments, and skip classes—these are the typical signs of student withdrawal. Similarly, when you become dissatisfied with a job, you want to withdraw from your task assignments and the organization. Rather than give in to temptation, however, you should critically evaluate your goals and attitudes or, perhaps, begin a job search.

For example, Sharon worked for her company as an administrative assistant for 5 years, through "thick and thin"—from the uncertainty of its inception and through the early years when it struggled for stability. She had stayed after work for another hour or two at least twice a week, worked an occasional Saturday, and frequently took work home—all for no additional compensation. But Sharon was "burning out," and in spite of the hiring of a new employee to take on many of her responsibilities, she grew apathetic, was late or left work early with no explanation, and often displayed an "I-couldn't-care-less" attitude. Her new supervisor was particularly concerned because her negative behaviors were apparent to the new employee and were starting to affect the work. In spite of counseling sessions that produced some changes in her assignments, Sharon's behavior continued to deteriorate over several weeks. External/personal issues did not seem to contribute to her general attitude. Finally, her employment was terminated. In spite of her earlier commitments and important contributions to the organization, her performance during the final months made it impossible for her supervisor, and even the CEO to whom she reported during her early years, to write a favorable letter of recommendation. In short, given her unwillingness to modify her attitude and behaviors or seek new employment in a timely manner, Sharon's years of constructive service to the organization were negated. The moral of this story is this: Circumstances may lead you to *feel* justified in expressing negative attitudes toward your job, but be aware of how the consequences of your behavior can influence your future work opportunities.

By now, you should know that negative attitudes may be found in almost any social situation. You encounter negative attitudes in college, and you will encounter them in the workplace—negative attitudes others may have toward you and negative attitudes you may have toward others. Let's briefly review a few additional concepts you probably acquired in your earlier psychology courses (Greenberg, 2010): prejudice, stereotypes, and discrimination.

Prejudice refers to negative feelings an individual has toward people who belong to a certain group, such as ethnic, gender, racial, religious, age, physical condition, or political groups. A prejudicial attitude—like attitudes in general—contains a belief, feeling, and behavioral predisposition component. *Stereotypes* refer to a false set of beliefs or assumptions that all members of a particular group possess the same characteristics. If a coworker does not like you simply because you are a new college graduate and because he believes all new college graduates are alike, he is expressing a stereotype based on age, education, or both. Similarly, if you distrust a coworker who is 60 years old or older simply because of that person's age, you are expressing an age stereotype. If either you or that 60-year-old coworker is not promoted simply because of age, then your employer has *discriminated* (i.e., behaved on the basis of a prejudicial attitude).

Thanks to nonpreferential affirmative-action plans and diversity-management programs, prejudice and discrimination in the workplace can be avoided somewhat. But the reality is, these conditions exist, and you should expect to encounter negative attitudes to some degree in your future workplaces. Become familiar with your organization's policies and procedures regarding prejudice, discrimination, and harassment. As for stereotypes, some people may change their attitudes toward a particular group based on how individuals in that group perform; others will retain their stereotypes regardless of a person's performance achievements.

In almost any organization, there are policies and practices that become irritating. In *They Don't Teach Corporate in College*, Alexandra Levit (2009) identified several annoyances in the corporate world that can contribute to negative attitudes:

Hierarchies: You can get in trouble for speaking with someone at a higher level without first going through proper channels.

Denigration: The younger you are, the less respect you receive.

Bureaucracy: Lengthy approval processes are common because of the numerous levels of oversight involved.

Hypocrisy: Sometimes the company does not practice the values it preaches.

Micromanagement: Some managers are critically involved with every miniscule stage of a project.

As an employee, your frustration may be justified, but you must learn to respond maturely.

> Negativity might be a natural reaction to frustration, but that doesn't mean it's the right one. Pessimistic twenty-somethings waste a lot of energy being unhappy. They're unpopular with their colleagues because they suck the life out of everyone around them, and their corporate personas suffer because they are perceived as immature. (Levit, 2009, p. 169)

To maintain a positive attitude, Levit (2009) suggested that you learn to "adjust your thoughts, let go of irrational expectations, and manage your emotions to banish anger, worry, and stress [and] you will genuinely become a happier and more peaceful person" (p. 169). In addition, we recommend you practice the methods of stress reduction offered in Chapter 12.

Time Out: Exercise

In Chapter 5, we summarized the results of the Collegiate Employment Research Institute report (Chao & Gardner, 2007b) about job characteristics young adults seek. We adapted some characteristics of this survey and added a few of our own to create a short job satisfaction instrument you can apply to your job (current or previous). Keep in mind that if you are only a part-time employee, some characteristics may be difficult to achieve. If you are not achieving your goals in a part-time job, the fact that you experience the absence of these qualities can be instructive as you prepare for full-time employment. Indicate below the extent of your satisfaction with each of the following characteristics, where 1 = *very dissatisfied,* 2 = *dissatisfied,* 3 = *not sure,* 4 = *satisfied,* and 5 = *very satisfied.*

- – Opportunities to learn new skills
- – Limited job stress
- – Job security/steady employment
- – Pay/salary
- – Interesting work
- – Flexible work hours
- – Opportunity to develop positive relationships with others
- – Your supervisor
- – Chances for promotion
- – Recognition or reward for work well done

Sum your scores for each item, and calculate the average rating.

1. To what extent does your average score accurately reflect your level of job satisfaction?

2. What reasonable or realistic changes in your job would increase your satisfaction if you had the power to change them?

3. To what extent could a change in your attitude (recalling William James's observation) improve your satisfaction?

4. How applicable to your situation are each of the three approaches to job satisfaction—value theory, social information processing, and dispositional model?

The Many Faces of Organizational Justice

Have you ever completed a course expecting a particular grade—for example, a B—but instead received a disappointing C or an unexpected A? Chances are you had no trouble dealing with the A, but you probably muttered, "What did I do to *justify* the C?" and subsequently e-mailed the instructor. Justice is also an important concept in the workplace, because your attitudes, satisfaction, and performance, as in the classroom, are influenced by your expectations and perceptions of justice and equity. Organizational justice is concerned with an individual's perceptions of and reactions to fairness and unfairness in the workplace; it may focus on individuals (e.g., a supervisor or manager) or the organization as a whole (Greenberg, 2010).

The concept of justice is abstract, so let's describe the forms of organizational justice with concrete examples. *Distributive justice* focuses on "people's beliefs that they have received fair amounts of valued work-related outcomes" (Greenberg, 2010, p. 37), such as pay, recognition, and benefits—or, in the example above, a fair grade. Distributive justice is concerned with an equitable relationship between your performance and the rewards you receive. Your perceptions (notice, our focus is on perceptions, not on external standards) of fairness or unfairness will influence your feelings about your overall job satisfaction. For example, let's say you are the eager new hire who works productively, willingly labors extra hours, and volunteers for tasks others avoid. One day, you notice the behavior of two coworkers who were hired a few weeks before you and at higher pay. Every 2 or 3 weeks, they slow their work pace, socialize continuously, and spend little time at their computers for a day or two before returning to their normal work routine. Their behavior irritates you, and you conclude that the rewards for good work in your department are unfairly distributed.

Another form of organizational justice is called *informational justice* because it is concerned with the way an individual perceives the fairness of the information received (i.e., its accuracy or completeness) for making decisions; it focuses on the openness and thoroughness of communications in the organization (Greenberg, 2010). Returning to the example above, the distributive injustice you perceive toward your coworkers irritates you so much that you complain to your supervisor. If your supervisor curtly dismisses your concern and says the situation is none of your business and you should not worry, you may also experience informational injustice. That is, you would feel devalued because your supervisor's response would be meaningless, giving you no true information about your concern. Instead, however, the supervisor patiently points out that your coworkers were hired 2 weeks before the organization declared a companywide bonus, and what appears to be slacking is due to their efficiency in completing tasks before the supervisor can assign new ones. Hearing this information might cause you to feel less irritated, because it is a fair explanation and certainly better than none at all. The lesson for you in this example is to withhold judgment about the apparent unfairness of a situation until you gain sufficient information to render a judgment. Informational justice is enhanced when important information, decisions, policies, and procedures are explained clearly to all involved.

In this example, we also encounter a third form of organizational justice—namely, *interpersonal justice,* which characterizes a person's perception regarding the extent to which she or he is treated fairly by others. The supervisor who senses your dissatisfaction and understands (but not necessarily agrees with) your perceptions of the distributive injustice is showing respect by listening to your concerns and offering explanations for your perceptions. The extent to which you are treated (and you treat others) with dignity and respect, apart from one's level of agreement on a particular issue, is a strong determiner of interpersonal justice. Finally, *procedural justice* refers to an individual's perceptions about the fairness of procedures and policies used to determine the outcomes he or she receives (Greenberg, 2010).

If the coworkers entered the organization just before the distribution of a companywide bonus determined in advance by an acceptable procedure, that was their good fortune; it was your misfortune to have missed the bonus. Was the supervisor obligated to explain (i.e., follow a procedure) why your coworkers earn more than you and why they appear to be slacking at their jobs? Perhaps not. Clear procedures are important in establishing salary and benefits, promotions, performance reviews, and similar issues. Procedural justice is improved in situations where members have a voice in decisions that affect them, where companywide rules and policies are applied consistently, and where decision makers operate without bias (Greenberg, 2010).

You may have noticed that the four types of organizational justice are not completely independent of one another. Criteria for distributive justice are often tied to procedures, procedures rely on information, and information can be communicated in a positive or negative interpersonal manner. Nevertheless, keeping these distinctions in mind can help you begin to understand the various faces of organizational justice. Determining justice or injustice is a complex process in an organization. You do not want to be treated unjustly or exploited because you are a new employee, but as a new hire you do not have knowledge of or experience with the organization's culture, policies and procedures, or members. Furthermore, if your past work experience is minimal, you have little or no basis for comparison. During your orientation to a new job, learn as much as you can about the organization, especially its policies and procedures on issues such as performance reviews, salary, promotions, benefits, and other work-related outcomes. If you encounter situations that appear to be unjust, try to see issues from different perspectives, seek information, and give yourself plenty of time to form judgments. Consulting with a trusted mentor or mature coworker is a helpful way to explore the issues.

Let's return to that unexpected low grade you received. Before you meet with the teacher, carefully review the course syllabus and the notes you took during the first day of class—perhaps the most important class of the term—as well as your other notes. Also consider the particular days you were absent or late. Your syllabus and notes should reflect *information* and *procedures* that explain how outcomes of your work are *distributed* in relation to the grade you receive, such as the weights for exams, papers, and other assignments; attendance policies; and required texts. Good teachers will provide you with substantial (but do not expect complete) information that promotes the forms of justice summarized above. Remember, however, that unlike a product you purchase—where its quality and your satisfaction depend primarily on the manufacturer and seller—the quality of your education depends primarily on what you (not the teacher) have contributed or not contributed to it. And when you meet with your teacher, express your concerns in such a way (i.e., do your part) that *interpersonal* justice prevails.

Time Out: Reflective Questions

Spend a few minutes reflecting on your current or past job as it relates to organizational justice.

1. To what extent is/was your overall satisfaction with the job related to . . .
    a. distributive justice?
    b. procedural justice?
    c. informational justice?
    d. interpersonal justice?

2. To what extent are/were the forms of justice related in that job?

Work Motivation

Motives and attitudes interact with each other in complex and often interdependent ways. From the many theories of work motivation discussed in the literature, we summarize two theories that can be applied to several situations you are likely to encounter. Motivation refers to those processes that arouse, direct, and maintain your behavior toward a particular goal (Greenberg, 2010). At a mention of the name Maslow, you are likely to recall a diagram of his needs hierarchy as it appeared in your general psychology text: physiological, safety, social, self-esteem, and self-actualization—with physiological needs placed at the bottom of the pyramid and self-actualization placed in the pointy top of the pyramid. Whereas research over the years has revealed flaws with the Maslow hierarchy, the theory remains popular in organizational training and motivation sessions, with this basic message: Your job should fulfill the first two levels, satisfy many of your social needs, promote self-esteem (assuming you enjoy your work), and could lead to self-actualization (some trainers may proclaim). As there are occasions when all of us feel motivated or unmotivated to work, we explore two perspectives to help you understand how your motives may operate; each incorporates fundamental concepts of psychology with which you are likely familiar.

Expectancy Theory in Motivation and Performance

Expectancy theory maintains that people are motivated to work when they believe their efforts will help them achieve their goals. Developed by Porter and Lawler (1968; as cited in Greenberg, 2010), the theory asserts that a person's motivation consists of three beliefs:

Expectancy: A person's *effort* will influence *performance.*

Instrumentality: The *performance* will be *rewarded* (i.e., performance is instrumental to receiving a reward).

Valence: The *rewards* have a particular value to the individual.

Although this theory postulates that the relationships among these components are multiplicative, we focus only on its basic elements. Motivation is a central but not sole component of performance; a person's abilities, traits, role perceptions, and opportunities also contribute. Motivation depends on one's *beliefs,* which may or may not reflect the reality of a situation. Companies that use merit pay plans or pay-for-performance plans are linking expectancy, instrumentality, and valence beliefs (Greenberg, 2010).

Chances are you have applied the expectancy theory often to allocate your time and efforts to assignments and activities. For example, Jared has only 2 days during the final week of classes to write a paper for Art History and to prepare a 10-minute presentation for his capstone psychology course. Each assignment counts for 20% of the final grade, but his motivation to complete them differs. He knows the art history assignment will require considerable time just to write an above-average paper, and he knows the teacher is a tough grader; although the class has been enjoyable, he does not believe the course will benefit him much in the long run. In short, he believes that his efforts may not contribute to a high level of performance (expectancy), that his performance will not be rewarded by a high grade (instrumentality), and that the knowledge acquired from writing the paper will not be particularly useful in the future (valence). The 10-minute talk required for his capstone course has a different motivating effect. Jared has performed well in the course and expects to continue at this level (expectancy); he likes to give oral presentations and knows the teacher is lenient on grading them (instrumentality); and he knows a high grade in his capstone course will make his transcript a little more attractive to a potential employer or graduate school (valence).

Let's examine the three belief systems in expectancy theory as they apply to obtaining a job, working backward with the concepts. Before and during a job interview process, you should obtain clear information about the nature of the work, opportunities for advancement, pay, and job benefits and similar rewards. Many companies offer cafeteria-style benefit plans that allow employees to choose from several alternative benefits (valence). In accepting the job, you will probably presume (believe) performance will be rewarded appropriately through timely feedback and an evaluation system that is implemented fairly (instrumentality). To the extent this information is clearly understood, both you and the company will benefit.

Variability and uncertainty reside in the expectancy beliefs. If you have performed the same or similar tasks in previous jobs in similar settings, your expectancy belief is likely to be high—that is, effort will lead to successful performance. If all or most of the tasks are new for you or if you have limited prior work experience, your expectancy set of beliefs may not be strong and you will probably be willing to work hard to strengthen the needed skills.

A Digression: Expectancy Theory Applied to Your Expectations

College students have high expectations for using their expensive and time-intensive college educations to establish careers and enrich their lives. You expend considerable financial, intellectual, emotional, and physical resources for 4 or more years to acquire the knowledge and skills that culminate in a bachelor's degree. Probably, you have been conditioned to this expectation since elementary or high school. You also firmly believe that your college education will be well rewarded: It is instrumental to receiving the numerous rewards you have dreamed about. Finally, you believe the rewards for achieving higher education have strong and lasting value (valence), including advancement, a rewarding career, healthy relationships, financial security, and other components of "the good life."

Such expectations may be readily met when the U.S. economy is strong, when unemployment is low, when challenge and advancement in a job are readily accessible, and when employment benefits are generous. However, during an economic downturn, soaring national debt, domestic and international conflicts, and other serious problems our country is facing in the second decade of the 21st century, the expectations of many college graduates are being shattered. Jobs are scarce, graduates have debts to pay, many new grads must trade their prized independence for living inexpensively at home again, and many college seniors and graduates feel discouraged. In short, the motivation for some college students to complete their education decreases in the face of high loan debt, poor job opportunities after graduation, and undeveloped skill sets. As a result, some students are dropping out or stopping out to seek full-time work—any job that provides income. They fear accumulating debt, as all of us do. However, it is very important for students to keep debt in perspective. According to the Project on Student Debt (Institute for College Access and Success, 2010), the average 2009 graduate began post-college life with about $24,000 in loans to repay (it can be much higher if you attend a private institution). This average debt sounds like a heavy burden until you realize that if you were to buy a car for $20,000 (a low-end model), signing for a 3- to 5-year loan for that amount would be standard—an amount most people do not fear. Your car may be a necessity, but it is an expense and not an investment, because after 5 years, its trade-in value may be less than half what you paid.

In contrast, your college loan debt is an investment—it's good debt, representing an asset that will (presumably) increase in value over the years; it amounts to only about 1% of lifetime earnings for typical graduates (Settersten & Ray, 2010). Individuals with only a high school diploma have estimated lifetime earnings of $1.2 million; those with a bachelor's degree, $2.1 million; and those with a professional degree, $4.4 million (Tanner & Arnett, 2011). These amounts may differ from survey to survey, and the gaps between education and pay levels may differ from occupation to occupation (Network on Transitions to Adulthood, 2011). Not only does your college degree enable you to achieve a high level of lifetime earnings (and enjoy the good life), but without it you do not have access to graduate or professional programs you may seek after a few years in the workplace.

When an individual drops out of college to join the workforce, it is easy to forget the importance of higher education, accumulate unnecessary material goods (that lead to further debt), and become caught up in a lifestyle that may exclude further education. If finances force you to consider dropping out of college or you do not believe your psychology major (or any other liberal arts major) will lead to a satisfying job, consider the kinds of educational options—for example, certificate or technical programs—discussed in Chapter 2, but do not drop out unless absolutely necessary. Whatever option you choose, higher education—whether in a 4-year liberal arts or professional/applied program—is always an investment in your future, regardless of the economy and labor market you face upon graduation.

As former Harvard President Derek Bok remarked, "If you think education is expensive, try ignorance." In the long run, your expectancy beliefs will be confirmed. History shows that the economy always recovers sooner or later. The current generation of college graduates may have to wait a few years longer than their predecessors did to achieve their career goals, but with education, a strong work ethic, and the willingness to pursue a zigzag course to your career, the goals are likely to be attained. In the meantime, *you must be persistent, patient, and proactive.* As Settersten and Ray (2010) pointed out, "The key . . . is to graduate. Those who drop out of college with student debt are not reaping the full payoff from a college degree, and yet they still have a college tuition bill to pay" (p. 34).

Time Out: Reflective Question

In what ways do the high costs of your education influence (a) your motivation to complete your degree and (b) your three expectancy beliefs?

Goal-Setting Theory of Work Motivation

We introduce you to goal-setting theory for three reasons: (a) Establishing goals is one of the most effective ways to motivate yourself, (b) many organizations apply goal-setting theory to motivate and evaluate their employees, and (c) you probably apply goal-setting concepts to your behavior. Based on the work of Edwin Locke and Gary Latham (1990), goal-setting theory is based on the notion that you become motivated to achieve a particular goal when you are able to compare your present performance to a standard or outcome you seek. Chances are you set goals implicitly or explicitly for many of your activities: to establish a positive relationship with a roommate, friend, or significant other; to work effectively in your job and be acknowledged by your supervisor; to make the intramural or varsity team; to become an officer in Psi Chi or other campus organizations; to receive a high grade in Dr. Curmudgeon's notoriously hard psychology course. The major concepts of the Locke and Latham goal-setting theory include

- recognition that achieving the goal poses a challenge;
- assessment of one's level of personal commitment to the goal, which is a function of one's desire to attain the goal and perceived probability of reaching it; and
- assessment of one's self-efficacy beliefs (belief in one's ability to perform a task; Greenberg, 2010).

When the levels of personal commitment and self-efficacy beliefs are high, the individual is motivated to perform at the goal level he or she established. For example, perhaps you want to find a job after graduation that tests your potential interest in pursuing a graduate degree in applied developmental psychology. You believe it will be challenging (but possible) to find such a job, and you believe the pay will barely sustain you, but it is important to discover the work you want to build a career around. Your strong *desire* to find that job combined with your belief (*perception*) that finding that job is attainable (using the job-search tools described in Chapter 7) reflect your *commitment to the goal*—that is, your determination to reach it. Although the goal poses a real challenge, your commitment is high, meaning you are more likely to achieve it than if your commitment were low. Finally, past successes in your psychology courses plus your volunteer work with developmentally disabled children have created high levels of *self-efficacy;* that is, you strongly believe that you can succeed in finding the job you seek. Knowing the conceptual ingredients of goal-setting theory is important, but achieving your goals requires the application of three principles: establishing specific goals, establishing challenging but acceptable goals, and obtaining feedback about your goals.

Establishing Specific Goals

If your goal is simply "I want to work with kids," you might find yourself interviewing for jobs in a day-care center, as a camp counselor at your local YMCA, or simply babysitting—jobs that are a waste of time given the particular experience you seek. Be specific when you articulate your goal: "I will actively seek a full-time job where I can work with children under 13 who have either a developmental, emotional, or physical disability." An additional goal might include "I want to work in a setting with diverse professional staff from whom I can learn." You may have to expend considerable effort to locate an organization that meets your goals, but you are likely to be more satisfied in reaching your specific goals than if you accepted a less-desirable job based on vague goals.

Establishing Challenging but Acceptable Goals

When goals are not challenging enough, there is little incentive to reach them; when goals are too difficult, they are rejected as unattainable. In such situations, motivation deteriorates. Sometimes it is difficult to know when a goal is challenging but attainable. If your goal in the example above is restricted to seeking a full-time job that pays $35,000 per year and involves working a regular shift in a hospital or similar facility that cares for children with bipolar disorders, you might never achieve that goal; it probably is too specific and unrealistic. Be willing to reevaluate, adjust, and adapt your goals to the realities of the situation. For example, if you can't obtain a full-time job, would you settle for working two part-time jobs in similar agencies? If the nature of your work is satisfying but the schedule requires you to work night shifts and most weekends, are you willing to make that adjustment? If the salary barely covers your living expenses, will you accept that challenge to get the job you seek? The old saying that "beggars can't be choosers" applies when your options are limited. If you truly want the experience of working with a population of special children to test your interests in graduate school, be prepared to modify your goals and expectations to achieve satisfactory results.

Obtaining Feedback About Your Goals

As a psychology major, you know the importance of feedback for changing performance. In the example above, you decided to seek a particular kind of job to test your interest in pursuing a graduate degree. You set a specific and challenging goal, and with persistence and good job-search skills, you found the job you believed would provide the opportunity you need for an important career decision. After you start working, you will search for feedback almost continuously: How well do I like working with this population of children? What do I like and dislike about this organization? What insights am I gaining from the staff? What aspects of the organizational atmosphere make it a positive or negative experience? What opportunities exist to broaden my experiences and skill sets? If you answer these and similar questions, you are likely to achieve the goal you originally established; your answer may reveal itself in a matter of weeks. The process of establishing specific and challenging goals for your immediate post-college experiences and obtaining thoughtful feedback is a motivational force that enables you to answer an important career decision.

You have applied the concepts of goal-setting theory: You compared the information you possessed as a senior to the information and experiences you sought and obtained several months later. And by implementing the principles of goal specificity, challenging goals, and obtaining feedback, you accomplished your goals successfully. When you enter the workplace, chances are you will encounter goal setting or one of its variants, such as S.M.A.R.T. (Simple, Measurable, Attainable, Realistic, and Timely) as a self-assessment technique in performance reviews or as a project management procedure (J. Keil, personal communications, September 12, 2011).

Intrinsic Motivation

As an astute psychology major, you probably noticed the concept of reinforcement embedded in each of the two previous theories of work motivation: the expectation of reward and valence in the expectancy theory and feedback in the goal-setting theory. You may also recall that reward theories have been criticized as inadequate to explain all motivated behavior; intrinsic motivation promotes some behaviors that external rewards do not. Pink (2009) would agree with this, and he argued persuasively from empirical studies that most business organizations operate primarily on carrot-and-stick external motivators, or what he calls the Motivation 2.0 operating system (Motivation 1.0 refers to our basic biological drives), when they should be using Motivation 3.0. Pink's concept of a Motivation 3.0 system is derived primarily from the research of Ryan and Deci (2000) on self-determination theory, which postulates the three innate needs of autonomy, competence, and relatedness. Pink connects to these investigations the work of psychologists Seligman, Csikszentmihalyi, Dweck, Amabile, Gardner, and Sternberg, and economists Benabou and Fry. Throughout his book, Pink drew on many examples from business organizations to illustrate his ideas.

At the risk of oversimplifying complex behaviors to make his points, Pink (2009) discusses Type I (Intrinsic) and Type X (Extrinsic) behaviors.

> Type I behavior: A way of thinking and an approach to life built around intrinsic, rather than extrinsic, motivators. It is powered by our innate need to direct our own lives to learn and create new things, and to do better by ourselves and our world. (p. 226)

In contrast, Type X behavior is "fueled more by extrinsic desires than intrinsic ones and . . . concerns itself less with the inherent satisfaction of an activity and more with the external rewards to which that activity leads" (p. 226).

Differences between types X and I are not mutually exclusive (Type I persons can enjoy rewards, and Type X persons can enjoy what they do), but they do exist. First, although external rewards can produce a high rate of responding in the short term, Pink (2009) believes that Type I individuals nearly always outperform Type X individuals in the long run (Type I persons persist through difficulties because of their internal motivation). Second, Type X and Type I individuals are each concerned about money, but once they achieve an adequate level of compensation, Type I persons become more concerned about the inner satisfaction their efforts produce, including feedback, whereas Type X persons seek compensation and recognition as an end in itself. Third, Type I behavior is a "renewable resource" that keeps giving and growing, whereas Type X behavior requires larger and more frequent rewards. Fourth, the intrinsic motivation of Type I behavior promotes self-esteem, healthy relationships, and better well-being in comparison with Type X behavior.

What are the elements that fuel Type I behavior? Again, drawing on the work of Ryan and Deci (2000) and the others mentioned above, Pink (2009) identified the key elements as *autonomy, mastery,* and *purpose*—elements addressed in the second sentence of his definition above. He anchored his concept of *autonomy* to that of Ryan and Deci, who view this quality as acting with full volition. Autonomy is not a go-it-alone individualism and independence; it is acting with choice. A person can be both autonomous and interdependent with others. Pink (2009) also stated that "autonomous motivation promotes greater conceptual understanding, better grades, enhanced persistence at school and in sporting activities, higher productivity, less burnout, and greater levels of psychological well-being" (pp. 88–89). If organizations want employees to act autonomously, they must find ways to give them control of their *tasks* (what they do), the *time* (when they can do it), the *team* (individuals with whom they do it), and the *technique* (how they do it; Pink, 2009).

Whereas Motivation 2.0 uses an "if–then" reward system to produce mastery of tasks in the workplace, Motivation 3.0 seeks *engagement* (the second element of Type I behavior) by the employee. Pink (2009) uses Csikszentmihalyi's (2000) concept of flow as a foundation for mastery. Flow refers to the highly satisfying, self-rewarding, optimal experiences that occur when the challenges a person faces are well matched to that person's abilities. This occurs, for example, when the athlete performs a "career best" in a playoff game or when the highly prepared student leaves the demanding final exam supremely confident in having achieved an A. But flow is a special experience that is hard to achieve in daily activities; flow occurs in moments, but mastery can require months or years, depending on the demands of the task.

According to Pink (2009), *mastery* operates by three rules. First, it is a mind-set that requires the individuals to view their abilities as infinitely improvable, not finite or limited; this mind-set is not easily achieved. Second, mastery is a pain. Mastery requires an irrevocable commitment to practice. Gladwell (2008) argued persuasively that many individuals we regard as the best in their professions may be very talented but achieved their greatness through long hours and years of practice, not by talent alone. For instance, before coming to the United States in 1964, the Beatles had played together since 1957, including many long (8-hour), "hard-day's-night," 7-day-per-week engagements in Hamburg, Germany. Bill Gates did real-time programming as an eighth-grader in 1968 and is said to have lived in a computer room after that. Violin soloists considered "elite" in their profession now had practiced about 10,000 hours by age 20 (Gladwell, 2008). Finally, remember what we have been told since childhood, that practice makes perfect (with feedback, of course).

The third rule for achieving mastery is to realize that mastery is an asymptote, which means you can get close to perfection but never reach it. "You can approach it. You can home in on it. You can get really, really, really close to it . . . .. Mastery is impossible to realize fully" (Pink, 2009, p. 125). It may be frustrating to know you cannot fully reach mastery, but you may be allured into pursuing it anyway.

The third element of Type I motivation is *purpose*. Autonomous people are able to achieve a high level of mastery to the extent that they operate with a purpose—they have goals. Pink (2009) believes that the current generation of young workers is helping change organizations insofar as their goals include a variety of non-monetary factors, not simply compensation and profit maximization. In Chapter 5, we summarized a study by Chao and Gardner (2007b) that shows "interesting work" tops benefits and job security as the most sought-after quality in a job. Pink referred to workers' preference for nonmonetary factors as "purpose maximization" and regards it as a significant aspect of Motivation 3.0. Other factors that promote purpose maximization on par with profit maximization include an emphasis on using language that devalues self-interest and organization policies that permit employees to pursue purpose on their own terms (Pink, 2009).

Time Out: Reflective Questions

What does this exploration of Type I and Type X behavior mean for you as a student and as a freshman in the workplace?

Intrinsic motivation is difficult to achieve—some might even say idealistic. Do you need your teachers or your boss to clearly define the consequences of arriving late or doing substandard work (Type X behavior) to motivate you? Or are you intrinsically motivated to arrive at class and your job on time for the satisfaction it provides you, without the threat of punishment, even if your job and classes are routine?

If you are like most students, you should be in the process, as you mature through college, of becoming less dependent on external contingencies for reinforcement and more self-starting and intrinsically motivated, at least for the more important aspects of your life. As for being the new employee—a freshman in the workplace—you might enter a company and work for a supervisor who relies on Motivation 2.0. That's OK if you operate on the Motivation 2.0 system. If your entry-level job consists primarily of routine, sometimes mind-deadening tasks (expect them in most entry-level jobs), the rewards you receive (e.g., keeping your job, receiving your pay and benefits) may be the only reason you can think of to do those tasks correctly without being totally bored, ineffective, and fired. As a suggestion for reducing boredom, Pink (2009) recommended that you (a) admit to yourself that the task is boring, (b) understand the rationale and necessity for performing it (your supervisor might not communicate that), and (c) obtain some freedom to do it your way—probably at your supervisor's discretion (Pink, 2009). If you are a Type X student, you may operate successfully as a Type X employee, though as you progress, ideally, your responsibilities will become more challenging and you will mature to a Type I person. If, however, you accept a job in an organization that is trying to operate on the Motivation 3.0 system, will you be ready for the challenge to grow? If you are mostly Type I now, you are likely to enjoy the challenge and advance.

Motivation: Concluding Comments

In this section, we endeavored to show the role motivation plays in the workplace. You are motivated by the expectations you bring to your job and by the goals you establish. Motivation derives *from you*, but your motivation is strongly influenced by the particular work you do and the organizational environment in which you do it.

Time Out: Exercise

In the list of statements below (Hettich, 1998), mark whether the reasons for attending college were *mostly true (T)* or *mostly false (F)* when you *began* college, and mark them again according to how you perceive them *now*. Be honest with yourself!

Reasons for Attending College	*Beginning*	*Now*
1. To prepare for a personally satisfying career.	_____	_____
2. Because my family wanted me to go.	_____	_____
3. To learn about history, culture, science, and the world in which I live.	_____	_____
4. To be on equal status with my high school friends who attend college.	_____	_____
5. To meet the many personal challenges that college offers.	_____	_____
6. To avoid having to enter the workplace.	_____	_____
7. To learn more about myself and to mature.	_____	_____
8. To satisfy the concerns of friends and family.	_____	_____
9. To develop intellectual, social, moral, and emotional skills.	_____	_____
10. To meet other people my age.	_____	_____

Now sum the number of Ts you marked for all the *odd*-numbered items for each column. Do the same for the *even*-numbered items. Also, note the changes between the time periods.

Intrinsic motives are those that originate primarily within the individual, not primarily from external influences. College is a period of growth and change when many of your motives for doing important things in your life should be evolving from primarily extrinsic to intrinsic. As you summed your answers across all even- and odd-numbered items, you may have noticed that the odd-numbered reasons represent mostly intrinsic motives, while the even-numbered items reflect mostly extrinsic motives.

1. When you began college, were you primarily extrinsically or intrinsically motivated?

2. Based on these self-report items, how would you characterize your motives now?

3. What have you experienced during college that may have shifted your motives from one type to the other (ideally, from extrinsic to intrinsic)?

Work Centrality

We devoted a substantial portion of this chapter to essential concepts of work-related attitudes and motivation because these concepts help you understand how such seminal psychological processes shape your thoughts, feelings, and behavior. But how important *is* work to you? Many readers belong to a generation (the Millennials) that is viewed by many in the workforce with suspicion and sometimes disdain because of a perceived lack of work ethic. Consequently, you may want to become particularly aware of your attitudes and motivation toward work. One of the most central attitudes potential employers want to ascertain is how important work (your job) is to your life. According to Chao and Gardner (2007a),

> More than previous generations, they [young adults] are looking for more than a steady job and good career. They value a high quality of life that views work as one role in a variety of roles that contribute to a good life. Attitudes and values about work can shape how young adults choose careers and commit to specific jobs. Work centrality is an important concept because it describes how involved people are with their work. People who view work as central to their lives are generally more motivated toward high performance and are more satisfied with their work. (p. 3)

Chao and Gardner (2007a) analyzed data collected in a 2005 MonsterTRAK survey of 10,000 young adults between the ages 18 and 28. Work centrality was measured on a 6-point rating scale ranging from *strongly agree* to *strongly disagree*, using a 1982 survey by Kanungo that contained these six items:

1. The most important things that happen in life involve work.

2. Work is something people should get involved in most of the time.

3. Work should be only a small part of one's life.

4. Work should be considered central to life.

5. In my view, an individual's personal life goals should be work-oriented.

6. Life is worth living only when people get absorbed in work.

When the 1982 and 2005 samples were compared, the most pronounced differences were found for questions 6, 4, and 1 (in that order), with lower ratings on work centrality found in the 2005 sample. Similarly, when responses for the combined six items were compared, the 2005 sample showed significantly lower work centrality than did the 1982 sample. In addition, statistically significant differences between men and women were found on all six items, with men showing higher levels of work centrality than did women, although both groups responded in generally similar ways to the items.

Twelve scales were created to compare persons who were rated high, medium, or low on work centrality. Three related factors were job surfing (willingness to try out different jobs to find one that matches one's interests and abilities), career/life vision (no well-defined career plan or vision of a career in 10 years), and delayed marriage (marriage was not a high priority at this time). On the career/life vision and delayed marriage subscales, high-work-centrality persons scored highest, followed by medium- and low-work-centrality individuals, respectively. That is, where work centrality is high, young adults tend to have a clearer career and life vision and greater willingness to delay marriage than do the other two groups. Job surfing was strongest among low-centrality and weakest among high-centrality young adults (Chao & Gardner, 2007a).

Two additional scales tapped personality dimensions: a superior factor (belief that a person is superior to or can excel over others) and a goal instability factor (doubts about one's self and ability to follow through on goals related to work). Individuals high in work centrality held statistically higher superior beliefs than did the medium-centrality group, which felt more superior to low-centrality adults. No significant differences were found on the goal instability factor (Chao & Gardner, 2007a).

Three scales measured attitudes toward business, government, and religious leaders. In general, the Chao and Gardner (2007a) sample demonstrated the most trust in religious leaders, followed by business and then government leaders. Level of centrality was not important in the religion category, but in comparisons between government and business, centrality levels were statistically significant. High-centrality persons expressed greater trust in business (followed by government) than did medium-centrality persons; low-centrality adults were the least trusting across the three organizations. The authors suggested that high-work-centrality adults are able to find role models that can help them develop positive work roles. In contrast, the low-work-centrality adults were the least trusting. "Perhaps those young adults who hold low opinions on current leaders are less likely to be influenced by them and thus less likely to hold conventional attitudes and values toward work" (p. 9).

Finally, the three work-centrality groups were compared on four scales that reflect the importance of job characteristics young adults seek: interesting work (work flexibility and independence, travel, and interesting work), security (good benefits, opportunity to learn new skills, location, and job security), low stress (limited overtime, regular hours, annual vacations of at least 1 week, and limited job stress), and success (high income, prestigious company, and chances for promotion). The analyses revealed no significant differences among the three groups for the importance of security and interesting work. However, low-work-centrality adults rated the low stress factor significantly higher in importance than did the medium-centrality group, which assigned it greater importance than did high-centrality adults. Finally, success was significantly more important to high- and medium-centrality adults than to low-centrality adults. Chao and Gardner (2007a) concluded their analyses with this observation:

> The results in this report suggest that the current generation of young adults
> is drifting away from conventional values of work as a central life interest.
> They are looking for more balance between work and non-work ("non-work"
> includes all roles/activities outside a person's job—e.g., family, recreation,
> religion, civic activities, etc.). (p. 11)

Time Out: Exercise

Briefly review the findings of Chao and Gardner (2007a) above.

1. After answering the six scale questions, would you group yourself with the high-, medium-, or low-work-centrality groups?

2. What do you believe your current employer would think about the findings on work centrality?

3. Beginning with the economic recession in 2008, numerous organizations across the country have reduced their workforces and required the remaining employees to shoulder an increased workload, usually without additional compensation. Assuming that situation generally characterizes the workplace you will enter, what are implications of the Chao and Gardner findings for you as you enter the workplace? For example, if your work centrality is high, what can you expect of yourself from employers who demand long work hours, perhaps with minimal benefits and few opportunities for advancement? If your work centrality is medium or low, how well are you likely to adapt? What are your options?

4. To what extent are your attitudes and motives toward work important to understand in such situations?

Closing Comments

We began this chapter with William James's observation that you can alter your life by altering your attitude. We explored basic dimensions of workplace attitudes, summarized three theories of workplace motivation, and examined survey results of workplace centrality. We repeat our advice from past chapters to become actively involved in college activities that promote workplace readiness, examine your skills in-depth, take steps to plan your career, develop strong communication and interpersonal skills, and critically study other issues we address. Ultimately, it is up to you to critically examine your work-related attitudes and motives and decide how they can be strengthened, knowing well that if you can change your mind, you can change your life.

Getting Involved

Journal Starters

1. What are the most significant insights you gained from this chapter?

2. Think about a specific project or activity in which you are now or were recently engaged where your motivation wavered or deteriorated (e.g., a group project,

a campus organization you joined, your job, a relationship, or other activity to which you made commitments and subsequently felt left down).

a. Analyze this activity (Why not outline or diagram it?) in terms of your expectancy, instrumentality, and valence beliefs. To what extent are these belief systems being met? To what extent do your abilities, role perceptions, and opportunities influence your performance and overall motivation?

b. Use the concepts and principles of goal-setting theory to improve the situation you described above. What resources and barriers can affect the change?

3. Relate Pink's (2009) concepts of autonomy, mastery, and purpose to your responses on the checklist. To what extent do you believe you are autonomous? Achieving mastery? Operating with purpose?

Projects

1. Review the literature on either the goal-setting or expectancy theory of work motivation, with emphasis on its applicability to entering the workforce.

2. Design a study that tests the connection between expectancy theory and dissatisfaction with entry-level jobs.

3. Conduct a survey of students in your class regarding their levels of work centrality, and report its findings to your class.

Additional Resources

URL	Brief Website Description
http://transitions.s410.sureserver.com/	The Network on Transitions to Adulthood
http://www.ourtime.org	Our Time is a "national non-profit network of young Americans . . . [that] leverages pop culture, retail partnerships, and online organizing to promote thoughtful consumerism and civic engagement."

References

Chao, G. T., & Gardner, P. D. (2007a, May). *How central is work to young adults?* (White paper prepared for MonsterTRAK). East Lansing: Michigan State University Collegiate Employment Research Institute. Retrieved from http://www.ceri.msu.edu/publications/pdf/work_young_adults.pdf

Chao, G. T., & Gardner, P. D. (2007b, Winter). *Important characteristics of early career jobs: What do young adults want?* (White paper prepared for MonsterTRAK). East Lansing: Michigan State University Collegiate Employment Research Institute. Retrieved from http:www.ceri.msu.edu/publications/pdf/JobChar4-16.pdf

Csikszentmihalyi, M. (2000). *Beyond boredom and anxiety: Experiencing flow in work and play.* San Francisco, CA: Jossey-Bass.

Gladwell, M. (2008). *Outliers: The story of success.* New York, NY: Little, Brown.

Greenberg, J. (2010). *Managing behavior in organizations* (5th ed.). Upper Saddle River, NJ: Prentice Hall.

Hettich, P. (1998). *Learning skills for college and career* (2nd ed.). Pacific Grove, CA: Brooks/Cole.

Institute for College Access and Success. (2010, October). *Student debt and the class of 2009.* Oakland, CA: Author. Retrieved from http://projectonstudentdebt.org/files/pub/classof2009.pdf

Levit, A. (2009). *They don't teach corporate in college: A twenty-something's guide to the business world.* Franklin Lakes, NJ: Career Press.

Locke, E. A., & Latham, G. P. (1990). *A theory of goal setting and task performance.* Upper Saddle River, NJ: Prentice Hall.

Network on Transitions to Adulthood. (2011, August 8). Education still pays, but the devil is in the details. Retrieved from http://transitions2adulthood.com/?s=education+still+pays%2C +but+the+devil+is+in+the details

Pink, D. H. (2009). *Drive: The surprising truth about what motivates us.* New York, NY: Riverhead Books.

Ryan, R. M., & Deci, E. L. (2000). Self-determination theory and the facilitation of intrinsic motivation, social development, and well-being. *American Psychologist, 55,* 68–78.

Settersten, R., & Ray, B. E. (2010). *Not quite adults: Why 20-somethings are choosing a slower path to adulthood, and why it's good for everyone.* New York, NY: Bantam Books Trade Paperbacks.

Tanner, J. L., & Arnett, J. J. (2011). Presenting "emerging adulthood": What makes it developmentally distinctive? In J. J. Arnett, M. Kloep, L. B. Hendry, & J. L. Tanner (Eds.), *Debating emerging adulthood: Stage or process?* (pp. 13–30). New York, NY: Oxford University Press.

CHAPTER 9

Your First Real Job? It's Primarily About Communicating

*Work is an extension of personality: It is achievement. It is one of the ways
in which a person defines himself, measures his worth, and his humanity.*

—Peter F. Drucker (1974), management consultant and author

rucker's remarks reflect a high ideal and the attainable goal of integrating one's work and personality, at least to some extent. His comments may not reflect your early post-college job experiences, especially during a tight labor market, but those experiences will exert influence on your identity, your perceptions of self-efficacy, how you relate to others, and your achievements. The positive outcomes of your early experiences will be enhanced to the extent that you were prepared to navigate your organization's communications and collaborative environment; the negative outcomes are opportunities for self-reflection, change, and growth. An essential component of how you define yourself, whether through your job or personal relationships, is your ability to communicate and work with other people. Kathy Kane, senior vice president for Talent Management at New York-based staffing firm Adecco, observed:

> This generation has more reason than others before it to think they can come into the workplace and change it, that they can become CEO in five years. What's funny is that many of them are actually so good with technology and innovative thinking that they really can change things for the better. But they

need to work on their interpersonal skills first so they can use that talent more effectively. (McIlvaine, 2011, para. 7)

Communications Concepts for College and Career

By graduation, you probably will have completed at least two courses in writing, learned the basics of writing American Psychological Association style, and given several oral presentations in class. However, do not feel complacent about your communication skills, even if you receive high grades for your writing, because the National Association of Colleges and Employers (NACE, 2011) survey of employers reports that communication, including written and verbal skills, is simultaneously the skill set employers value most and college graduates are most deficient in. Landrum, Hettich, and Wilner (2010) identified "work well with others" and "meet the needs of others, such as clients or customers" among the top five skills employers expected of graduates. You can acquire written, verbal, and presentation skills primarily through your coursework. To the extent you complete several courses that require challenging group projects, you may be able to work well with others. To meet the needs of others, you'll likely need to have the appropriate job experiences. In this chapter, we address fundamental concepts of workplace communications and interpersonal skills employers expect you to possess when you *begin* your job, and we introduce you to emotional intelligence. These concepts may also be applied to the job you currently hold, to the in-class and extracurricular groups to which you belong, and to your day-to-day interactions with friends, family, and classmates.

The Direction of Communications

Formal communication in an organization travels upward, downward, and horizontally. In downward communications, executives, managers, and supervisors transmit information in the form of directives, policy, instructions, and feedback to be followed by lower-level employees. Sometimes when this information travels through several levels downward, it may become distorted, unless it is transmitted to large numbers of people simultaneously at different levels. In upward communication, information such as data, status reports, or recommendations is conveyed, often formally, from lower-level employees to supervisors and their managers. Upward communication is also open to inaccuracies and distortion, especially if mistakes or other negative information is omitted to keep a lower-level employee from looking bad. In horizontal communication, information is transmitted laterally and often casually between equal hierarchical levels of the organization and usually involves the coordination of efforts by members of different departments (Greenberg, 2010).

If you hold a job, you may understand how the directions of communication operate in your organization, but communications in college and workplace settings may differ substantially. On a typical day, most of your communication is likely to be horizontal and informal with your peers, though not necessarily to coordinate activities. In classes or meetings with your teachers, advisor, or administrative staff, you generally communicate upward and somewhat formally and measured. Formality in upward communication is very important in the workplace. According to Keil (Hettich, 2010), your boss will expect you to communicate professionally orally and in writing—that is, clearly, concisely, expressing complete thoughts, and with a minimum of abbreviated or slang terminology. As your e-mails may be kept on a company server, you will think carefully about what you write. Your manner of self-presentation (e.g., dress, posture, and similar nonverbal cues) will influence your overall message. You will not be in college anymore, where unprofessional speech, dress, and manner of communication were tolerated even by some faculty and staff. And do not expect a diploma to automatically delete substandard habits (if you possess any) and substitute the professionalism expected of graduates.

Finally, become aware of your company's span of control or chain of command, the organizational chart of the hierarchical structure of who reports to whom. In most situations, your upward and downward communications are exclusively with your supervisor and seldom with your supervisor's boss or counterpart in another department. On those occasions when you might communicate with anyone above or on the same level as your supervisor, think carefully about what you say. If a supervisor is ignoring complaints of bullying, harassment, discrimination, or other serious personnel issues, it is appropriate for you to seek assistance through the organization's human resources department. If your complaints pertain to task-related matters or inappropriate or obnoxious behavior by coworkers, consider meeting with your supervisor (after your attempts to communicate with coworkers have failed and you have carefully explored all aspects of the situation). As a new employee, however, you may not understand the full context of the issues and your organizational culture, so we advise you to seek the views of a respected coworker or mentor before you initiate action. Different situations will require different responses.

Media Richness

Assume for a few minutes that you work in a large, not-for-profit community organization as the training director of a department that prepares volunteers to work on diverse neighborhood projects in a major urban area. You supervise two full-time employees and four interns, all of whom are present. You begin the day with a very demanding workload, but your boss interrupts and insists you deal immediately with three "critical" items: a new two-page directive from the local fire department regarding next month's fire drill, a notice that planned budget cuts are likely to result next week in the layoffs of one of your employees and two interns, and some sort of volunteer data that are needed by the CEO before she addresses board members that evening. Given your tight schedule and your reputation for efficiency, you decide to e-mail a copy of the fire drill directive to your staff, along with a sentence or two about the personnel cuts; e-mail your recent comprehensive, 30-page report on the agency's volunteers to the CEO; and then get on with your day's workload.

Time Out: Exercise

1. How would you evaluate the training director's decisions about transmitting this information?

2. What would you do differently?

3. Why would you choose that action?

Communications media differ in form along a continuum of richness in which print media such as memos, employee handbooks, and bulletins represent *lean* (one-way and noninteractive) communications, whereas phone and face-to-face discussions represent *rich* (two-way and interactive) communications (Greenberg, 2010). With modern technology, we can include video conferencing as a rich medium, as well as websites, e-mails, and texting, assuming interactive communication is expected. The effectiveness of the training director's message will depend on the form chosen to convey it and on the director's ability to understand the message's audience.

Unfortunately, the director decided to use e-mail for all three messages. As the new fire department directive is a one-way, downward (the organization must comply) message regarding next month's fire drill, an e-mail was the appropriate medium to use. The other two messages, however, require two-way communication and empathy (the ability to share another person's thoughts and feelings). Put yourself in the CEO's shoes: She does not have time to peruse the training director's detailed, 30-page report on volunteers, in spite of the director's hard work and pride in the document. Because it's not clear what particular information she needs, the training director should have phoned the CEO's office and asked about the specific parameters needed. Finally, the unfortunate and uncertain news about next week's layoffs will devastate the director's staff. If the director is truly concerned about them, genuine empathy and a face-to-face meeting are necessary—preferably a half hour before they end their day's work.

In short, the choice of a medium that best fits the nature of the message and your ability to anticipate the receiver's reaction to it will exert considerable influence on the manner in which a message is received. The CEO will appreciate having specific information she can present, not a cumbersome, 30-page report; the fire drill policy can be discussed on a day with less pressing agendas; and the employees will appreciate a frank discussion of next week's layoffs, even if the situation is clouded with uncertainties.

In an age of ever-increasing convenient communications technology, you may be tempted to use the medium of least resistance. Tweeting your instructor that you missed an important exam because an automobile accident tied up morning traffic, without asking to meet, is not a sufficient response to the situation. E-mailing or texting a parent or significant other after a major argument is not going to resolve the issue adequately. E-mailing a two-sentence group "thank you" to presenters who took time from their busy schedules—including one presenter who drove 130 miles round trip—to speak pro bono at a psychology club meeting is simply rude (this happened to one of the authors). Furthermore, we recommend against conducting your Psychology Club/Psi Chi officers' meetings via the Internet. Such "leadership experiences" are not truly preparing you for the face-to-face interactions you will encounter in your next job, where interpreting the richness of verbal and nonverbal cues is an essential component of effective communications. In essence, if you wish to be a successful communicator, be prepared to thoughtfully match the medium to your message, however inconvenient the medium may be to use.

Working in Groups and Teams

Throughout college, most of what you learn is assessed by individual measures such as exams, papers, and reports, and a great deal less by group projects. In contrast, a good deal of your daily activity in the workplace is likely to be part of a *group* or *team* effort. These terms are often used interchangeably but are defined differently. By *group*, we mean a collection of "two or more interacting individuals with a stable pattern of relationships between them who share common goals and who perceive themselves as being a group" (Greenberg, 2010, p. 252). The friends from your residence hall who have lunch between classes on a regular basis form a group. The term *team* is commonly used in the workplace and refers to a "group whose members have complementary skills and are committed to a common purpose or set of performance goals for which they hold themselves mutually accountable" (p. 262). Members of your sports team or fellow club officers may be considered a team. Thus, teams are a type of group where members possess complementary skills and are accountable to one another.

Groups and teams operate according to *norms,* which are a set of assumptions or rules that represent the procedures, values, and beliefs that guide the communications and actions of the group. Some norms are crucial, such as on-time attendance, use of cell phones, or expectations regarding individual contributions, whereas other norms may be peripheral, such as where you sit or an occasional digression. When norms are violated, the group may react depending on the importance of the norm. Individuals should become aware of the diversity within the group—that is, the cultures, gender, age, education, religions, and work experiences represented. Depending on the goals, tasks, and situations, the group's norms may be imposed by a leader or developed and modified by the members (Harris & Sherblom, 2011). As a new employee, especially if your college experiences in work groups are limited, it is crucial to develop a keen awareness of the explicit and implicit norms of your group and the diversity of its individual members.

Members often occupy a particular *role* within a group—that is, a position or status that reflects certain behaviors or responsibilities. Some people occupy a *task* role, one that relates to moving the job to completion, such as initiating new ideas, clarifying or summarizing the discussion, or critiquing ideas. Other members occupy *socioemotional* or maintenance roles such as encouraging or supporting a member's contributions, harmonizing, or keeping the group's communications open. Still others reveal a personal agenda by blocking discussion, persistent criticism, aggressive behavior, withdrawing, interrupting, or self-promotion. One person may take on several roles (Harris & Sherblom, 2011).

As a new member of a work group, expect your role to be ambiguous and confusing during your early meetings. You will probably be expected to contribute, yet your lack of experience with the task leaves you little to offer. Your fellow group members know this but are interested in how you behave. In college, your teachers also expect you to contribute your knowledge and ideas; they praise you for your positive input, wait patiently for your response, and are probably not very harsh in their criticisms. One approach to surviving in a new group is to express an eagerness to learn and humility in your lack of experience (your college degree does not confer expertise in workplace groups). Think carefully about what you want to say, have the courage to jump into the discussion when you should (sooner or later, you have to), and cultivate the resilience to recover if your remarks crash. Most likely, a coworker will find something positive in your remarks, and another member, something to criticize. Just as you learned to recover from a shoddy class presentation, you can recover from your early group experiences, provided you learn from your mistakes. The dynamics of how groups and teams operate are complex, vary among organizations, and are beyond the scope of this book. Below are additional concepts you can apply to the current and future groups in which you will participate.

Group Cohesiveness

You want the groups to which you belong to be cohesive; that is, you want group members to remain in the group and willing to contribute their time and ideas toward the successful completion of the group's goals. Groups can tolerate differences among their members and remain cohesive if members are satisfied with the tasks they perform, if their patterns of communication are generally positive, if they enjoyed past successes to some degree, and when there is pressure to conform to the group's standards. Under these conditions, the group can be productive, generate good decisions, and experience personal and group satisfaction (Harris & Sherblom, 2011). Still, problems can occur.

Groupthink

Cohesiveness is an important characteristic of productive groups. However, when members of highly cohesive groups are so committed to remaining in agreement or so fiercely loyal (or apprehensive) that they fail to critique one another's ideas or they isolate themselves from outside information and then make faulty decisions, the group commits the error called *groupthink*. You may have heard the term applied to the 1986 *Challenger* and 2004 *Columbia* space shuttle tragedies, where poor decisions were made because members apparently failed to adequately critique their own decision-making process. You may never be involved in a decision as critical as launching a space shuttle, but you still do not want to be duped by an avoidable group process gone wrong.

Groupthink is often hard to recognize from inside the group, but there are strategies for reducing its intrusion. First, the group leader should promote open inquiry and skepticism, even encourage members to play devil's advocate. Second, be willing to admit the group is open to shortcomings, limitations, and imperfect decisions. Third, when issues are complex and open to different interpretations, opposing subgroups can be formed to further examine their respective positions; further disagreement between the subgroups will raise important issues, but agreement would likely signal the absence of groupthink. Fourth, before implementing a decision, hold a *second-chance meeting* to let members express any doubts or propose new ideas (Greenberg, 2010). In short, group cohesiveness is important, but in extremes it debilitates the group and group decisions.

Time Out: Reflective Questions

Think about an important group in which you are currently involved or one from the past.

1. Using our definition of cohesiveness, to what extent was/is this group truly cohesive?

2. Given this level of cohesiveness, to what extent was/is it a productive group (i.e., meeting its goals)?

3. To what extent did/does the group meet the description of groupthink?

Social Loafing

Have you ever complained about doing a group project because you fear the possibility of working with classmates who either dominate the project or contribute less work to the group effort than if they were working alone? The latter phenomenon is known as *social loafing*, but it can be reduced or eliminated by incorporating these suggestions into the group's work.

First, try to design the project components to be interesting and meaningful for each member. If there are stimulating and dull tasks to be done, try to distribute responsibilities such that each classmate does a little of both tasks, or encourage them to negotiate the tasks. Loafing is less likely to occur when tasks are enjoyable. Second, agree to publicize the specific task responsibilities accepted by each member in writing or on your Internet discussion site. Requiring a weekly progress report from each member also enhances individual public accountability and participation. Third, reward progress with praise and show how individual accomplishments contribute to the final goal. Fourth, work constructively with the social loafer and threaten punitive action if necessary (Greenberg, 2010). For example, if legitimate reasons exist for why a member cannot meet with the group or falls behind on a task, find out why and try to resolve the problem; perhaps exchanging assignments will help. If the classmate shows clear signs of loafing and is unwilling to explain his or her actions, members can request that the loafer join them in a meeting with the teacher to resolve the problem before the assignment is due. Some teachers incorporate peer evaluation (usually a survey) as part of a group grade. In the workplace, social loafers are likely to lose their jobs quickly, a consequence far more punitive than receiving a poor grade in a group project.

Taking Charge

In contrast to the social loafer is the person who takes control of the group without the group's permission. The individual could be the supervisor, who has legitimate power to head the group. It may be a person with considerable experience in groups who mistakenly perceives other members as timid and unwilling to lead. Or the "take-charge" member may be an authoritarian individual with a strong need to control other people.

For example, Deborah was a returning adult student, an active volunteer in nonprofit organizations, assertive, accustomed to taking the lead, and had good intentions to contribute to the group experiment for her research methods class. During the first meeting, she began to identify and organize the group's tasks but did not seek input from the other four group members. She continued in this manner during most of the second group meeting, unaware of the looks exchanged by the other students, their constant shifting in their chairs, and their general silence occasionally punctuated by curt comments. Finally, one member objected strongly to Deborah's "taking over the show," a remark that was quickly affirmed by other students. A heated discussion followed but was terminated when the class period ended. During the third group meeting, however, Deborah was apprehensive, generally quiet, and let her classmates express their ideas. During the fourth meeting, she contributed a suggestion the group supported, but she did not attempt to dominate the discussion. The instructor was not aware of the early tensions because the group's collaborative efforts ultimately merited an A+ grade. Years later, at an alumni event, Deborah related her experience with this group to her former instructor. She described her early tendency to take charge, the rebuff she received, the subsequent positive changes in her behavior, and her gradual acceptance by the group as the class progressed. She also acknowledged (to the teacher's surprise) that her experience in that group was one of the most positive learning outcomes of her college education. Had Deborah "read" the skill levels and feelings exhibited by her group members during the early meetings and been less domineering, she would have avoided the negative feedback (but possibly missed an important insight into her behavior). This example illustrates three points: Some persons who are quick to take charge are unaware of their behavior and the resources other members bring to a project; group members are responsible for providing constructive criticism as soon as a problem develops; and conflict can be resolved and a project brought to successful completion without the teacher's intervention.

Dealing With Conflict

As this example demonstrates, whenever people interact, there is the potential for conflict, a process or condition where one person believes another individual will act or has acted in a manner incompatible with that person's interests. From your own experience with groups, you may have observed that conflict is difficult to understand and resolve because it is multifaceted. Let us explore some key dimensions: types of conflict, causes of conflict, the role of criticism, conflict-management styles, and tips for managing conflict.

Types of Conflict

Dirks and McLean Parks (cited in Greenberg, 2010) identified three major types of conflict. In *substantive conflict,* the perceived incompatibility between individuals arises from different philosophies, perspectives, or opinions regarding decisions the group must make. Substantive differences are often the result of diverse cultural, socioeconomic, and religious backgrounds. For instance, Republican and Democratic members of Congress may strongly desire to reduce budget deficits, resolve serious social issues, and address global problems, but their differing political philosophies often create incompatible solutions. Substantive conflict can be constructive when it forces each party to clearly articulate its perspectives. When serious differences lead to emotional outbursts, personality clashes, and mutual demonizing, the public becomes witness to *affective conflict,* the presence of which renders substantive conflict resolution even more difficult. In *process conflict,* incompatible interests become focused on the procedures for operating the group, the allocation of resources, and the assignment of responsibilities for completing the group's objectives. In Congress, existing procedures permit the members of the majority party to chair the various government committees, set the agenda, and allocate resources for addressing issues, but debate over procedures and resources is ongoing, frequently fierce, and often slows the resolution of substantive conflicts.

Causes of Conflict and the Role of Criticism

Several individual factors that exacerbate conflict include personal grudges, distrust, malevolent attributions, competition for the same resources, and destructive criticism. Criticism may be constructive or destructive depending on several factors. *Constructive criticism* does not contain threats, is motivated by the desire to help a person, shows consideration for the person's self-esteem, and focuses only on specific aspects of an individual's performance. In contrast, *destructive criticism* may contain threats, is motivated by the desire to dominate or gain revenge on the individual, expresses harshness and inconsiderate feelings, and makes sweeping attributions of the individual's inferior performance to lack of effort or ability (Greenberg, 2010).

When Shaun Cowman, the director of institutional research at a small Midwestern college was asked for his advice to psychology students preparing for the workplace, he responded,

> If you are not used to constructive criticism then make it a point to receive as much as you can before entering the workforce. I was lucky enough to have a mentor in graduate school who was no stranger to *constructive* criticism. Some of my fellow students were not so lucky and often expected to be put on a pedestal. This does not happen very often in the workforce so get used to criticism. (Hettich, 2011, p. 11)

Cowman's advice is reflected by Huma Cruaz, president and CEO of Alpaytac Marketing Communications/Public Relations, who believes that "young people often have difficulty accepting constructive criticism" (Frink, 2011, p. 14). Cruaz described a situation in which she told a young employee (a straight-A student) that although she excelled in nearly every area of her job, her writing skills were low. In response to this feedback, the employee began to cry. In spite of her many strengths, she was unable to deal with the one area in which she did not excel. Cruaz speculated that such behavior is possibly due to the experiences of many young people growing up in a culture of constant reinforcement, where they are often consoled for their mistakes and do not experience the consequences of their errors. Cruaz noted that the same employee was promoted and given a new title at a later time due to the overall quality of her work (Frink, 2011).

Perhaps the inability to deal with criticism is a common experience. For example, Megan was an excellent student, a personable individual, a conscientious department assistant, and a super tutor. She never made any significant mistakes, and her minor slip-ups were sometimes overlooked by her supervisor (perhaps unwisely). In short, she had never experienced criticism for the work she performed while in college. Two years after graduation, when Megan was working in a research position for a consulting company, her former college supervisor asked her about her initial months with her employer. She replied that her overall adjustment was good but her major problem was that she was too sensitive to her boss's criticism; she did not go into detail. Megan was a resilient person and gradually learned to accept negative feedback from her boss and remained at the company for another year.

Time Out: Reflective Questions

Recall recent instances when you were criticized for your work or a task you were performing.

1. Using the distinctions above, was the criticism constructive or destructive? Explain your answer.

2. How well or poorly do you generally deal with constructive criticism? What can you do to improve?

Conflict-Management Styles

Some persons exhibit one of five styles or orientations to dealing with conflict, depending on their levels of assertiveness (the importance of completing the task) and cooperativeness (the need to maintain relationships within the group). Individuals who are highly assertive but low on cooperativeness tend to *compete* during the process of conflict resolution, while highly assertive individuals who are also high on cooperativeness tend to *collaborate*. Persons who are low on assertiveness and cooperativeness tend to *avoid* or withdraw from the conflict, while an individual low on assertiveness but high on cooperativeness may be likely to *accommodate*. Finally, persons who occupy the midrange of assertiveness and cooperativeness tend to *compromise*. Different situations may call for different styles. The orientations that value completing the task and maintaining relationships (collaboration and compromise), however, are more likely to move the group forward to constructive conflict and satisfactory solutions (Harris & Sherblom, 2011). We emphasize that these five styles refer to orientations and tendencies found in some individuals; they are not clear distinctions within the population. Nevertheless, you may benefit from becoming aware of the intensity of your involvement and concern for relationships in a conflict-resolution situation.

Tips for Managing Conflict

Although collaboration is highly desired, sometimes you may have to settle for compromise or accommodation for an acceptable solution. On other occasions, perhaps you may have to compete hard or even withdraw from the situation to obtain a temporary solution. The following are steps that groups can pursue to reduce or manage conflict effectively:

- Before the group begins a task, discuss and agree on a process for making decisions, such as following the steps of a standard problem-solving model (e.g., define the problem, define objectives, generate and evaluate alternatives, formulate and implement decision, and follow up).
- Periodically clarify each member's tasks, responsibilities, and deadlines.
- Recognize that some conflicts, such as deadlines or meeting times, may be built into the structure and limitations of the larger group and cannot be resolved by the group.
- Acknowledge the potential emotional reactions to conflict and the problems they create for subsequent decision making.
- If conflict is becoming apparent, deal with it; don't pretend it doesn't exist.

These suggestions are neither bulletproof nor cure-alls for eliminating conflict, but if they are discussed as a group begins its work, the advice they contain should improve the chances of a successful project.

In this section, we explored the essential components of several communication concepts that you can apply to your group experiences during and after college. To make them work for you, however, you must consciously apply them. The exercise below and those provided at the end of the chapter offer a few opportunities to practice these steps.

Time Out: Exercise

1. From this list of concepts, identify those that would have been most helpful to you in a previous group project had you known about them.

2. If you are currently collaborating on a group project, which concepts will be most important for a successful outcome? Why?

The direction of communication	Media richness	Group norms and roles
Cohesiveness	Groupthink	Social loafing and taking charge
Types of conflict	Causes of conflict	Destructive/constructive criticism
Conflict-management styles	Steps to manage conflict	

Emotional Intelligence

So often, we hear about people who behave inappropriately, even stupidly: the politician who has an extramarital affair, the robbery performed in full view of security cameras, crimes of passion, the employee who lashes out at the boss over minor criticism, the couple who argue intensely over trivial issues, the student who succumbs to an evening of irresponsible drinking, the student who explodes when the teacher returns a paper marked "C," or the unwanted pregnancy. Why do allegedly intelligent people lose control over their emotions? Multiple hypotheses can be generated to explain such phenomena, even when the facts are known in each instance.

The notion of emotional intelligence (EI) was first proposed in 1990. Early conceptions generated considerable research over the years that yielded differing perspectives, definitions, methods of assessment, wide-ranging applications, critics and adherents alike, and a continuous refinement of concepts and measures. Psychologist Daniel Goleman popularized EI with his 1995 bestselling book, *Emotional Intelligence.* He discussed an earlier model of EI developed by John Mayer and Peter Salovey but expanded it to include several personality traits they had not endorsed. Enthusiasm for applying EI to the workplace, schools, relationships, and other situations created a proliferation of books, training formats, and assessment tools by psychologists and nonpsychologists alike. Our intent is to summarize the basic elements of EI in the Mayer and Salovey framework (which we consider to be solidly anchored in empirical evidence) because we believe the concept is relevant to understanding and controlling everyday behavior.

> EI includes the ability to engage in sophisticated information processing about one's own and others' emotions and the ability to use this information as a guide to thinking and behavior. That is, individuals high in EI pay attention to, use, understand, and manage emotions, and these skills serve adaptive functions that potentially benefit themselves and others. . . . As we use the term, emotional intelligence is an instance of a standard intelligence that can enrich the discussion of human capacities. (Mayer, Salovey, & Caruso, 2008, p. 503)

EI is an important concept. First, emotions are signals that act as a source of important information about what is happening at a particular time, as in the

Emotional intelligence: Sets of skills from higher to lower levels that comprise EI

- *Managing* emotions so as to attain specific goals
- *Understanding* emotions, emotional language, and the signals conveyed by emotions
- *Using* emotions to facilitate thinking
- *Perceiving* emotions accurately in oneself and others

Note: Each branch describes a set of skills that make up overall emotional intelligence. Each branch has its own developmental trajectory proceeding from relatively easy skills to more sophisticated ones. For example, Perceiving Emotions typically begins with the ability to perceive basic emotions in faces and voice tones and may progress to the accurate perception of emotional blends and to the detection of emotional microexpressions in the face.

Source: Mayer et al. (2008, p. 507). Reprinted with permission of the American Psychological Association, Washington, DC.

Figure 9.1 The Four-Branch Model of Emotional Intelligence

examples above. Second, when integrated with our thinking, emotions can promote positive self-management. Third, the concept of EI can modify the traditional perception of human nature as divided into thinking versus feeling. Finally, EI expands our understanding of the nature and measurement of intelligence (Ciarrochi, Forgas, & Mayer, 2006).

In the approach to EI represented in the Four-Branch Model of Emotional Intelligence (see Figure 9.1), emotional abilities are viewed as operating on a continuum, from those functioning on a lower level in carrying out basic psychological functions (e.g., perceiving emotions) to the developmentally complex ability to manage one's emotions maturely (Mayer et al., 2008). The Consortium for Research on Emotional Intelligence in Organizations website (http://www.eiconsortium.org/) lists the books and test materials developed by Mayer, Salovey, and Caruso and contains links that describe each of the four abilities.

Perceiving Emotions

The most basic EI skill of the Mayer et al. (2008) model is the ability to identify or recognize emotions accurately.

The better the emotional read you have on a situation, the more appropriately you can respond to it. It is difficult, if not impossible, to recover from faulty emotional data; basing actions on incorrect information is a recipe for disaster. You need to be aware of your own and others' feelings and emotions in order to have accurate data and information about the world around you. Being aware of others' emotions is critical to building a successful workplace environment and quality interpersonal relationships. Imagine what it would be like to work with a colleague or be in a romantic relationship with someone who is oblivious to your feelings—never noticing them, never asking about them. (EI Skills Group, 2005–2012)

Using Emotions

At the next-highest level of the model is the ability to use emotions to facilitate thought.

How we feel influences how we think. Using or generating emotions refers to knowing which moods are best for different situations, and "getting in the right mood." More specifically, this skill allows you to employ your feelings to enhance the cognitive system (thinking) and, as such, can be harnessed for more effective problem-solving, reasoning, decision-making, and creative endeavors. Of course, cognition can be *disrupted* by extreme negative emotions such as anxiety and fear, but emotions also can prioritize the cognitive system to attend to what is important and even focus on what does best in a given mood. By way of example, if you are feeling sad, you may view the world one way, while if you feel happy, you will interpret the same events differently. Indeed research shows that people in a sad or negative mood tend to focus on details and search for errors, whereas those in a more positive mood are better at generating new ideas and novel solutions to problems. (EI Skills Group, 2005–2012)

Consider another example: When the media report a serious accident such as a building collapse, we may see people fleeing in fear as a natural response to eminent harm; however, we may also witness other individuals who subordinate their fear and risk their lives to rush to the site to save those involved in the accident. Each individual witnesses the same situation, but everyone uses their emotions according to the way they prioritize the responses that are best for them.

Understanding Emotions

Our ability to understand and think about the information that emotions contain is important in our daily life.

The first component of understanding emotions includes knowledge of the emotional lexicon, including simple and complex emotion terms, and the ways in which emotions combine (anger and disgust form contempt), progress (annoyance to anger to rage), and transition to one another. This skill also involves the capacity to analyze emotions and their causes and the ability to predict how people will feel and react in different situations. This skill answers such questions as: *Why* are we feeling anxious; If I say this to my friend, *how* will he feel; *What* will happen if I say that to her? (EI Skills Group, 2005–2012)

Managing Emotions

The fourth and highest domain in the model is the ability to regulate moods and manage your emotions and those in other people.

When managing one's own feelings, people must be able to monitor, discriminate, and label their feelings accurately, believe that they can improve or otherwise modify these feelings, employ strategies that will alter their feelings, and assess the effectiveness of these strategies. If emotions contain information, then ignoring this information means that we may end up making a poor decision. At times, we need to stay open to our feelings, learn from them, and use them to take appropriate action. Other times, however, it is better to disengage from an emotion and return to it later. For instance, anger, like many emotions, is a misunderstood emotion. Anger is not necessarily a bad thing to feel. (EI Skills Group, 2005–2012)

If you are insulted by a remark directed at your race, gender, or religious affiliation, you will likely become angry. Your anger may motivate you to back away and take proper steps to deal with the slur. If, however, your anger blinds you and causes you to lash out at the individual physically or with inappropriate language, you may regret the mismanagement of your emotion.

To illustrate a negative instance of EI followed by a positive example, we return to Deborah, the student who tried to take charge of her research methods group. Deborah was a bright, twentysomething, returning adult student with a family, and a respected volunteer in a nonprofit organization that supported developmentally disabled youngsters. She was assertive, effective, and accustomed to taking a leadership role, but her prior experiences with other groups (perhaps with passive and unassertive members) and inability to *perceive* the feelings of classmates likely contributed to her confrontation with a classmate in the second group meeting. Her fellow students were of similar age, had probably participated in other groups, possessed relevant skills (they were businesspeople and nurses), and were willing to share ideas and accept responsibilities. Deborah, however, did not *perceive* her classmates as equally talented or experienced, nor did she perceive the rising emotional tensions caused by her domineering behavior. Because Deborah subordinated (whether consciously or inadvertently) the role of her classmates, there were no positive emotions in the group for anyone to *use* that might facilitate progress. She did not *understand* the meanings of the emotions expressed in her classmates' glances, curt remarks, and other signals until after the confrontation occurred, so there was no way the group's emotions could be *managed* productively at that time.

But the situation changed after Deborah was rebuffed; she learned quickly (a positive instance of EI). By the next meeting, she had retrospectively and accurately *perceived* the hostile feelings of her classmates and her own feelings of being rebuked (perceiving—the lowest branch of EI skills). We can infer that she also recognized that completing the group project was an essential part of her final grade and that joining another group was not feasible (using emotions to facilitate thinking—the second branch). In this process and in subsequent meetings, chances are Deborah also began to understand the emotions and nonverbal communications of her classmates in their initial negative response to her and their gradual acceptance in subsequent meetings of her new role as a contributing member of the group (third branch—understanding emotions, emotional language, and signals).

By the end of the course, the students had become a collaborative and cohesive group in which individual and group emotions were productively managed (top branch) in service of the group's goals. This summary of an actual classroom situation, some of it inferred, does not begin to capture all the thoughts, feelings, and verbal and nonverbal behaviors of the group members, particularly Deborah's. Yet it illustrates a common conflict that exists with a task-oriented student trying to "lead" a group, whether formed in a classroom, campus organization, or office—namely, how the perception, use, understanding, and managing of emotions can lead to either positive or negative outcomes, or both. Research may ultimately clarify whether phenomena such as those in the example above should be called emotional intelligence, a personality characteristic, or something else. In the meantime, it is important for us to learn how to become aware of, reason with, and understand our own and others' emotions, and ultimately to manage our emotions for the achievement of our individual and group goals.

Time Out: Exercise

Recall a positive or negative instance of a situation (at school, work, or in a relationship) that happened to you recently, and apply the Four-Branch Model of Emotional Intelligence to analyze how the situation developed, ended, and could have been improved.

Closing Comments

We encourage you to complete courses that focus on small-group behavior and interpersonal communication skills offered by your psychology, communications, business, or other departments. Depending on the instructor's goals, the course will provide a combination of time spent on theories and concepts, and practical applications through class exercises and projects. Because such courses must fit into the structure of class meetings and the academic calendar, they may not match the realities of the workplace, but they can serve as a valuable opportunity to understand, develop, and practice communication skills before you graduate. We also suggest you complete a course on public speaking/speech that enables you to develop abilities and confidence in presenting information persuasively and using technology effectively.

Throughout this book, we emphasize the value of becoming actively involved in extracurricular activities that provide dynamic opportunities to work in groups and develop leadership and EI abilities. We emphasize "dynamic" because some campus organizations operate at a low energy level where officers do just enough to get by so they can create a line for "leadership" on their résumés. Either avoid or decide to change such organizations through your participation. If time permits, join more than one organization with the intention of seeking a leadership position during your junior and senior years. You might not use your leadership skills directly during your early career jobs, but the skill sets will be invaluable as you work your way upward through your career. Campus organizations, resident assistant positions, and athletics provide excellent occasions for you to observe and participate in the dynamics of how groups function while simultaneously learning leader and follower (yes, learning to be a good follower is important) behaviors. Often, learning "happens" by painful trial and error through miscommunication, arguments, criticism, and other behaviors, but learning can and does occur. It is far easier on your ego and self-confidence to learn from your mistakes in the generally supportive environment of a college organization or classroom than to begin mastering communication skills and EI on the job, where poor interpersonal skills lead to career setbacks or loss of a job. According to Gardner (2007), ineffectiveness in teams, failure to follow instructions, and the inability to communicate effectively orally and in writing are among the most common reasons for disciplining new hires.

Also, seek opportunities to improve your communication skills and EI through your school's administrative departments. For instance, the office of admissions may have openings for touring prospective students and will train you how to interact with them. Consider becoming a residence hall assistant, where you are likely to be trained in a variety of skills (e.g., interpersonal, conflict management, stress management, decision making, planning, advocacy, and time management) and will practice them by assisting and supervising fellow students in diverse and sometimes emotionally charged situations.

If you have a job, use it to strengthen your communication, group, and EI skills. Observe how you and your fellow workers and supervisors interact orally and in writing. What aspects of communications operate well? Why? How could communications be improved? What situations cause conflict, and how is it resolved? What role do the company's standards of communication play in the overall quality of its organizational culture? Your job is not just a source of income, it is a laboratory for applying communications concepts and developing skill sets.

Finally, many employment recruiters maintain that because most tasks an individual performs on the job can be taught, they seek applicants who possess necessary qualities and skills that are less amenable to training, including communication and group skills. In the opening quotation, Drucker maintains that as an extension of your personality, work is an index of your achievement, self-identity, self-worth, and humanity. We hope this chapter demonstrates that your ability to communicate, whether at work or in your personal life, is also an integral extension of your personality.

Getting Involved

Journal Starters

1. What are the most significant insights you acquired from reading this chapter?

2. Every family has patterns of communication that its members carry outside the home to other venues. (a) What aspects of your communication skills can you trace to your family's patterns of interacting? (b) What concepts presented in this chapter can help you understand and influence those patterns?

3. If you are currently in a significant relationship with another person, what concepts and suggestions contained in this chapter could be applied to strengthen the relationship?

Projects

1. Construct a survey of the value of group projects, including questions regarding (but not limited to) the aspects of group projects that are most and least helpful, ways group projects can be improved, and the extent to which the work you perform in your job and group participation interact.

2. Groupthink is regarded by some social psychologists as a major factor contributing to the crashes of the 1986 *Challenger* and the 2004 *Columbia* space shuttles, as well as other disasters. Survey the literature for other historic events in which groupthink may have played a major role. What do the critics of groupthink say about these phenomena?

3. Research on emotional intelligence (EI) has generated several theoretical perspectives and methods of assessment. (a) Survey the research literature to identify these differences, or (b) discuss what current research literature says about applying EI to the workplace, schools, relationships, and other settings.

4. The research of Bernardo Carducci (2005; see "Additional Resources" below) indicates that about 40% of the general population regard themselves as shy and that 95% know firsthand what it means to be shy in various situations. What concepts or situations presented in this chapter (and in previous chapters) would a genuinely shy person have to contend with that make the transition from college to the workplace especially challenging? In either a classroom or workplace setting, how do the behaviors of a genuinely shy person differ from those who act listless or apathetic? Are these distinctions of importance to the employee, coworkers, and supervisor?

Additional Resources

Google the term *netiquette* to acquire helpful tips on how to compose e-mail messages.

- Appleby, D. C. (2005). *Career-related skills that can be developed by Psi Chi officers.* Paper presented to Psi Chi at the annual meeting of the American Psychological Association, Washington, DC.
- Carducci, B. J. (2000). The successfully shy worker. In *Shyness: A bold new approach* (pp. 308–337). New York, NY: Quill/Harper Collins.
- Carducci, B. J. (2005). *The shyness workbook: 30 days to dealing effectively with shyness.* Champaign, IL: Research Press.
- Levit, A. (2009). *They don't teach corporate in college: A twenty-something's guide to the business world* (2nd ed.). Franklin Lakes, NJ: Career Press.

■ Rubin, R. S., Bommer, W. H., & Baldwin, T. T. (2002). Using extracurricular activity as an indicator of interpersonal skill: Prudent evaluation or recruiting malpractice? *Human Resource Management, 41,* 441–454.

References

Ciarrochi, J., Forgas, J. P., & Mayer, J. D. (Eds.). (2006). *Emotional intelligence in everyday life* (2nd ed.). New York, NY: Psychology Press.

EI Skills Group. (2005–2012). *Ability model of emotional intelligence.* Retrieved from http://www.eiskills.com

Frink, S. (2011, October 9). Doing things differently: Generational characteristics becoming more obvious at work. *Chicago Tribune,* Section 2, p. 14.

Gardner, P. (2007). *Moving up or moving out of the company? Factors that influence the promoting or firing of new college hires* (CERI Research Brief 1-2007). East Lansing: Michigan State University Collegiate Employment Research Institute. Retrieved from http://ceri.msu.edu/publications/pdf/brief1-07.pdf

Goleman, D. (1995). *Emotional intelligence: Why it can matter more than IQ.* New York, NY: Bantam Books.

Greenberg, J. (2010). *Managing behavior in organizations* (5th ed.). Upper Saddle River, NJ: Prentice Hall.

Harris, T. E., & Sherblom, J. C. (2011). *Small group and team communication* (5th ed.). Boston, MA: Pearson Education.

Hettich, P. (2010, Fall). "What we've got here is a failure to communicate." *Eye on Psi Chi, 15*(1), 8–9.

Hettich, P. (2011, Fall). Connecting graduate degrees to the workplace: A diverse sample of three. *Eye on Psi Chi, 16*(1), 10–11.

Landrum, R. E., Hettich, P. I., & Wilner, A. (2010). Alumni perceptions of workforce readiness. *Teaching of Psychology, 37,* 97–106.

Mayer, J. D., Salovey, P., & Caruso, D. R. (2008). Emotional intelligence: New ability or eclectic traits? *American Psychologist, 63,* 503–517. doi:10.1037/0003-066X.63.6.503

McIlvaine, A. R. (2011, May 26). Reaching out to college students. *Human Resources Executive Online.* Retrieved from http://www.hreonline.com/HRE/story.jsp?storyId=533338166

National Association of Colleges and Employers. (2011). *Job outlook 2011.* Bethlehem, PA: Author.

CHAPTER 10

Avoid False Expectations

Onboarding and Your First 90 Days

Choose a job you love, and you will never have to work a day in your life.

—Confucius

This book is all about making the successful transition from your undergraduate career as a psychology student to the next phase of your life. If you are going to graduate school first, after that important detour, you will eventually seek employment with your graduate degree. In either scenario, there are multiple transitions in your future, and this chapter is about how to avoid false expectations and survive and thrive in the first 90 days of your new job.

Expectations

One of the most common expectations recent graduates hold regarding the workplace is that it will pretty much operate in the same way as college. Wrong! The organizational cultures of colleges and corporations are vastly different. An organization's culture consists of those assumptions, beliefs, expectations, and core values shared by the organization's members. These cognitions typically exert considerable influence over organization members in positive, and sometimes negative, ways

(Greenberg, 2010). By the time you graduate, you will have spent at least 16 years in a sequence of educational organizations that have instilled—*conditioned* is more accurate—countless expectations, assumptions, values, and beliefs about other individuals and procedures and customs that define the school. Recall the cognitive changes when you began college, transferred to another college, or began a new job. Perhaps you didn't understand why things were so different in your new situation; maybe you reacted negatively to some changes but adapted to your new environment. The organizational differences between college and the workplace are a frequently overlooked but critical element of workplace preparedness. Holton and Naquin (2001) persuasively articulated the vast disparities between college and corporate cultures:

> College and work are fundamentally different. The *knowledge* you acquired in college will be critical to your success, but the *process* of succeeding in school is very different from the process of succeeding at work. Certain aspects of your education may have prepared you to be a professional, but evidence from the workplace indicates that this is not enough for professional success. . . . Worse yet, the culture of education is so different from the culture of work that if you continue to have the same expectations of your employer that you did of your college and professors, you'll be greatly disappointed with your job and make costly career mistakes. (p. 7)

As you study the general differences between college and the workplace in Table 10.1, reflect on the extract above. Notice also the particular expectations, assumptions, beliefs, or core values *embedded* in each dimension; each can influence the process of your succeeding or failing in the often radically different environment of the workplace. In short, college expectations (left column) often clash with workplace realities (right column), and the clash can become overwhelming if you are not prepared.

Feedback

In the typical full-time semester load of four or five courses, chances are you *expect* to receive at least five specific measures of your performance (e.g., midterm and final exams, papers and projects) in each course, resulting in at least 20 assessments of your performance over a 3- to 4-month period. In the workplace, you can *expect* far less concrete feedback, perhaps one or two formal reviews annually, and irregular, informal feedback, depending on your performance. Many new grads become rattled when they do not receive frequent concrete feedback from their supervisors.

Structure

Imagine taking a course without a syllabus, where the teacher might stop by once a week or biweekly during your regularly scheduled classes, give you an unclear assignment with little direction, and on some occasions demand you submit the

Table 10.1   Graduates' Perceived Differences Between College and Workplace

College	Workplace
1. Frequent and concrete feedback	Infrequent and less precise feedback
2. Flexible schedule; less structure	Structured schedule
3. Frequent breaks and time off	Limited time off
4. Choose your own performance level	A-level work required all the time
5. "Right" answers	Few "right" answers; much uncertainty
6. Less initiative required	Initiative and active participation required
7. Independence of ideas and thinking	Do it the organization's way
8. Personally supportive environment	Less personal support
9. Focus on your development	Focus on getting results for organization
10. Highly structured curriculum	Much less structure; fewer directions
11. Few significant changes in routine	Frequent and unexpected changes
12. Personal control over time, classes	Respond to others' directions and interests
13. Individual effort	Team effort
14. Intellectual challenge	Organizational and people challenges
15. Create and explore knowledge	Get results with your knowledge
16. Professors	Bosses

Source: Holton (1998, p. 102). Adapted with permission of John Wiley and Sons, Inc.

assignment the next day, or else. In this situation, a core value of formal education (receiving a somewhat detailed syllabus of readings and assignments, clear directions, and reasonable deadlines) clashes with a core value in the typical workplace. For example, when Gerardo was asked what made him most nervous as the newest member of a corporate training team, he replied that it was the constant uncertainties about the nature of his tasks, how they were to be done, and frequent changes in the department. Such perceptions are common to new hires.

Time Off

Unless you hold down a very flexible part-time job while attending college, you will sorely miss those fall, winter, and spring breaks and the change of pace that summer provides. Instead, you will have to *accrue* time off day by day and carefully plan your vacation, which may be only 1 week per year.

Control Over Time

During college, you are required to be in class about 15 to 20 hours per week and at your part-time job for the hours you commit to; the remaining time is under your control. In the workplace, you can expect your employer to control when you arrive, when you take breaks (and how long they are), when you leave, and everything in between.

Challenge

When Lauren was in college, she enjoyed the intellectual challenge of reading diverse theories of personality, searching for flaws in research studies, joining discussions, and discovering the exciting ways psychology is applied to social problems. In her first job out of college, however, Lauren manages (sometimes by herself) the second shift of the very busy copy center in a major office supply store, where she simultaneously services several customers (some whose first language is Spanish) with diverse copy-center needs. She operates up to four machines simultaneously, collates the materials, and bills the customers. Her challenges are far less intellectual and far more organizational. Lauren misses the intellectual challenges of her college courses, but her consistent superior performance in the copy center drew the attention of her supervisor, who recommended her for management training.

Choosing Your Performance Level

Have you ever decided at the beginning of a new term to work extra hard for an A in one class, do B-level work in other courses, and be content with a C in that unpopular general-education requirement? If you answered "Yes," do not expect to have that choice in the workplace, because your supervisor will expect A-level work in all tasks you are assigned. If you get criticized for submitting mediocre work, do not ask for a makeup assignment, unless you anticipate searching for a new job.

Focus

During college, you direct your time and efforts to *your* intellectual, cultural, social, spiritual, and emotional development. College is mostly about *you*. In the workplace, however, you focus your best efforts to get positive results for your organization, in short, to make your boss look good. Focus is a very important difference to which you must adjust. First, intrinsic motivation is much easier to maintain when you can direct it primarily to your personal goals and not your work tasks, especially if they provide little or no challenge. Second, because achievement in college is primarily an individual effort, the consequences of your behaviors affect you alone. For example, if you are absent or late to class or if you submit a mediocre assignment late, you alone pay the consequences. If you are absent from your job, fail to submit an assignment on time, or submit poor-quality work, the consequences of your behavior may affect your supervisor, coworkers, and department. The failure to shift focus from your individual goals to organizational goals may help explain why four of the six reasons new hires are terminated are lack of work ethic or commitment, failure to follow instructions, missing assignments and deadlines, and being late for work (unethical behavior and inappropriate use of technology are the other reasons for dismissal; Gardner, 2007).

Knowledge

Holton and Naquin (2001) remarked that the knowledge you attain in college will be essential to your success. In most positions, do not expect to "create and explore" your knowledge of psychology often unless you enter a graduate or professional program. Employers may expect you to *apply* elements of your coursework, such as aspects of your quantitative courses. As your psychology major shapes a particular perspective on human behavior, chances are the perspective, more than specific coursework, will be valued most by you and your employer.

Even with a graduate degree, specific information you acquire from your courses may have limited application to your job. When your primary author served as a U.S. Army personnel psychologist (a position that required at least a baccalaureate in psychology) at an Armed Forces Entrance and Examining Station where physical and mental tests were administered, the only course that directly applied to his job was his undergraduate "tests and measurements" course. Yet the unique perspective on human behavior his psychology major created helped him understand and manage the young civilians he encountered and the enlisted personnel he supervised. In two subsequent positions that required a doctorate, he was a program evaluator at a federally funded education lab and an applied scientist in a corporate setting. In each venue, only his coursework in research methodology and statistics was used directly, but his other graduate courses presented a general context for approaching his work.

Individual Versus Team Effort

As college is primarily about your individual development, most of what you learn is assessed through individual measures. Few college courses devote a significant proportion of a final grade to group work. Yet teamwork and interpersonal skills are among the major qualities employers prize most (National Association of Colleges and Employers [NACE], 2012). In many organizations, teams and teamwork are the basic mechanism of daily operations; performance evaluations in these settings are usually based in part on team performance. If a person cannot function as a team player (regardless of a high GPA and a winning personality) that individual is cut from the group and sometimes from the job. Many college courses do not lend themselves to group projects, and in courses that do, realistic group projects may be difficult to design. When you enroll in courses that contain group projects, take the assignments seriously and learn (the hard way, if necessary) how to deal with your group members, especially the "social loafer" who lets others do the work or the "take charge" member who dominates the project. To gain solid team skills, join campus organizations and volunteer activities; seek leadership positions where the give-and-take of interpersonal communication can shape positive team skills you need before you graduate.

Right Answers

How comfortable do you feel when a teacher does not provide the correct answers during a test review? Or when an instructor argues multiple perspectives on a complex behavioral issue, such as an ethical dilemma, and then asks your opinion? The certainties you are conditioned to expect throughout your formal education are not the rule in the workplace, depending on the organization and its tasks. Contemporary successful organizations are in varying degrees dynamic, organic entities of ongoing change; "right" answers to new and complex problems are typically not the rule.

Professors Versus Bosses

This dimension is open to so much personal interpretation and variability of individuals involved that we will let you judge the differences.

Independent Thinking and Initiative

We group these aspects of culture together because the information about them appears contradictory. Webster's dictionary defines *initiative* as the act of taking the first step or move, or the characteristic of originating new ideas or methods (Agnes, 2009). Your teachers expect you to be independent thinkers, but the workplace side of Table 10.1 declares, "Do it the company way." Yet, in a survey of employers conducted by NACE (2012), initiative ranked 8th out of 14 attributes that at least 50% of the employer respondents deemed most important. In a survey of employers conducted by Gardner (2007), taking initiative was the No. 1 reason for promoting or making new assignments, whereas failure to take initiative was a major reason for disciplining new hires.

The apparent contradiction might be due to the nature of your responsibilities and the organization you work for. Many entry-level jobs for college graduates, especially during an economic decline, involve mindless, routine procedures that supervisors want performed a certain way for reasons they understand but may not explain. If you are convinced of a better way to do the job, first follow the advice we have heard from managers and supervisors. Express your eagerness to learn, humility regarding your lack of experience, and openness to new ideas and information, but refrain from sharing your opinions, knowledge, and suggestions until you have first studied the organization's culture, mastered your department's standard operating procedures (often referred to as the SOP), and climbed inside your supervisor's head. Or, as you may have heard a parent exclaim, "Don't open your mouth until you know what you are talking about." As you acquire experience, skills, and respect, your boss is likely to listen. Organizations that are worth working for do value the energy, talent, and creativity of college graduates, and managers do value independent thinking, but you should thoroughly understand the situation in which you want your independent thinking to be welcomed.

The above comparisons of college and the workplace are not exhaustive; below are four more that were suggested by managers and students with full-time jobs.

- In college, you can usually choose your partner for a group project; in the workplace, you might be assigned to team up with the least likable coworker.
- In college, the day-to-day physical demands of attending class and a part-time job and taking leisurely walks through campus will not prepare you for rising at 6:00 a.m., commuting to a continuous and often intense 8- to 9-hour slog at the office, and commuting again to arrive home at 6:00 p.m. or later, maybe with more work to do and family responsibilities waiting for you.
- Day-to-day interactions during college seldom require 100% professional behavior, but expect to maintain that level of professionalism from beginning to end of your workday.
- Time management is more crucial in the workplace, where serious deadlines can be frequent and assigned with short notice.

Understanding and (more important) adapting to the cultural and procedural expectations of the workplace are critical to your success; feedback we receive from employers and students with full-time jobs consistently and cogently affirms this. Recognize that in spite of the many skills and rich areas of knowledge you gain from your education, college has generally *not* prepared you for these aspects of the workplace. In fact, it may be argued that college has *counter-prepared* you (taught you to expect the opposite of what employers expect) by conditioning a repertoire of expectations and assumptions (e.g., feedback, structure, focus) that contradicts the cultures and operations of the workplace. Perhaps your greatest challenge in the transition to the workplace will be to assess, modify, and manage your expectations and assumptions.

So what steps can you take to improve your odds of cultural adjustment in your first post-college job? First, pay close attention to these dimensions in the job you currently hold (if you have never held a job, get one before you graduate!), even if you never want to perform that work again. In short, take Table 10.1 to work. Identify the extent to which each dimension on the right side of the table fits or does not fit your company. Second, discuss these issues with family and friends to obtain their perspective on these comparisons, and ask about additional distinctions. When one of your coauthors presented the Holton table at two corporate summer intern programs, supervisors from each company approached him afterward, enthusiastically endorsed the value of the information, and indicated that they were going to send a copy to their college-age son or daughter. That's affirmation!

As an undergraduate student, one of your explicit goals is to place yourself in situations, whether overtly or covertly, where you can acquire, practice, and hone these expected skill sets. If you avoid the difficult classes and the high standards of challenging instructors, you are just setting yourself up for future struggles ("pay me now or pay me later"). How do these skills relate to your first job after graduation? Are there generational differences between today's young adults and young adults from previous generations—and does it matter? As it turns out, it may be that the process of starting a new job—what many businesses call onboarding—may be more important than any generational differences that do exist.

Time Out: Reflective Questions

1. Based on your work experience, which of Holton's (1998) dimensions are most and least important for new employees to adapt to in order to succeed in a new job?

2. To what extent can you agree or disagree that your many years of schooling since childhood have "conditioned" a set of expectations regarding the ways you work and relate to those in authority (e.g., teachers, supervisors)?

3. To what extent do specific myths and realities hold true in your work experience?

4. Are there more myths or more realities in your work environment?

Onboarding

Here, we introduce a term used in the business world, which you should become familiar with. In *Onboarding: How to Get Your New Employees Up to Speed in Half the Time*, executive consultants George Bradt and Mary Vonnegut (2009) define onboarding as "the process of *acquiring, accommodating, assimilating,* and *accelerating* new team members, whether they come from the outside or inside the organization" (p. 3). They believe that onboarding is one of the most important aspects of creating long-term success of individuals or a team. In short, it's as important to the organization as it is to you that those first days, weeks, and months of your employment are a success.

If a new employee does not succeed in the onboarding process, it's usually a result of one or more failures: (1) a role failure due to unclear or misaligned expectations about the job or resources available to do it; (2) a personal failure due to a lack of strengths in the position, lack of motivation, or a poor fit with the organization that was overlooked in the recruiting process; (3) a relationship failure resulting from mistakes made early in the employment (e.g., when a new employee aggressively challenges a coworker or supervisor without fully understanding the situation); or (4) an engagement failure, such as inadequate orientation by a supervisor who was absent when the new hire began (Bradt & Vonnegut, 2009).

In formal onboarding programs, the process of bringing a new employee into the organization starts at what is called "Day Zero," or the day the applicant accepts the job offer (Levin, 2008). A successful onboarding enterprise can provide an employee-retention advantage for the employer; Fritz, Kaestner, and Bergmann (2010) reported one study that indicated that "new employees are 69 percent more likely to stay at a job after three years if they've experienced a well-structured onboarding program" (p. 15). So to be precise, just what is onboarding? Additional perspectives of onboarding are offered by authors and researchers, including that onboarding is

- an act of transformational leadership where hiring managers transform new employees while new employees transform their new organizations (Bradt, 2010);
- the process of integrating new employees into the workforce (Losey, 2008);
- the process where new employees transition from being organizational outsiders to becoming organizational insiders (Bauer & Erdogan, 2011);
- "a holistic approach combining people, process and technology to optimize the impact a new hire has on the organization with an emphasis on both effectiveness and efficiency" (D'Aurizio, 2007, p. 228);
- "the bridge between the promise of new employee talent and the attainment of actual productivity" (Snell, 2006, p. 32); and
- the process of assisting new employees in becoming productive members of the organization (Baumann, 2010).

If you step back and think about this from either the employee or employer perspective, there is much at risk from Day Zero, when the applicant is hired, to Day 1 on the job, and in keeping the employee productive and gainfully employed for as long as the relationship is mutually beneficial. Because the details of onboarding programs are often proprietary in nature, not much is revealed about the contents of such programs, but Table 10.2 provides an overview of the descriptions available in the literature.

Table 10.2   Brief Descriptions of the Design and Contents of Onboarding Programs

Source	Description of Onboarding Program
Snell (2006)	Four components:
	1. Process analysis
	2. Implementation
	3. Integration
	4. Reporting
Fritz et al. (2010)	Four steps:
	1. Self-study/prepare for tomorrow
	2. Experience
	3. Debrief
	4. Assessment

(Continued)

Table 10.2   (Continued)

Source	Description of Onboarding Program
Johnson and Senges (2010)	Process review: 1. Recruiting and pre-start preparation 2. Two-week face-to-face training and orientation 3. Online training 4. Mentoring program from support community 5. On-the-job training 6. Practice-based learning

Given that new hires often make the decision to stay within the first 6 months of employment, and considering the costs incurred by employers regarding training, performance, turnover, etc., it is important to get this process as right as can be. In fact, during your interviews, you might inquire about the extent to which onboarding programs exist—certainly, employers who invest in onboarding are investing in your future as well as the organization's future. Baumann (2010) recommended these steps for new employees to consider when participating in onboarding programs:

■ Communicate, communicate, and communicate.
■ Get the forms completed so you can orient more on "orientation."
■ Provide and take advantage of multiple training opportunities, extended over time.
■ Seek out mentoring relationships.
■ Make connections, and continue to network.

At this point in the onboarding process, you must recognize that being hired is one event; succeeding in the job is another. You can feel rightfully proud that you were *the* candidate from the large pool of applicants that successfully completed the interviewing obstacle course. When you begin the job on Day 1, however, you begin a new process—as a freshman again—and you cannot rest on the laurels of being the applicant that was hired.

Organizations are groups of people, and just because you have been hired does not mean that you have been accepted by those people as "one of them." Acceptance is earned, as are respect and credibility. Your colleagues will not automatically respect you, your expertise, or the contributions you make. Although success in college enabled you to be hired, it, by itself, is not enough on the job. You have to prove yourself all over again. (Holton & Naquin, 2001, p. 12)

Time Out: Reflective Questions

Reflect on your current job or one you held in the past. Think back to those first days. Chances are no one said you were being "onboarded," but perhaps someone mentioned "orientation."

1. To what extent were you onboarded or oriented by your supervisor or coworker, and how much did his or her instruction influence (positively or negatively) your adjustment to the job?

2. To what extent did you ask questions, seek information (i.e., communicate), and act proactively?

3. How could the onboarding process have been improved?

4. What's the connection between your orientation to college in your first weeks and onboarding as described above?

First-Day Strategies

Because of the high individual differences between employers, organizational environments, company culture, expectations, etc., it is difficult to provide specific advice on how to survive Day 1 on the job (remembering the words of Holton and Naquin, 2001, above is a good start), but Ellis (2009) offered the following general recommendations, as listed in Table 10.3. Some suggestions should be familiar to you from our discussion of the job-search process.

Table 10.3   Strategies for Your First Day on the Job

Dress the part.	First impressions are important, and they do last. On your first day, it is better to err on the side of overdressed than underdressed. You will soon figure out the organizational norms of the dress code, casual days, etc.
Arrive early.	Remember that you might have a new commute or have to check in with a security office or even find the correct parking lot. Being at work early on the first day also sends a positive first impression that you are dependable and you plan to work hard. Being late on your first day is absolutely unacceptable.

(Continued)

Table 10.3   (Continued)

Notice your nonverbals.	Be sure to make eye contact when being introduced to new coworkers, and use a firm handshake. Say hello in a friendly voice. Remember that you are "on" today, your first day, and your coworkers will be watching how you carry yourself (e.g., posture, attitude).
Remember names.	Depending on the size of the work environment, you may not be able to learn all your coworkers' names on the first day. Concentrate on just two to three key names, or concentrate on learning first names only at first, and pick up last names later. If you can obtain a group photo of the employees, making a caption for the photo with names might speed your learning.
Take notes.	Even with an effective onboarding program, you are likely to be bombarded by essential information on your first day—key codes to the copy machine, your username and password, phone and fax numbers, etc. Carry some paper with you so you can take notes and you do not need to memorize everything on your first day.
Pack a briefcase.	This is another element that shows your professionalism and attention to detail. You are likely to be bombarded by papers to read and review on your first day, so being prepared with a briefcase sends a good professional signal.
Go easy on yourself.	Give yourself a break—you're good enough, you're smart enough, and gosh darn it, people like you. Avoid self-talk such as, "How long until they figure out I'm just faking it?" There will be a learning curve, so there is no need to be hypercritical about your performance on the first day. But take the job seriously.
Don't say, "That's not how we did it at my last job."	Even if this is your first job as a college graduate, you have likely worked in other environments. Take a while to get the lay of the land. You can make suggestions based on your previous experiences, but when you phrase your statement this way, people are drawn to asking you, "Then why did you leave that job?"

To this list, we emphatically add, "Ask questions!" Chances are your assignments will be more involved than they appear during the explanation given you. The popular cliché, "The devil is in the details," will hold true even for many apparently simple assignments, much less the truly complicated tasks. You are expected to ask questions, and if you do not, your supervisor or coworkers may grow suspicious. Be sure to heed the suggestion of carrying a notepad to record the answers to your questions. One of your authors vividly recalls his first day of work in a corporate setting when his boss, an industrial psychologist, spewed out a series of tasks to be accomplished, but the new hire (with his new PhD) had not taken a notebook and found it necessary later in the day, highly embarrassed but with notebook in hand, to ask his boss to repeat the instructions.

Of course, you will need to adjust the suggestions in Table 10.3 to fit the particular needs of the organization, so do as much homework as you can, think analytically, and "follow your gut." Learning to trust your instincts, combined with thoughtful and reflective mentoring, helps you grow more confident in your new job with each passing day.

Time Out: Reflective Questions

Reverse the roles of supervisor and employee.

1. If you were the boss, what would you want from a new employee?

2. What qualities would you look for in a person who will perform increasingly important assignments and responsibilities, especially since your reputation as the manager is on the line?

3. What new employee behaviors will garner you respect?

4. When you realize that you will want to advance up the corporate ladder someday, these questions are not simply an exercise. In short, learn to become the employee you want to have working for you.

Mentoring

One of the most recommended strategies for new employee success is to seek a mentor, usually an experienced, older, highly respected individual who can serve as an adviser or counselor in your professional development. You, the protégé, can benefit from mentoring in several ways. A mentor can provide emotional support and confidence, which is especially important during the early weeks and months of your employment. A mentor can help you adjust to your new environment, especially its organizational culture; advise you on practices to develop and pitfalls to avoid; and provide feedback on your concerns (Greenberg, 2010).

However, don't select your mentor your first day or even your first week on the job. Study the environment of your department and the interrelationships among its members. Perhaps the preferred potential mentor may work in another department. Take time to search actively for someone you believe fits the qualities mentioned above, someone you believe will enjoy a mutually beneficial professional relationship. Think carefully about what you want from the relationship, and be flexible. Levit (2009, p. 106) identified several tips, developed by Michael Alexander of FindAMentor (www.findamentor.org), for making the most of a mentor–protégé relationship:

- Ask questions.
- Practice listening.
- Answer questions truthfully. (When the truth is withheld—even a little—the information provided by your mentor may not be accurate.)
- Filter information consciously before accepting it as true and right for you.
- Understand your mentor's desire to help, and take feedback you don't like in stride.
- Respect your mentor's time constraints and other commitments.

Mentoring relationships require time, thoughtful planning, and your best interpersonal skills. It is normal for mentoring relationships to change over time (months or years) as you gain experience, confidence, and skills. Your authors can relate experiences of serving as advisors to individuals as students, continuing the advising/mentoring after those students graduated (but less as teachers to students), and becoming their peers as they matured into their careers. Just as you needed (but may or may not have found) a wise advisor when you began college and declared your major, you will likely need a wise mentor/advisor as you begin your freshman year in the workplace.

A Primer on Office Politics

> Playing politics is like having sex. Almost everybody does it, but nobody is comfortable discussing exactly what they do. We will talk for hours, however, about what other people might be doing. Typically, we use the term "playing politics" only to describe our colleagues' behavior—never our own. *They* are sucking up, scheming, and manipulating, but *we* are building relationships, developing strategies, and opening communication channels. (McIntyre, 2005, p. 3)

You may claim you do not like to "play politics" or be involved in politics, but you have likely engaged in politics, knowingly or unknowingly, if you accept McIntyre's (2005) definition that "'politics' is what naturally happens whenever people with different goals, interests, and personalities try to work together" (p. 3). Certainly, you have been in that situation before, and you likely wanted to win. Politics are not inherently bad—when people with different goals try to work together, results can be constructive—and they are pervasive in most organizations.

When McIntyre (2005) surveyed 220 people from business and government organizations about their views on office politics, she received 20 different responses to the question, "When people are good at politics, what are they able to do?" Half of those responses were as follows: They are able to (a) get their projects moved up the priority list, (b) influence management, (c) bypass normal procedures, (d) advance quickly, (e) help bring about changes, (f) get more money in their budget, (g) have their own office, (h) stay out of trouble, (i) survive changes, and (j) have their ideas heard.

Are these good or bad outcomes? It depends, because often there are winners and losers in the struggle to be heard. On the first day of a new job, someone in your office is probably engaged in politics. Do not be surprised if you soon find yourself in conversations in which a coworker tries to influence your judgment about an organizational policy or a fellow coworker or supervisor. Indicate that you are new, unfamiliar with all the issues, and would rather not take a stand on such issues at this time. At some point in your career, however, you will likely develop the political savvy to influence decisions.

Time and space do not allow us to discuss office politics at length, but it is important to keep in mind the Political Golden Rule: "Never advance your own interests by harming the business or hurting other people" (McIntyre, 2005, p. 17). In addition, be aware of this workplace dimension in the broader context of your organization, and heed a few words of advice from the INROADS Guide to Corporate Survival Training Module, adapted for *Job Choices 2012* (NACE, 2011).

1. Know the company culture. Quickly become aware of your organization's customs and expectations, from dress codes to decision making, and behaviors to avoid and emulate.

2. Never make the boss look bad. Recall that in college, your focus is primarily on your personal development, but in the workplace, one of your major responsibilities is to make your boss look good.

3. Identify the people with power. Consult an organizational psychology or communications textbook to differentiate the different kinds of power; it is important for you to learn who the movers and shakers are in your organization and try to establish a good (authentic, not forced) relationship with them.

4. Be a straight shooter. That is, follow through on the commitments you make, and be loyal to those you work with.

5. Be visible. Become involved in activities that make you visible to management; be willing to stay late to increase that visibility.

6. Be indispensable. Seek and succeed at important assignments so your supervisor can't imagine the department being successful without you.

7. Be accountable. Accept responsibility for your role in the tasks you perform; avoid blaming others for errors unless the mistakes were clearly not your fault.

8. Handle criticism constructively. You will make mistakes, so listen to the criticism and try to learn from it. Most of the time, it is your behavior, not you, being criticized.

9. Listen more than you speak. Listening leads to learning, and it gains respect from others.

10. Treat everyone with respect and consideration, not only your supervisor and peers but also subordinates.

Performance and Feedback

Most college students expect frequent and specific feedback from their professors (recall the Table 10.1 comparisons between college and workplace); you will probably want feedback daily on your performance during the first weeks of your new job but may not receive any. Wilner and Stocker (2005) offer some tips for finding out how you are doing.

1. If your organization does not have a system for reviewing new hires early in their employ, ask your supervisor if you can schedule a review on an informal level, such as when you complete a particular project.

2. When you ask for a review, try not to schedule it during a particularly busy or stressful time for your supervisor.

3. If the supervisor seems reluctant to provide a review or to provide negative feedback, which you sense a meeting may contain, acknowledge that you know the review may be uncomfortable but are truly interested in improving and advancing in the company.

4. If you do not receive regular reviews, search for nonverbal cues such as eye contact and voice quality (provided you know what they signify) over a period of days or weeks.

5. Don't jump to conclusions if you do not receive feedback, because it is customary in most organizations to refrain from offering it unless the employee has failed in some significant manner. In this case, silence may be good news.

6. Remember that your peers can often offer constructive feedback and suggestions.

Because you cannot expect feedback to the degree you wish, you may have to provide it yourself. As subjective as it may be, your self-feedback is usually better than none. There is, however, an alternative. The research of industrial and organizational psychologist John Campbell (2011) and his associates produced a general model of occupational performance that he calls a taxonomy of higher-order performance components. He defines performance as "behavior at work that is judged to be relevant for the organizer's goals. Also, such behaviors, or actions, can be scaled in terms of how much they contribute to the attainment of such goals" (p. 248). The assessment of an employee's performance focuses on observable actions that are under the employee's control. The consequences of those actions, however, are not considered synonymous with that person's performance if they depend on variables that are not under the individual's control. For example, two air-conditioner salespersons should not be judged by the total revenues each generated if one was working in central Texas and the other in northern Idaho.

Campbell (2011) and his associates developed an "eight-component model for describing the basic composition of work performance in the entire labor force" (p. 249), summarized below. Not all components pertain to all occupations, but, frequently, more of them apply than is apparent. When you are yearning for feedback about your job performance, you may find Campbell's taxonomy helpful, but only to the extent that you critically reflect on your work situation as objectively as you can. Some components are familiar to you as skills and behaviors employers seek.

1. *Job-specific task proficiency* is the extent to which an employee performs the central substantive or technical tasks that make up that person's job. (What are the specific central tasks of your job? How well do you perform each?)

2. *Non-job-specific task proficiency.* In most organizations, employees are assigned some tasks that are not central to their job but must be completed by someone, often by new hires or those at the bottom of the hierarchy. (What are the nonspecific tasks you perform? How well do you perform them, whether or not you want to?)

3. *Written and oral communication* refers to the employee's proficiency in performing written assignments or oral presentations for audiences of any size, independent of one's subject-matter expertise. (What are your strengths and weaknesses in these areas? How can you improve?)

4. *Demonstrating effort* answers the questions, How often does an employee spend extra time when a task requires it? How willing is the employee to continue working under adverse conditions?

5. *Counterproductive work behavior* is concerned about the extent to which an employee avoids negative behaviors such as violating rules, excessive absenteeism, and substance abuse. (In what aspects of your job is it easy or hard to comply with the formal and informal rules?)

6. *Facilitating peer and team performance.* To what extent does the employee support peers, help them with job problems, and facilitate group functioning?

The two components below describe qualities to look for in supervisors and management.

1. *Supervision/leadership* is concerned with the extent to which supervisors influence the performance of their subordinates through face-to-face interaction and such actions as providing support, modeling appropriate behaviors, setting goals, and teaching.

2. *Management/administration* pertains to performance elements that are distinct from direct supervision. They include abilities such as organizing employees and resources to attain the unit's goals, monitoring progress, controlling expenditures, and representing the unit in its relations with other units.

Time Out: Exercise

Apply the first six components of Campbell's (2011) taxonomy to your current or former job. Transform each into a 7-point scale, where 0 = *not at all proficient*, 4 = *moderately proficient*, and 7 = *highly proficient*. Rate yourself on each component. Be thoughtful and honest with yourself. For example, to what extent are you proficient at

- your job-specific tasks? __
- your non-job-specific tasks? __
- your written and oral communications? __
- demonstrating effort? __
- avoiding counterproductive work behaviors? __
- facilitating peer and team performance (if relevant)? __

Another perspective on monitoring your performance derives from a series of suggestions for building a track record, adapted from the INROADS Guide to Corporate Survival Training Module and summarized in *Job Choices 2012* (NACE, 2011).

1. Continually strive to develop unequaled and transferable skills, especially uncommon skills or those that have broad application.

2. Learn about your industry by listening to what others say and reading industry and trade-related newsletters and journals.

3. Similarly, position yourself properly. That is, take advantage of new opportunities in your organization when you can; remain current on new developments in the company, including technology.

4. Solicit feedback on how you can improve, and be willing to provide carefully considered feedback and solutions regarding organizational problems.

5. Pack your "parachute." That is, always be prepared to face the possibility that you could lose your job anytime.

Closing Comments

Your first full-time job after graduation may be a few months or a few years after you read these words, but it is important to become familiar with issues you will confront before you begin that job, with time enough to establish realistic expectations about the workplace. Recall from Chapter 3, the first opportunity we discussed for improving workplace preparedness was your part-time job. This chapter elaborates on that point by identifying specific dimensions of the workplace you should attend to. We offer you considerable information and advice (we hope you didn't mind all the lists!) for applying yourself and these concepts. Now, as always, the rest is up to you.

Getting Involved

Journal Starters

1. What was the most significant insight you gained regarding the differences between college and corporate cultures?

2. Which of the dimensions of workplace culture from the Holton (1998) study will be the easiest and most difficult to adjust to? Why?

3. Reflect for a couple of minutes on those individuals who have served as your mentors. In what aspect of your life did these mentors serve you well, or not so well? What could you have done to strengthen the mentor–protégé relationship?

Projects

1. Our discussion focused on the right side of Table 10.1 and emphasized the differences students will encounter in the workplace compared with college. But how true are the dimensions attributed to the left side—the organizational culture of your institution? Choose four to six of the dimensions, and design a survey containing clear and unambiguous questions that enable you to confirm or disconfirm Holton's (1998) characterization of college.

2. Interview individuals you know with full-time jobs and ask each to identify (a) the four to six most important dimensions of Table 10.1 as they pertain to their organizations and (b) additional qualities that distinguish college from their workplaces.

Additional Resources

URL	Brief Website Description
www.jobSTART101.org	Free online tutorial hosted by Alexandra Levit and developed with the Business Roundtable and the HR Policy Association. It offers advice on communication, problem solving, and developing a professional persona.

- Bennington, E., & Lineberg, S. (2010). *Effective immediately: How to fit in, stand out, and move up at your first real job.* Berkeley, CA: Ten Speed Press.
- Meister, J. C., & Willyerd, K. (2010). Mentoring Millennials. *Harvard Business Review, 88,* 68–72.

References

Agnes, M. (Ed.). (2009). *Webster's new world college dictionary* (4th ed.). Cleveland, OH: Wiley.

Bauer, T. N., & Erdogan, B. (2011). Organizational socialization: The effective onboarding of new employees. In S. Zedeck (Ed.), *APA handbook of industrial and organizational psychology* (Vol. 3, pp. 51–64). Washington, DC: American Psychological Association.

Baumann, K. (2010, July 20). *5 effective steps for easy onboarding.* Retrieved from http://campus-to-career.com/2010/07/20/5-effective-steps-for-easy-onboarding/

Bradt, G. (2010). Onboarding: An act of transformational leadership. *People and Strategy, 33,* 4–5.

Bradt, G., & Vonnegut, M. (2009). *Onboarding: How to get your new employees up to speed in half the time.* Hoboken, NJ: John Wiley.

Campbell, J. P. (2011). Individual occupational performance: The blood supply of our work life. In M. A. Gernsbacher, R. W. Pew, L. M. Hough, & J. R. Pomerantz (Eds.), *Psychology and the real world: Essays illustrating fundamental contributions to society* (pp. 246–254). New York, NY: Worth.

D'Aurizio, P. (2007). Onboarding: Delivering on the promise. *Nursing Economics, 25,* 228–229.

Ellis, D. (2009). *From master student to master employee: Annotated instructor's edition* (2nd ed.). St. Charles, IL: College Survival/Houghton Mifflin.

Fritz, K., Kaestner, M., & Bergmann, M. (2010). Coca-Cola Enterprises invests in on-boarding at the front lines to benefit the bottom line. *Global Business and Organizational Excellence, 29,* 15–22. doi:10.1002/joe.20325

Gardner, P. (2007). *Moving up or moving out of the company? Factors that influence the promoting or firing of new college hires* (CERI Research Brief 1-2007). East Lansing: Michigan State University Collegiate Employment Research Institute. Retrieved from ceri.msu.edu/publications/pdf/brief1-07.pdf

Greenberg, J. (2010). *Managing behavior in organizations* (5th ed.). Upper Saddle River, NJ: Pearson Prentice Hall.

Holton, E. F., III (1998). Are college seniors prepared to work? In J. N. Gardner, G. Van der Veer, and Associates (Eds.), *The senior year experience: Facilitating integration, reflection, closure, and transition* (pp. 95–115). San Francisco, CA: Jossey-Bass.

Holton, E. F., III, & Naquin, S. (2001). *How to succeed in your first job: Tips for new college graduates.* San Francisco, CA: Berrett-Koehler.

Johnson, M., & Senges, M. (2010). Learning to be a programmer in a complex organization: A case study on practice-based learning during the onboarding process at Google. *Journal of Workplace Learning, 22,* 180–194. doi:10.1108/13665621011028620

Levin, B. (2008, Summer). On-demand workforce-communications technologies help organizations meet critical business goals. *Employment Relations Today, 35,* 43–50. doi:10.1002/ert20200

Levit, A. (2009). *They don't teach corporate in college: A twenty-something guide to the business world.* Franklin Lakes, NJ: Career Press.

Losey, S. (2008, June 9). First day on the job, first step to retention: HR managers work to smooth the way for new employees. *Federal Times, 44*(17), 16.

McIntyre, M. G. (2005). *Secrets to winning office politics: How to achieve your goals and increase your influence at work.* New York, NY: St. Martin's Griffin.

National Association of Colleges and Employers. (2011). *Job choices 2012.* Bethlehem, PA: Author.

National Association of Colleges and Employers. (2012). *Job outlook 2012*. Bethlehem, PA: Author.

Snell, A. (2006). Researching onboarding best practice. *Strategic HR Review, 5,* 32–35.

Wilner, A., & Stocker, C. (2005). *The quarterlifer's companion: How to get on the right career path, control your finances, and find the support network you need to thrive.* New York, NY: McGraw-Hill.

PART IV

I Graduated and Got a Job: What's Next?

CHAPTER 11

Your Personal Life Changes After College

by Abby (Wilner) Miller, MA

Friendship is the hardest thing in the world to explain. It's not something you learn in school. But if you haven't learned the meaning of friendship, you really haven't learned anything.

—Muhammad Ali (1942), boxer

The Changing Social Landscape for New College Graduates

Like most students, my graduation from college to the "real world" marked not only a major change in my role from student to employee but also a major shift in my social life. When I discovered there were few resources to help college graduates deal with typical transitional issues, I applied the knowledge and skills I acquired as a psychology major to researching what seemed to be a common phenomenon, a major life transition that I termed the *quarterlife crisis*. After interviewing dozens of recent graduates who all seemed to be facing similar personal, financial, and career struggles in their 20s, I documented these challenges and coauthored a best-selling book that many other twentysomethings felt they could relate to (Robbins & Wilner, 2001).

The literature supports the occurrence of personal transitional challenges during young adulthood. Marcia Baxter Magolda (2009), in her ongoing seminal longitudinal study of college graduates, found that while the 20s and 30s are a time of career exploration and difficult decisions, "personal life choices were equally

salient" among her subjects (p. 22). The twentysomething years following graduation, also known as emerging adulthood (Arnett, 1998), encompass a transitional
period of evolving identities, values, roles in society, and, subsequently, new friendships, jobs, living situations, and romantic relationships. Even our hobbies and the
way we spend our free time can change during this critical period when we officially
become adults.

Changing Identities, Values, and Roles in Society

Your twentysomething years often comprise a formative phase of evolving identities, values, and roles in society. This now-prolonged transition to adulthood marks
a time of exploration when the typical graduate tries to determine the right fit in
a career and a spouse. The exploration can sometimes have negative consequences
such as stress or anxiety when individuals feel conflicted by the growing number
of options related to careers, relationships, and living arrangements (Schwartz,
2005). College coursework does not always give students a good sense of what jobs
will really be like. Therefore, graduates "try out" an average of eight jobs before the
age of 32 (Bureau of Labor Statistics, 2002). The age to get married, start a family,
and become financially independent has also increased (Furstenburg, Kennedy,
McCloyd, Rumbaut, & Settersten, 2003).

Recall our exploration of emerging adulthood in Chapter 5. Arnett (1998) found
not only financial independence but also the ability to accept responsibility and
make decisions to be indicators of moving into full adulthood. During the phase
of emerging adulthood, twenty- and thirtysomethings are continually adapting
their roles as family members, employees, and friends. Baxter Magolda (2009)
described a struggle we experience during this time involving internal values that
underlie more outward challenges such as jobs and relationships. In other words,
deciding on a career and a life partner is further compounded by struggles with
one's evolving identity, and the former cannot be easily resolved without exploring the latter. Baxter Magolda (2009) maintains that finding one's internal voice is
critical to "withstand the uncertainties and complexities of life in the twenty-first
century society" (p. 10). The individuals she interviewed over the past 20 years
faced—in addition to the normal adjustments of work, personal relationships, and
parenting—a multitude of health problems, family tragedies, and career upheaval.
She found that establishing good company—whether coworkers, friends, or family—helped the subjects establish internal foundations critical to development.

The twentysomething years are also a time when one experiences a shift in
political and societal values (Pew Research Center for the People and the Press,
2010). Contentious issues such as social security, taxes, and the national budget take on new meaning when you experience the effects personally through a
paycheck and "real-world" financial responsibilities. Students may often express
liberal, idealistic views in college (Lee, 2006) and may have altruistic notions of
saving the environment and world peace. Certainly, the core of these values may
not change. But the recent graduate may take on a more practical or realistic stance
once he or she has a greater understanding of the limits and complexities that
financial constraints impose.

Due to all these internal and external changes, recent graduates may also notice changes in the way they interact with others. Real-world interactions with peers often take on a more formal structure than those experienced in college keggers or dorms. You may feel like a fish out of water at first, trying to navigate the unfamiliar social settings of the real world, but like anything, making new friends in this new world just takes practice.

Time Out: Reflective Questions

Chances are you know someone who graduated from college within the past 5 years. What points or ideas mentioned above do you believe relate to his or her post-college experiences? If you do not know a recent college graduate, try to speculate how these points might apply to you.

New Friends in a New World

As a college graduate, you may not realize just how easy it was to make friends and form bonds over common interests in college until in the throes of a "dog-eat-dog" world where office friendships often carry risks and awkwardness. In college, fellow students share classes, activities, dorms, or at the very least the same institution. Further, as a college graduate, you may have no control over your residential destination depending on the job market, particularly in an unstable economy where you cannot exercise a great deal of control or selectivity over your newly adopted hometown.

Below are some examples of twentysomethings who initially found it difficult to navigate the social landscape and find new friends (www.quarterlifecrisis.com/forums):

I think it's been very difficult to make new friends after college, especially since I've relocated to a new city. I've made friends mostly from work, and then friends of their friends, and also a few of my neighbors. There just aren't as many opportunities to interact with people of your same age range, along with those that have similar interests, in a non-school environment.—"Lisa"

I think one of the biggest problems with my current job situation is there are NO young people. At first I thought working with a bunch of 40+ people would be a rewarding experience and there would be less drama. But now I have found that it's just as depressing. I get up, go to work for 9 hours with people who are as old as my parents, and then head home to my empty apartment. The thing is, I'm an incredibly outgoing person and made several great friends during college. However, I now find myself regressing back to my high school years . . . traveling home on the weekends, going to dinner and a movie with my mom, and just bumming around. It's really pathetic. I always thought when I was in my twenties I would have this fabulous life. . . . I'm really praying that I'm only in a post-college rut, and that this won't be my life in a year or two.—"Jeremy"

When I first left college, I was in a new city at grad school—it was very tough. Everyone had their own agenda. My college friends were about an hour away, but they were busy too. I later left grad school after one semester and returned to my hometown. At first I was really upset when my friends from high school (who had also moved back home) couldn't get together because they had established their lives. I did give it time and we reconnected. I have met one new friend, actually via online message boards. I am fairly friendly with a few people at work, but not super tight like the friendships I had in high school and in college.—"Jennifer"

Friendships are important on a deeper level than merely providing weekend plans—friendships are actually beneficial to our health. Positive relationships, including friendships, have the power to shape our identities and even boost our immune systems (Bonior, 2011). Friends help us cope with feelings of anxiety or depression simply by providing company and acting as sounding boards to our greatest challenges and insecurities.

Despite promises to maintain the tight-knit bonds formed in college, doing so can often be difficult due simply to growing geographic distances from college friends. College is often a time of intense friendships formed over all-nighters with roommates. It is hard to imagine one day forgetting the inside jokes and common experiences that made the friendship so close. It is also difficult to imagine forming such a tight bond with anyone in the real world with whom one does not share a dorm room. Yet, often due to jobs and post-college plans that require moving to separate cities, friendships can grow apart. These close friendships may never end, but they don't always maintain that same level of intense, daily contact. Recent graduates must look to new outlets to form new friendships with fellow "almost adults."

Beyond Bars: Creative Social Outlets

Many recent graduates find that bars are not the best outlet to meet long-lasting friends. Bars are a natural hangout for recent college graduates who socialized in similar settings during their senior year in college. However, bars are also very loud and do not typically lend themselves to conversation. Moreover, intoxication is not really the best state in which to form a meaningful friendship or relationship. Recent graduates quickly learn that they must look beyond the bar scene to form quality, lasting friendships like those they built in college.

One great way to meet others who share your interests is by getting involved in the community and volunteering. Most cities offer numerous opportunities to give back to the community while socializing. Just a few examples are soup kitchens, housing rehabilitation programs, retirement homes, tutoring programs in low-income neighborhoods, and park cleanups. Both national websites and regional organizations consolidate the listings for you in one central location and send regular e-mail updates, so you don't even have to do the work to seek out opportunities (see the "Additional Resources" at the end of this chapter). Your college or university may also provide opportunities for alumni to connect off campus. Many alumni associations have regional chapters in cities around the country and organize various events and activities such as outings to baseball games or professional-development seminars.

In fact, meeting people through such activities can lead not only to friendships or romances but also to networking opportunities for future jobs. Keep this suggestion in mind as you explore new outlets for making connections—you never know whom someone else might know, or who could end up being a potential employer or spouse in the future. For this reason, it's important never to turn down opportunities to get involved, never to burn bridges, and to do your best to stay in touch with new contacts. You never know what might blossom from a chance meeting.

Most geographical areas offer a plethora of organizations that bring people together based on common interests, such as sports or the arts, and provide excellent opportunities for getting involved in the community and meeting new people. Taking a class at a local community college or university is also a great way to explore fields of interest before committing to a degree while meeting new people who share those interests. Even if unrelated to your work, you may wish to take a language class for fun or to prepare for an upcoming vacation abroad. Or perhaps you simply want to learn more about art history and choose to audit a class at night. Libraries, museums, and community centers often offer interesting classes and lectures as well. Take advantage of all the resources available in your community, especially those funded by taxpayer dollars now that you are a taxpayer.

For twentysomethings with religious beliefs, becoming involved in community-based religious organizations can be beneficial. Researchers report that although involvement in religious and other community-based organizations often declines among young adults, it is positively associated with identity development (Hardy, Pratt, Pancer, Olsen, & Lawford, 2011). This conclusion supports Erikson's (1968) theory that adopting ideological beliefs can help young adults form identities. Through increased levels of community involvement, social interconnectedness, and an emphasis on values and ideologies, involvement with a religious organization can provide a valuable support system for twentysomethings who possess or are interested in exploring religious beliefs.

Initially, getting involved in the community may take more initiative on your part than did joining organizations in college through orientations or activity fairs. Similarly, attending a new activity on your own can be intimidating, but making yourself slightly uncomfortable for a few minutes pays great dividends in the long run. Finding new, creative outlets to make new contacts requires putting yourself in some unfamiliar and uncomfortable situations, but these activities do not necessarily have to be entirely new. In fact, identifying extracurriculars as an adult gives you the opportunity to reconnect with some of your childhood hobbies you may have forgotten in the throes of college all-nighters.

Time Out: Exercise

Take a moment to think about the hobbies you truly enjoyed as a kid before you started to think about padding a résumé for college applications. Then look for opportunities to engage in these hobbies through the community—or if the opportunity doesn't exist, start something! Surely other recent graduates share your nostalgia for childhood hobbies.

1. What activities did you enjoy in grade school or high school simply because they were fun that might help make you feel at ease in new social situations?

2. What extracurricular activities do you most enjoy in college that you want to continue after graduation?

Blurry Boundaries Between Work and Fun

In one sense, work seems like a logical place for recent graduates to find new friends with whom they share common interests. Individuals are often drawn to specific workplaces for similar reasons. For example, many graduates today choose to work at nonprofit organizations to fight for causes about which they feel strongly—be it saving the environment or providing health care access to the poor. They likely find much in common with coworkers who share similar passions and interests. Further, simply based on the sheer amount of time spent with coworkers (more waking hours than with anyone else in our lives) it is inevitable that coworkers will get to know one another, no matter their backgrounds.

Yet, despite the fact that forming friendships or even romances might seem logical to recent graduates new to the workforce, they quickly realize that these relationships carry risks. Often, twentysomething coworkers will get together for after-work happy-hour drinks—and sometimes, after a few drinks, they end up regretting things they said or did that could later be reported to management.

Workplace friendships are normally healthy but often take time to develop, because we are concerned with acting professionally and don't always let our guards down, with good reason. Sometimes, workplace friendships take years to develop but then last a lifetime. Other times, workplace friendships may develop very quickly but then disappear after we move on to the next job. Just like any friendship, the deeper bonds carry greater returns.

Clinical psychologist Andrea Bonior (2011) recommended approaching workplace friendships with caution so you don't become overly attached to any one coworker. Moreover, do not let workplace friendships impede the quality of your work by spending excessive amounts of time away from the office together when you should be working on a project. Also, try to restrain yourself when it comes to revealing personal details and gossiping about other coworkers. A little chitchat is fine, but don't let it get in the way of your professional demeanor, and remember that workplace friendships do not replace close friends. It's better to think of friends in the workplace as a supplement to, rather than a substitute for, your social circle.

Whereas workplace friendships are typically innocuous, romances carry greater risks in the office. Office romances can sometimes turn rocky and sometimes end on nonspeaking terms that cause a great deal of tension or discomfort in the workplace—not only for those involved but for all officemates who share work or workspace with the former couple. For this reason, some workplaces put policies in place that restrict office romances and strive to keep workplace relationships professional. Alexandra Levit (2009), who writes about corporate survival skills for twentysomethings, advised avoiding inner-office dating entirely, particularly within your immediate team—and never with a supervisor. Instead, she recommends asking colleagues to make introductions to their eligible single friends who may be a good match for you.

Socializing in a Digital World

Social-networking sites such as Facebook and Twitter have opened up a whole new slew of potential interactions—and pitfalls—with friends. These websites have spiked in popularity enormously over recent years, to the point that not only college students but their parents connect with friends online. In many ways, this powerful technology has changed the dynamics of friendships. Now we can observe our friends' conversations with others, and we can see where they are or where they are planning on going, even if we have not been invited.

Friendships through social-networking sites can also be misleading. The mere term *friend* is used quite liberally and does not necessarily mean you will ever talk to the person but, rather, can include them in your total count of friends. Bonior (2011) advised avoiding sending what should be personal messages to the masses; remember that about 3,000 other friends can view your posts. Be sensitive to commenting on personal news such as engagements or breakups until the friends they pertain to have already made a public statement about such events. Also, become familiar with privacy settings so your coworkers don't have access to all your personal posts and photos. And be cautious of becoming overly dependent on, even addicted to, social-networking websites such as Facebook. Although online exchanges can provide some entertainment, they should not act as replacements for real-life interactions.

Maintaining Lasting Friendships

Because this is a transition period, we are busy exploring new activities, starting new ventures, and managing real-life responsibilities, often for the first time. We are building the foundation of our adult lives: trying to meet new people, becoming settled in a new city, and developing our careers. While settling into this new and hectic life, it is comforting to maintain the friendships we have treasured so much up until this point. Holding on to old friends, however, can also be difficult given that we are all moving in different directions. Getting together may become more like a chore—we have to schedule appointments to see our friends rather than simply dropping by a dorm room. But keeping friends close is critical during times of stress, because the people who really know you also know how to help.

Some friendships simply fade as you grow and develop separate interests. In these cases, try to nurture friendships to the best of your ability, because even though a friendship may go dormant, one or both of you may need the revival and support of that relationship in the future. For example, Erica and Beth were very good friends during most of college, but friction grew from a disagreement during the last months of their senior year, and their graduation goodbyes were somewhat cold. Years later, they saw each other's names on the list of alumni attending their 5-year reunion, and when they met they put aside their previous differences and renewed their friendship.

Romantic Interference

Interestingly, as romantic relationships improve, friendships can sometimes grow apart. One friend who remains single can start to feel lonely or even resentful while the other spends more and more time with his or her significant other. Personality clashes between the friend and significant other can cause additional tension. Below is an example of a twentysomething who was not exactly crazy about her roommate's boyfriend, which made for a difficult living situation (www .quarterlifecrisis.com/forums):

> I probably would never say anything, but one of the significant others I don't get along with is a bit more of a difficult situation because it's my roommate's boyfriend. My roommate and I have been very good friends for years and she moved in at the start of the year because she took a job near my home. It was going to be a temporary situation; she was going to look for a place to live. But it's been going well living together so we agreed that there wasn't an urgency in her moving. However, at that time she wasn't serious with this guy. In the past 4 months, she has broken up with him twice. . . . A couple weeks ago they got back together and I was honest with her that I see it as a major red flag that she's broken up with him twice in a span of a few months, and that she has so many things about him that she wants him to change. She said she understands, she's just not done with him. I totally get that, but I don't see why she's wasting her time. If we didn't live together, I wouldn't care at all. It would just work itself out. But seeing as he is in my home all the time—MY home, my small apartment—I'm going crazy! I don't even want to come out of my room when he's over, and it's making me angry because I'm 29 years old, have put THOUSANDS of dollars into my place, I've lived there for almost 6 years, and now I feel like I'm sharing it with someone I can't stand (him, not her). So that changes things, I know. And there are other friends whose boyfriends I don't like, but this is the one that's getting to me most because I'm around it all the time.—"Taylor"

The above anecdote may be an extreme situation, because a roommate's significant other is simply unavoidable, and this particular relationship is perhaps not the healthiest. Should such a situation occur with your roommate, you would need to have a very frank talk, since the problem is beyond an annoyance and is a hindrance to one's lifestyle. Further, when you are paying the rent, this situation is simply not fair. In general, however, when friendships grow apart either because of drifting interests or romantic interference in the form of engagements and marriage, the best advice sometimes is to let go of the past. This does not mean letting go of a friendship altogether but, rather, letting go of the closeness you might have once held and the surrogate-family role your friends once provided when you were all young and single and living in the same apartment building. As much as we might like to hang on to the way things are in our cozy, intimate circles of friends, people will move, they will get married, our interests and values will change, and so, too, will the dynamics of friendships.

Maintaining closeness with certain friends as an adult may be impossible; growing apart is inevitable as individuals grow and change. However, as we move on and get married, maintaining friendships from school becomes increasingly meaningful to provide us with grounding and stability. Do your best not to burn bridges or cut ties with old friends, and stay in touch, even if that just means the occasional Facebook update. Friends who really know you and care about you can act as surrogate family members as you adapt to life as an adult. When we feel lost about our future direction, we often become increasingly sentimental about our pasts and in need of the comfort and support that only old friends can provide.

Dating Dos and Don'ts

Many recent graduates say they never went on a "real" date until after college. Most opted for—or naturally fell into—hooking up at parties or hanging out in the dorms. Thus, many twentysomethings have yet to master the nuances of checks and dining: who pays, where to meet, what to say, and how to end the night.

Even more so than with friendships, researchers report that romantic relationship qualities correlate positively with adult identity achievement. Specifically, companionship, worth, affection, and emotional support help emerging adults establish their identities (Barry, Madsen, Nelson, Carroll, & Badger, 2009). Baxter Magolda (2009) emphasized the importance of additional relationship qualities, including mutual respect, understanding, constructive listening, and problem solving, as being beneficial during this transition.

Many twentysomethings and thirtysomethings seek the close companionship and support of a relationship, and they are not always single by choice—in many cases, they simply have not met the right partner yet. "Debbie" is an example of this (www.quarterlifecrisis.com/forums):

Basically, I am starting to get to a point in life where I feel very strongly that I want to be married. I have dated a lot and I want to experience the stability of having one special person in my life. I'm dating someone I really like right now, although it's a pretty new relationship. However, it is so scary for me because I feel that I'm starting "late" on everything . . . career, marriage, kids (if I decide to have them). I feel that everyone else has had a head start on me. I was so focused on "having fun" for so long and now suddenly I'm not in my 20s anymore. It's not that 30 is so old but I feel that I want to settle down and if not now, when? I'm not totally set on having kids, so that is not so much of the issue. It's more a feeling of when is "it all going to happen" for me like it seems to for everybody else? There has been a lot of upheaval in my life recently. . . . I feel very uprooted and just wish to put down more roots. It's hard to be alone and to not really have anyone to count on other than yourself.

You can follow the same guidelines for meeting prospective romantic partners as you would for finding friends (see above); those common-interest activities in the community serve to connect you with prospective partners as well as friends, since you want to spend the most time with those who share your interests and values. In fact, the most successful romantic relationships often start out as friendships.

Each relationship is unique and impossible to measure against a set of benchmarks (unlike standardized test scores and starting salaries); thus, no set of official guidelines exists that one can follow for beginning a relationship and making sure the first date goes smoothly. Like most things we learn, real-world dating takes practice and will involve some trial and error. Below are two examples of first-date concerns and advice shared by recent graduates (www.quarterlifecrisis.com/forums):

I've never fully understood exactly what to talk about on a first date. I'm a great conversationalist once you get to know me, but I've wondered if maybe I'm showing a lack of confidence not knowing what to talk about on a first date. But I'm wondering what would be some good things to talk about on a first date. I definitely know not to talk about certain things: politics, religion, sex, bodily functions, etc. I seem to spend a lot of time on dates trying to figure out what to say. My mind works by tangents; my train of thought runs from food to sex to sports to politics in a matter of minutes. I always worry about saying the wrong thing, but that just doesn't work, so I'm trying to figure out something else.—"Paul"

Another twentysomething, "Diane" provided her antidote to that concern:

The best first dates I've been on were the ones where I didn't feel like we were just asking questions back and forth. We started out talking about basic stuff (jobs, where we grew up, siblings, college, etc.), and then conversation just flowed naturally. I'm kind of shy until I'm comfortable with someone, so if I can talk to a guy about pretty much anything, that's how I know I might be able to date him. But, then again, since I'm rather quiet at first, I don't mind if a guy asks me questions. I just don't like to feel as though I'm being interrogated. That conveys nervousness and discomfort.

Once you move past the first-date awkwardness into relationship territory, things can get more serious—and scarier. In college, you were probably not used to thinking about relationships on a permanent level but were more focused on enjoying the moment. Even after college, we often need some time to explore before settling down, and that's perfectly healthy. However, it's important that in a relationship you and your partner are on the same page when it comes to future plans.

It could be that one of you is ready to think about marriage, whereas the other is in no rush to leave the dating scene; there is a lot more at stake in the real world. When considering marriage, you have to think about a lot more than just what movie you want to see next—for instance, whether or not your attitudes on big issues such as family and finances are a good match. Bonior (2011) advises against a checklist mentality where you approach each relationship with a standard set of generic qualities you hope to find in a mate. Rather, you will have to rely on your feelings and gut instincts to some extent to test the long-term compatibility of each unique relationship.

Twentysomething Habitat

Yet another adjustment for recent graduates is one's living arrangements. Rooming with friends in college—either on or off campus—or staying at home with the family was an easy and often affordable arrangement that didn't require a great deal of thought. Once you begin earning a salary, however, you may seek greater independence. You may eventually decide you are ready to live on your own. Or you may decide to join the millions of young adults returning home to live with their parents to save money for the future. Regardless of which arrangement is the best fit, exploring housing alternatives requires a great deal of research, planning, and consideration of many options.

You will likely need to prioritize your housing requirements and decide which features are most important to you. Location, cost, safety, roommates, space, amenities, and parking are just some examples of the considerations we make in housing decisions. If you work in a big city and want a short commute, for example, you may have to sacrifice space. And you may need the help of a roommate to afford a place in the trendy neighborhood downtown near the nightlife. In terms of cost, one general guideline is not to spend more than half your monthly take-home pay (that's after taxes) on rent and utilities (Wilner & Stocker, 2005). For example, if you make $35,000 per year, this may equate to nearly $3,000 per month. But once you take into account benefits, taxes, and Social Security, the take-home pay, in reality, is closer to $2,000 a month. Therefore, you would need to find a place you can rent for $1,000 a month. This way, you will have some money left for personal expenses and future savings. It's amazing how quickly that paycheck can disappear.

Another housing consideration is roommates. The roommate relationship in the "real world" is a little different than in college. Once you are responsible adults with 9-to-5 schedules, you might have more appreciation for factors such as quiet and cleanliness. It is important when searching for a roommate to discuss and establish guidelines concerning matters such as paying bills, coordinating schedules, and habits such as smoking that might impede your lifestyle or even your health. Your roommate may or may not turn out to be a close friend, but it's most important that you be open and honest with each other and respectful of your shared space.

Making the Most of Moving Back Home

According to the MacArthur Foundation's Research Network on Transitions to Adulthood, only about one third of men (31%) and less than half of women (46%) reached adulthood benchmarks—defined as moving from home and attaining financial stability—in 2000, compared with roughly twice as many (65% and 77%, respectively) 40 years earlier, in 1960 (Furstenburg et al., 2003). Therefore, an unstable job market has implications beyond one's career, affecting one's financial situation and, moreover, independence as a full-fledged adult (Furstenburg et al., 2003). Although moving back home with one's parents after graduation has become more common, it can still feel like taking a step backward after spending 4 years gaining what felt like independence on campus. Although it is normal in many cultures for adult "kids" to stay at home until they are married, this is a period of adjustment for some U.S. families (Gordon & Shaffer, 2004).

Moving back home does not have to be a bad experience. In fact, living with one's parents can be an excellent learning opportunity. It can, however, be difficult and awkward to adjust to life with your parents again. In college, you might have become accustomed to coming and going without anyone checking up on you. You really enjoyed that newfound freedom and independence, but back at home you may have a tough time adjusting to your parents' ground rules. Gordon and Shaffer (2004) recommended, above all, to communicate. Discuss the move before it takes place; establish expectations about rules and responsibilities that will be instated when you once again live under their roof. Also, establish a timeline in advance to begin the search for your own place after a certain number of weeks or months at home.

Time Out: Reflective Question

If you moved in with your family after college, what would life be like for you and your family in terms of the advantages and disadvantages of being together?

From 3 Hours of Class to 8+ Hours of Work: Time Management for Working Adults

The college environment is in many ways an isolated microcosm far removed from the reality of the workplace. Students attend class an average of 3 hours a day; the remainder—other than any hours required for work—is completely at the student's disposal. For traditional-aged students in particular who do not need to work or attend to family responsibilities while enrolled in college, ideal days are often spent throwing a Frisbee in the quad; studying may come in the form of reading Chaucer while sunbathing or carrying on deep, philosophical discussions with friends. Yet for 4 (or more) years, this is a reality for many students. Despite an apparent abundance of free time, most students are not aware of that luxury until they become bound to the standard 9-to-5 reality of working life.

You may realize once you are out in the workforce that you did not fully appreciate the extent of your freedom in college, now that your schedule is truly booked solid. Some of you may prefer the routine of 9-to-5 life. Either way, many recent graduates are initially surprised by the lack of free time for personal errands, such as going to the gym or doctor's appointments. Having to work in an office and commute for the majority of your waking hours, and facing far more serious consequences for skipping or sleeping in than you would in school, makes a recent graduate realize just how precious those few free hours are.

Below are some ways to maximize that scarce free time so you make the most use of it:

- *Kill two birds with one stone.* Get together with a friend at the gym, at the grocery store, or the Laundromat. That way, you make the errands more fun, and you can catch up with friends at the same time.

- *Maximize your lunch hour.* Don't get in the habit of eating lunch over your keyboard on a daily basis. If your employer allows you to take a full hour for lunch, take advantage and run as many errands as possible—visit the bank, make a doctor's appointment, or go for a walk and get some exercise. Also take some days to catch up with friends over a relaxed lunch or set up a lunch for networking or informational interviewing with a colleague (Wilner & Stocker, 2005).

Coping With Feelings of Loneliness, Anxiety, and Depression

For many, the twentysomething transition to adulthood is a stage of anxiety and complex decision making. For some, everyday worries can become more serious if not handled constructively. A natural consequence of exploration, new situations will not always be the right fit. In some cases, jobs or relationships that end abruptly cause much stress and inner conflict. Depending on one's predisposition, individuals may experience stress, anxiety, or even depression—often for the first time in their lives—due to stress associated with a tumultuous transition. Individuals may simply feel lost or lonely, not having a road map before them similar to that which guided them through their lives in school up until this point (Robbins & Wilner, 2001).

When the freshly minted college graduate is not prepared to face real-world challenges, however, the resulting insecurities, instability, and volatility can develop negatively into a state of turbulence, also known as the quarterlife crisis (Robbins & Wilner, 2001; Wilner & Stocker, 2005). When twentysomethings experience these feelings but keep them inside, they may not realize the commonality of this type of experience, and the stress then becomes even harder to manage.

The most important thing to realize, should you experience difficulty with this major life transition, is that it is normal to experience anxiety or even depression during this time. In fact, the twentysomething years are the most common for onset of major psychological disorders, including anxiety, depression, addiction, and obsessive-compulsiveness (Kessler et al., 2005). It is important to know that despite any images you may have developed in school of your post-college years, the 20s are rarely completely easy and carefree. Today in particular, we deal with identity issues our parents might have waited until midlife to explore (Rubenstein, 2002). Know that it is healthy to take your time to explore the various options and life pathways, and learn to embrace the freedom and independence that accompany your 20s. Most important, talk about your experiences—if not with friends or family, then anonymously on message boards or in support groups.

It is possible, since twentysomethings today are doing so much exploration and experimentation, moving between jobs and relationships, and taking their time to settle down, that perhaps we will not need to change careers or spouses at midlife as the previous generation did. Ideally, we will have experienced so much change by the time we turn 50 that we will not feel the need to go try additional options (Wilner & Stocker, 2005).

In fact, the AARP—a powerful advocacy group for seniors and midlifers—found that the 20s, rather than the 50s, is the most traumatic period: the begin-life crisis. Psychologist Alice Rossi, a specialist in the midlife period, adds:

> There is no midlife crisis. . . . Much more critical and traumatic events occur in early adulthood than in midlife. It's during their twenties and thirties that Americans are searching for the right partner, a suitable career and a sense of identity. The peak in depression and anxiety occurs in early adulthood, not in midlife. (as quoted in Rubenstein, 2002, p. 56)

The AARP study found that "Americans under the age of 35 experience negative feelings more often than older Americans. A majority of boomers often feel happy, capable and competent, truly alive and peaceful" (Rubenstein, 2002, p. 57).

Psychologist Jean Twenge, author of *Generation Me* (2006), identified a prevalence of depression and anxiety among twentysomethings of this generation in particular, due in part to increased expectations. She noted that, in general, Americans now are more depressed than were past generations, or at least are being diagnosed and treated at higher rates. Bonior (2011) stressed the importance of friendships in counteracting depression. In fact, friendships actually have physical and medicinal qualities that are beneficial to our well-being. The social support and emotional connection between friends can actually boost our immune systems and help create a state of euphoria through mutual understanding (Bonior, 2011). And surrounding yourself with friends who make healthy choices can positively influence your own habits.

It is important to take healthy, proactive steps to fight negative feelings, should they occur. Getting 8 hours of sleep, exposure to sunlight, at least 30 minutes of exercise three times a week, and a balanced diet are all steps you can take to reduce depression. Healthy social relationships, as noted, also have the power to help you stay positive. Adopting a positive outlook, adjusting expectations, and learning to accept that some things are beyond your control are all ways to feel more stable. If you feel that you need the assistance of a professional, therapy or another medical treatment may be helpful. Please visit the National Institute for Mental Health's website (listed in the additional resources at the end of this chapter) for guidelines about detecting and treating depression and other psychological disorders.

In earlier chapters, the authors emphasized the importance of using your campus counseling services to address personal issues you are currently experiencing, such as anxiety, depression, loneliness, alcohol or substance abuse, sex and sexuality issues, and similar concerns. Now is the time to develop resources to manage these conditions so they are not exacerbated by the many workplace stresses you are likely to encounter. Your tuition has already paid for your access to counseling services; after graduation, you will have far less time and fewer resources to pay for this help.

Closing Comments

Whereas career choices will certainly take up a good deal of energy and time in your 20s, it is important not to lose sight of your social life and to grow continually on a personal level. The twentysomething years are a time to adapt to a new social landscape, by expanding your social circle and going on "adult" dates. Getting involved in the community, volunteering, and joining common-interest groups are just some of the ways to meet new people that could lead not only to friendships or romances but also to networking opportunities for future jobs. This transition is also a time for an evolving habitat, which can sometimes entail moving back home before being financially stable enough to live on your own.

Finally, due to all the constant change, you may need to learn to cope with new feelings, such as anxiety. Remember that it is normal to experience stress or anxiety during this major life transition. Talk about your experiences, if not with friends or family, then anonymously on message boards or in support groups. If you feel that your stress has gotten serious, don't be afraid to seek out professional help to diagnose and treat your symptoms.

Getting Involved

Journal Starters

1. What are the most significant insights you gained from this chapter that you can apply to your college life?

2. If you have older siblings or friends who graduated a few years ago, what kinds of personal life changes did they face?

3. What are your biggest concerns regarding your social life after college? What concerns, if any, do your friends face?

Projects

1. Conduct a literature survey about the role of social media in establishing and influencing friendships.

2. Since many of you will return home after graduation, you will want to be prepared for your new relationship with your family. (a) Perform a literature review of research studies on this topic, or (b) survey a group of graduating seniors about their intentions and concerns regarding living at home again.

3. Conduct an online search of three cities where you could potentially live after graduating: (a) Search local classifieds for housing options to get a sense of the typical cost and amount of space you could realistically afford on an entry-level salary, and (b) search local websites (including your university's local alumni association) to compile a list of activities and events that appeal to your interests and hobbies, where you might be able to meet fellow twentysomethings.

Additional Resources

URL	*Brief Website Description*
www.quarterlifecrisis.com/forums	These message boards provide an online forum for recent graduates to connect with one another, share concerns, and provide support on a range of issues common among twentysomethings—from careers to finances to relationships.
www.meetup.com	Meetup provides a platform for groups to connect online and plan in-person meetings based on a range of common interests. Many geographic areas have Meetup groups for new residents to those particular locations.
www.volunteermatch.com	VolunteerMatch is a database of volunteer opportunities across the nation, allowing users to search for events by interest area and geographic location.
www.nimh.nih.gov	The National Institute of Mental Health provides resources across the nation, allowing users to search for events by interest area and geographic location.

References

Arnett, J. J. (1998). Learning to stand alone: The contemporary American transition to adult-hood in cultural and historical perspective. *Human Development, 41,* 295–315.

Barry, C. M., Madsen, S. D., Nelson, L. J., Carroll, J. S., & Badger, S. (2009). Friendship and romantic relationship qualities in emerging adulthood: Differential associations with identity development and achieved adulthood criteria. *Journal of Adult Development, 16,* 209–222.

Baxter Magolda, M. D. (2009). *Authoring your life: Developing an internal voice to navigate life's challenges.* Sterling, VA: Stylus.

Bonior, A. (2011). *The friendship fix: The complete guide to choosing, losing, and keeping up with your friends.* New York, NY: St. Martin's Griffin.

Bureau of Labor Statistics. (2002). *National longitudinal survey of youth, 1997–2000.* Washington, DC: U.S. Department of Labor.

Erikson, E. H. (1968). *Identity: Youth and crisis.* New York, NY: Norton.

Furstenburg, F. F., Jr., Kennedy, S., McCloyd, V. C., Rumbaut, R. G., & Settersten, R. A., Jr. (2003). *Between adolescence and adulthood: Expectations about the timing of adult-hood* (Research Network Working Paper No. 1). Chicago, IL: John D. and Catherine T. MacArthur Foundation.

Gordon, L. P., & Shaffer, S. M. (2004). *Mom, can I move back in with you? A survival guide for parents of twentysomethings.* New York, NY: Tarcher/Putnam.

Hardy, S. A., Pratt, M. W., Pancer, S. M., Olsen, J. A., & Lawford, H. L. (2011). Community and religious involvement as contexts of identity change across late adolescence and emerging adulthood. *International Journal of Behavioral Development, 35,* 125–135.

Kessler, R. C., Berglund, P., Demler, O., Jin, R., Merikangas, K. R., & Walters, E. E. (2005). Lifetime prevalence and age-of-onset distributions of DSM-IV disorders in the National Comorbidity Survey replication. *Archives of General Psychiatry, 62,* 593–603.

Lee, J. (2006). *The "faculty bias" studies: Science or propaganda?* Washington, DC: American Federation of Teachers.

Levit, A. (2009). *They don't teach corporate in college: A twenty-something's guide to the busi-ness world.* Franklin Lakes, NJ: Career Press.

Pew Research Center for the People and the Press. (2010). *A pro-government, socially liberal generation: Democrats' edge among Millennials slips.* Washington, DC: Author.

Robbins, A., & Wilner, A. (2001). *Quarterlife crisis: The unique challenges of life in your twen-ties.* New York, NY: Tarcher/Putnam.

Rubenstein, C. (2002, July–August). What turns you on? *My Generation,* 55–58.

Schwartz, B. (2005). *The paradox of choice: Why more is less.* New York, NY: Harper Perennial.

Twenge, J. M. (2006). *Generation me: Why today's young Americans are more confident, asser-tive, entitled—and more miserable than ever before.* New York, NY: Free Press.

Wilner, A., & Stocker, C. (2005). *The quarterlifer's companion: How to get on the right career path, control your finances, and find the support network you need to thrive.* New York, NY: McGraw-Hill.

CHAPTER 12

From Know Thyself to Manage Thyself

No bird soars too high, if he soars with his own wings.

—William Blake (1757–1827), poet

Throughout this book, we address several issues we believe will strengthen your preparedness for organizations you will enter after graduation. We encourage your focus on personal development, whereas your job will demand that you direct your talent, time, and energy to accomplishing the tasks and objectives assigned by your supervisor. However, you cannot neglect your personal needs. You must learn to manage yourself as well—even better than your work—because if you disregard the former, you will fail in the latter. Failure happens frequently to college grads who believe that a diploma will instantly transform bad lifestyle habits into productive behaviors (it does not). In this chapter, we address selected aspects of self-management (but some topics are so complex as to be beyond the scope of this book) that we believe are crucial for you to practice: stress, time, financial, and life/work balance. There are thoughtful and well-researched (as well as superficial) resources on each of these topics that you may consult, so we will provide you with information and advice that you may not be fully aware of.

Managing Your Stress

By way of review, the transition to the workplace is a major change in the lives of most college graduates, and this will likely be a period of high stress—stress that is *added* to existing personal stresses. You are very vulnerable during this transition, and you ardently want your first post-college job to be a successful beginning to a rewarding career. If you are experiencing the kinds of health problems, threats to personal safety, or stressors interfering with your academic performance that are described below, you *must* do your best to attend to them. *Do it now!* Do not wait and assume these conditions will disappear; most will not. In the nerve-racking environment of a new job (and perhaps a new residence), not only are stressful issues exacerbated, but you will also have to deal with them on your own time (non-working hours) and at your own cost. And procrastination has its consequences.

Common Stressors

Let's face it: College is a stressful time, from a number of perspectives. When the American College Health Association (ACHA, 2011) conducted its National College Health Assessment II with more than 30,000 college students in 2010, the most highly reported health issues by at least 10% of college students diagnosed by a professional for a particular health problem in the past 12 months included allergies, sinus infection, back pain, and strep throat.

College can clearly be a stressful time for one's physical health, which makes success all the more challenging. The concerns of everyday life are continuous for a student, including personal safety, potentially abusive relationships, and violence.

Of course, individuals in the general population also contend with physical health, mental health, and physical safety concerns. Our point here is, when the normal concerns of everyday life are coupled with the additional unique stressors of college, your life gets complicated. Table 12.1 presents the percentage of students who reported that a particular factor influenced *academic* performance at some point in the past year, specifically (a) receiving a lower grade on an exam or project, (b) receiving a lower course grade, (c) dropping the course or receiving an incomplete, or (d) experiencing a substantial disruption in a research or thesis project. Thinking about these conditions, might they also impact your work performance? What will you do differently after the transition to the workplace to keep yourself healthy?

Table 12.1 Student Self-Report of Factors That Negatively Impact Academic Performance

Health Problem	Percentage of College Students Reporting
Stress	25.4
Sleep difficulties	17.8
Anxiety	16.4
Cold/flu/sore throat	13.8
Internet use/computer games	11.6
Work	11.4
Concern for a troubled friend or family member	10.1

Depression	10.0
Relationship difficulties	9.6
Participation in extracurricular activities	8.8
Finances	6.3
Death of a friend or family member	5.1
Sexually transmitted disease/infection (STD/I)	4.9
Sinus infection/ear infection/bronchitis/strep throat	4.8
ADHD	4.5
Alcohol use	3.7
Homesickness	3.7
Chronic health problem or serious illness	3.0
Allergies	2.9
Learning disability	2.9
Chronic pain	2.4
Injury	2.1
Other	1.8
Drug use	1.6
Eating disorder/problem	1.1
Discrimination	1.0
Pregnancy (yours or partner's)	1.0
Assault (sexual)	0.9
Assault (physical)	0.7
Gambling	0.5

Source: American College Health Association (2011).

Not much information here should surprise you. College students face stressful situations like everyone else, tend to have high expectations of their education, are demanding of themselves, and may be away from home for the first time. Couple the adjustment to any new environment with balancing a job or jobs in college (or finances in general), romantic relationships, and new friendships, and the sources of stress are easy to identify (Hamaideh, 2011).

> Those stressors do not cause tension or stress by themselves. Instead, stress results from the interaction between stressors and students' perceptions and reaction to those stressors. . . . The amount of stress experienced by an individual may be influenced by one's ability to effectively react to stressful events and situations. (p. 70)

Seven Major Causes of Workplace Stress

An important step for dealing with stress is to identify its sources. One major cause is the particular demands of the job or *occupation*. Those demands pertain not only to safety-related factors that miners, policemen, and firemen face but also to jobs that involve constant monitoring of devices or materials, repeated exchanging of information with others, working in an unpleasant physical environment, and performing unstructured rather than structured tasks (Greenberg, 2010). Workplace violence can sometimes be a concern as well. We also include boring and repetitive tasks, such as certain data-entry jobs that do not require high-level skills but demand patience, accuracy, and attention. During economic crises, low-skill jobs are often the only ones available at the entry level for many new graduates. We hope you are able to avoid such jobs, but if you cannot, be prepared to experience stress if your primary tasks are tedious, repetitive, and involve little or no challenge.

A second major cause of stress is the conflict created by the interplay of work and nonwork activities, such as family obligations, that create *role conflict* and constant juggling of schedules; conflict resulting from holding more than one job; or conflict due to heavy course loads and jobs. *Role ambiguity,* a third cause, occurs when an employee is uncertain about the nature of her or his responsibilities, how to assign time to tasks, the organization's reporting structure, or specifically what is expected of him or her. Meet with your boss to clarify these issues, but recognize that some supervisors are not well organized or may be operating in an environment where ambiguity is systemic.

Work *overload* or *underload* is a fourth major stress factor. You can identify with overload, especially at the end of the academic term, but you may wonder how work underload (not enough work) can create strain. Just as boring and repetitive tasks create pressure, so does a lack of work. Sometimes there is a lull in one's workload, especially if the business's products or services are seasonal, and when a supervisor does not plan assignments well. Dealing with underload can be tricky: You do not want to be reprimanded or terminated if you are seen not working, nor do you want to succumb to the temptation of playing computer games or logging on to your social network during work hours (a cause for formal disciplinary action in many companies). We recommend you alert your supervisor to the situation and seek additional tasks either at the same level as your current assignments (i.e., job enlargement) or that are more challenging (i.e., job enrichment); either type may reduce the stress of underload (Greenberg, 2010), hopefully without leading to overload.

A fifth cause derives from being the victim of *bullying* or *sexual harassment.* Some companies provide training for resisting these unwanted behaviors, and all human resources departments should have written policies and procedures for dealing with them. Do not let yourself be a victim of these behaviors; if you are not sure how to respond, consult your mentor, supervisor, a trusted and experienced coworker, or meet with the person in Human Resources responsible for the organization's policies and procedures regarding these behaviors. Sixth, the *absence of social support* is stressful. Seeking support from friends and family can boost your self-confidence, provide direction, and serve as a diversion from work.

It may be a few years before you encounter the seventh major source of job-related stress—namely, the *burden of being responsible for others,* a pressure your supervisor experiences in addition to those stressors you may contend with (Greenberg, 2010).

Stress Reduction Strategies

According to Greenberg (2010) about two thirds of today's companies offer programs that help employees address problems they encounter in their personal lives. These services are generally called employee assistance programs (EAPs); typically, they provide assistance with financial and legal problems, substance abuse, and career planning. Company stress-management programs may involve training in relaxation techniques and meditation. Wellness programs promote healthy lifestyles through nutrition, exercise, and weight management. Companies incur significant costs to operate such programs because they know there are payoffs in reduced absenteeism, improved health, and higher employee productivity, and they expect employees who need program services to participate. Employers also promote EAPs to avoid the problem of *presentism,* the tendency of some employees to report to their jobs but feel too sick to work productively (Greenberg, 2010). Some teachers permit students to attend class sick, but do not be surprised if that behavior is discouraged by a supervisor.

What can you do to reduce the stresses and strains of work? Below, we summarize advice you have heard probably several times, but it remains true for most people and you have so much to lose if you fail to heed it.

1.   Get a good night's sleep—about 8 hours for most young adults. If you plan that 8 hours backward, you will discover bedtime is likely to be closer to 10:00 p.m. or 11:00 p.m., not midnight or later. If you do not get enough sleep, your boss will know. Relax before bedtime with a good book, soothing music, or whatever it takes (except habit-forming sleeping pills) to create a half-hour-or-so transition between complete wakefulness and sleep. Need we say more?

2.   Eat a healthy diet, and stay physically fit. You may be aware that food scientists and marketers know that the receptors for fat, salt, and sugar are part of the neural pathways to the pleasure centers of the brain. You should also know enough about the body to value the importance of regular exercise and its many forms. Convert that knowledge into good eating and exercise habits.

3.   Build time into your schedule for regular relaxation through meditation, yoga, hobbies, a walk in the forest preserve, or similar methods. View relaxation as a necessity, like eating and sleeping, not a luxury. Similarly, when you feel the tension rising in yourself or others at work, take a timeout, such as a short break to walk down the hall or outside, a trip to the bathroom, or other activities that create a brief breathing space.

4.   Another effective method for reducing stress is to avoid inappropriate self-talk (Greenberg, 2010) or distorted styles of thinking (Helkowski, 1998). For example, using the *mind reading* distorted style of thinking, you inappropriately believe you know what others are thinking and feeling about you and why they behave the way they do when, in fact, there is little data to support your beliefs. *Catastrophizing* is a form of distorted thinking in which you expect the worst outcomes from a

situation or you believe that positive events are only temporary even though there is little evidence to support that belief. For instance, you are probably exaggerating if you believe that your family will withdraw their support if you do not take the job they encouraged you to apply for or if you are not accepted into graduate school. In *emotional reasoning,* an individual disregards the facts of the situation and depends almost totally on his or her feelings to judge the outcome of an action. As an example, you might complete a task for your boss feeling you did a poor job even though there is no basis for predicting failure. Finally, *blaming* is a form of distorted thinking in which you hold others accountable for an action when you are the responsible agent. For instance, you might wake up late for work and blame your roommate for not waking you in time, when it was your responsibility to do so. Remember, the enemy that creates this form of stress is you, not other people or external events. Try to minimize *you* being the cause of your own stress.

5. When you use your time ineffectively, fall behind in your work, or feel overwhelmed by how much you have to do and how little time you have to do it in, you will feel stressed. Sometimes, however, you may have so many tasks to perform that even if you control your time well, you will feel the tension. Taking control of time is such an important survival skill that we devote the next section to this dimension of self-management.

Time Out: Reflective Questions

1. What specific actions do you take to manage your stress? Are some forms healthier (e.g., exercise, sports, or relaxation methods) than others (e.g., excessive drinking, smoking, or drugs)?

2. If you are not in the habit of healthy stress management, what techniques would be relatively easy for you to practice?

Time Management

Time is definitely one of those finite resources with which we must contend. Although we can increase our efforts to be healthy or to become a better employee, friend, or spouse, we cannot increase the amount of time in a day, so we are left with the strategy of becoming more efficient with the time we have.

Time Management: College Versus Corporate Settings

If you are a junior or senior with a fairly full schedule and good grades, chances are you manage your time reasonably well, at least for a college student. In the workplace, however, time management operates differently. Return to Chapter 10 and study Table 10.1, Holton's 16 comparisons between college and workplace, and mark those that relate to controlling time.

You should have marked dimensions 2, 3, 4, 6, 9, 10, 11, 12, 13, and 14, which are reproduced in Table 12.2. Yes, more than 60% of the general dimensions that distinguish college from corporate environments are related directly or indirectly to time. You would quickly agree that most of these elements pertain to time, but what about comparisons 4, 6, 9, 13, and 14?

At the risk of repeating remarks we made in Chapter 10, we contend that managing time is so critical to your success that you *must* understand the power your work environment exercises over you, even if you possess excellent time-management skills. For example, you have some freedom in college to set schedules for classes, work, and other activities. You are your own boss. You create a schedule around your needs, and you are accountable primarily to yourself. The workplace is different, and adjusting to this disparity is usually a major challenge. In general (differences may exist as a function of the tasks you perform), you have much less freedom over your schedule, even if you can work from home. Time off is limited to national holidays and vacation days that you accrue. There is no structured course syllabus with assignments and due dates listed, so you will need some form of scheduling technology, plus other techniques. Unlike college, which is about *your* development, you will perform the tasks your supervisor assigns you, often with little advance notice or direction, and sometimes with short deadlines you may deem impossible to meet.

In short, the way you distribute much of your time may no longer be your decision but your supervisor's. Expect uncertainty and ambiguity about tasks, instructions, procedures, and deadlines to be the rule, not the exception. Your challenges

Table 12.2   Differences Between College and Workplace That Influence Time Management

College	Workplace
2. Flexible schedule; less structure	Structured schedule
3. Frequent breaks and time off	Limited time off
4. Choose your own performance level	A-level work required all the time
6. Less initiative required	Initiative and active participation required
9. Focus on your development	Focus on getting results for organization
10. Highly structured curriculum	Much less structure; fewer directions
11. Few significant changes in routine	Frequent and unexpected changes
12. Personal control over time, classes	Respond to others' directions and interests
13. Individual effort	Team effort
14. Intellectual challenge	Organizational and people challenges

Source: From Holton (1998, p. 102). Adapted with permission of John Wiley and Sons, Inc.

are primarily organizational (of which time management is an essential part), not intellectual. Furthermore, your supervisor will expect you to be actively involved with your work continually (a warning to procrastinators and passive students) and will expect all your work to be performed excellently, not at the level of your choice. If you are part of a team, you must plan ahead to complete your contributions or get reprimanded by coworkers. You must view time management as a job-saving survival skill, as you would swimming if you were a lifeguard.

Because you probably possess at least some basic skills for controlling time, we want to heighten your awareness of time with these general suggestions for your current and future jobs; most remarks also apply to your college activities.

Establish Priorities

At the beginning of an academic term, some students take each course syllabus and enter the dates of exams and assignments on a monthly calendar or electronic device, along with their job schedule and extracurricular events, to create a big picture of what lies ahead. As the weeks unfold, students add tasks such as group projects and club meetings. In your job, you will also have several assignments to manage simultaneously, although most due dates are likely to be on an ASAP (as soon as possible) contingency, not a 4-month calendar. Your challenge, even if you are an accomplished multitasker, is to understand your priorities and act on them in a timely manner.

One useful method for establishing priorities is the Covey Time Management Matrix (Covey, 2004), in which tasks are viewed on two variables: urgency (urgent or nonurgent) and importance (important or nonimportant). In Quadrant I, you place tasks that are *urgent and important* that might cost you your job if you failed at them, such as meeting important deadlines or dealing with crises or pressing problems. In Quadrant II are the *nonurgent and important* tasks that promote your professional growth, such as attending a training session to learn new software or building a relationship with a colleague who could be instrumental in your advancement. Quadrant III tasks are those *urgent and nonimportant* activities, such as certain phone calls, e-mails, or meetings, that help maintain relationships. Quadrant IV tasks are *nonurgent and nonimportant* activities for which you could be disciplined if you are not careful—for example, avoidance behaviors such as excessively long breaks or playing games on your computer (Covey, 2004).

During your first weeks in a new job, you are likely to view most priorities as urgent and important, so expect to spend considerable time and commit errors of judgment before you clearly distinguish among the four quadrants. As you identify your Quadrant I, II, and III priorities, enter a time estimate for the time-consuming activities so that after you complete them you can compare the estimated and actual times required; the discrepancy between the two times is instructive for future planning of similar tasks.

Although the Covey Time Management Matrix (Covey, 2004) can be very useful, you will encounter additional challenges to distributing your time. For example, what should you do when you have a Quadrant I priority to finish that day and your supervisor assigns you another high-priority task to be done ASAP. Or what if you work for two supervisors and each wants you to complete his or her project ASAP? Levit (2009) noted that "*no* is a tricky word in business, because you always want to be perceived as a can-do employee. In general, you should try to preempt situations in which you will have to decline an assignment" (p. 138). For example, Levit advises first formalizing your assignments with your boss by identifying those members of your team who are authorized to delegate work to you and the kinds of tasks they can assign. If your supervisor assigns you two Quadrant I projects, ask which project has the higher priority. These situations are analogous to what you experience in college when a teacher piles one heavy assignment immediately on another and expects them to be completed within a short time frame, or when a teacher assigns a major project due on the same day as a big assignment for another class. Before you complain, just bite the bullet and recognize such situations prepare you for the real world.

A supplementary method for managing priorities is to create a DO List (or to-do list), a technique you might already practice. Using a small notepad or a digital device, begin your day with a list you constructed the night before or the morning of your work day. List those activities that must be completed, such as meetings, e-mails, and phone calls; priority projects to be completed and started; and personal chores you can complete during your lunch hour or after work. Variations on the DO List for the truly time-conscious person can include a star system to identify priority level (e.g., four stars for the highest and one star for the lowest) and time estimates for each. And you will experience a feeling of satisfaction when you cross out each task as you complete it.

Time Out: Exercise

Identify all the tasks you need to complete tomorrow or the next day, and apply the Covey Time Management Matrix for categorizing each. Although 1 day may not be sufficient for judging the usefulness of this system, evaluate its advantages and disadvantages.

Using Time More Efficiently

Even if you establish priorities for your assignments, you still have the challenge of using your time efficiently and avoiding time robbers. Hopper (n.d.) suggested that we seek out more time during any particular day by (a) doing the same tasks in less time—that is, becoming more efficient—and (b) making better use of wasted time through better planning, such that wasted time is minimized. For example, learn to prioritize your e-mails and become conscious of how much time you spend reading and responding to them, and keep phone calls on focus. Stay off Facebook and other social media sites during company time, and remember that many organizations monitor your computer activities. We do not recommend that you become antisocial, but get into the habit of monitoring the time you spend on breaks, in casual conversations, and on lunch hours.

Two of Hopper's (n.d.) best suggestions are to carry "pocket" work with you always and keep a date book/electronic calendar. There usually are occasions during the day (either in college or work) where you will have small stretches of time when you are doing nothing, such as waiting for a class or meeting to start or arriving at a destination early. Given the portability of modern work tools such as your iPhone, Android phone, iPad, other tablet devices, and laptops, you can take work with you. And if you want to go old school, you can do that, too, with venerable and time-tested portable tools such as paper, pencils, and books. If you make effective use of these small times during the day with your pocket work, you become more efficient and gain time that can be devoted to other tasks later. In the same vein, by keeping an up-to-date planner, you can avoid missing deadlines and prevent showing up for a meeting at the wrong place and/or time. Both strategies can help you be more efficient with the time you have and minimize wasted time. Finally, remember that when you create more time in your schedule, you create more freedom—freedom to accomplish more work or to pursue a little more balance in your life.

Managing Finances

Your college or university attempts to teach you so much during your career as an undergraduate student, but a common lament is that one of the areas higher education institutions do not attend to well is teaching financial literacy. Students need real-world financial knowledge, because real-world ramifications exist, such as the current 7% default rate on student loans (Bahls, 2011) and widespread poor credit scores. We strongly encourage you to search your school's offerings for a course (whether for credit or noncredit) or campus workshop on financial fitness. Contact your nearby universities or community colleges if your school does not offer training in this survival skill. The time and tuition you invest in acquiring such information will be paid back quickly and generously within a year of graduation.

As with health, nutrition, and exercise, numerous resources addressing finances are available. The Internet can be a wonderful resource, but remember to apply your critical thinking skills when evaluating the credibility of sources and websites. If you Google "college graduate finances" or use similar terms, you will discover an array of websites containing advice to view and evaluate. Because you have access to these resources, we will focus on just two of the more salient money-related topics (credit cards and saving), but we strongly encourage you to pursue related issues (e.g., insurance, student loans, and investments) on your own time.

Credit Cards

Ellis (2009) offered these suggestions for students and their prudent use of credit cards:

- Scrutinize credit card offers carefully, especially the fine print. Before you apply, call the company if you have any questions about their policies.
- Avoid cash advances, unless you enjoy paying ATM fees.

- Check your monthly statements (either online or paper) against your own records (either online or paper). Compare each statement charge to each of your receipts, and pay special attention to unexpected fees.
- Pay off the balance each month, not only to avoid interest charges but also to strengthen your credit rating. Our addendum to this advice: Don't buy what you can't pay for in 30 days.
- Use just one credit card, unless you travel widely and need to keep an additional card as a backup.
- Because you are entitled to receive one free copy of your credit report annually, be sure to obtain the copy and check the accuracy of the information; credit report companies do sometimes make mistakes.

In addition, make sure you understand the card company's annual fees, APR (annual percentage rate), credit limits, and the grace period. Be aware that missing a monthly payment or paying late may lower your credit rating and that credit ratings are used as a basis for charging interest on loans and other major services and products you purchase. Major changes involving credit card companies and users were enacted in 2011, some features of which the companies are arguing in court, so make sure you understand all existing and new regulations.

Saving

According to Mark Kantrowitz, publisher of FinAid.org and FastWeb.com (as cited in *TIME* magazine), the average student loan debt for 2011 graduates was $27,300 (Dell, 2011). If the loans taken out by parents for their children's education (which many graduates repay) are added, the debt rises to $34,400. If you are graduating from a private university, chances are your loan debt will be much higher. The article (Dell, 2011) also reported that 41% of the borrowers who began repayment of loans in 2005 became delinquent or defaulted within 5 years. As you know, failure to repay loans will lower that all-important credit score you want to raise continually. We know that you do not want to be reminded of this (the same article affirmed the employment and salary benefits of a college education), but debt is a reality most of you must face. If you graduate from college financially challenged, one way to compensate for less-than-desirable wages is to develop a proactive attitude about using money. We offer just a sampling of ways you can save and encourage you to search widely for additional resources.

Wilner and Stocker (2005) offered several useful suggestions for saving money:

1. Assess your spending. Note all expenses and keep all receipts for a week or two, and carefully analyze where your money is going. You may be surprised about how much you spend on certain items.

2. Limit your expenditures on things (tangibles), especially large furnishings you are likely to move from place to place. Think small.

3. Sell items you do not truly *need* or want at garage sales, on eBay, or by consignment, or trade them for items you do need. Not only do such items require space, but their value is not earning you anything.

4. Set a 5-year goal. Try to establish a realistic plan for when you can put a down payment on a new car, a condo, or that dream trip overseas.

5. Try to get side jobs. Can you baby-sit, mow yards, create websites, teach guitar lessons, or paint rooms or houses? Do you have any hobbies or skills that could be turned to profit? For example, do you know SPSS and its applications or similar software so thoroughly that you could become a tutor or an independent contractor?

6. Learn the basics of investing (many college business departments offer an investment course), and develop a savings plan, no matter how little you earn.

7. Take the 30-Day "Survivor" Spending Challenge. Wilner and Stocker (2005) suggest you try to go 1 month without such expenses as your favorite gourmet latté, appetizers or dessert with dinner when eating out, that extra drink, bottled water, taxis, and premium cable TV. Similarly, try to survive without late fees, cigarettes, lottery tickets, or parking tickets. Create a list of these items. For each, record your estimated monthly cost, and next to it leave space for the actual monthly cost. Does this sound Spartan? Yes, but consider how much you might save on nonnecessities, especially if you really cannot afford them.

In addition to these tips, your book's coauthor (PH) has used a resource for several decades (yes, decades!) that has not only saved him thousands of dollars but also has taught wise consumer decision-making skills while providing valuable information about products and services. That resource is the monthly magazine *Consumer Reports*, published by Consumers Union and available at many major newsstands, by subscription, and online. From this magazine, you will acquire information about specific products and services, the criteria used to judge quality, comparisons amongst brands, and prices. Due to the lag between product purchase, testing, and publication, some product models may no longer be available when the reader is ready to buy, nor can all models of all brands be tested. Overall, however, this magazine is an excellent resource for making decisions about a wide variety of products and services.

Perhaps the best tip we can provide about saving is to assess your basic attitudes toward thrift, saving, and owning, and make a critical distinction between wants and needs. What possessions do you truly *need*, especially with your limited resources, versus possessions you *want*? For example, everyone needs shoes, but how important is your owning a $150-pair of high-fashion shoes if you are working in a minimum-wage job, do not need expensive shoes, and cannot afford an expensive social life? Or do the expensive shoes really serve as a much-desired boost to low self-esteem? Is the $5 cup of gourmet coffee really necessary, or would the $1.70 variety suffice? If you buy that $30,000 car you really cannot afford, does that mean you won't have funds to purchase health insurance or begin a retirement account? Throughout this book, we have emphasized the importance of self-reflection. One important aspect of self-reflection is to have the clarity of thought, discipline, and courage to know and act on the distinction between your true needs and your wants.

For additional tips on college and post-college financial management and loan repayment issues, consult the "Additional Resources" section at the end of this chapter. As for online resources, some sites you might want to explore in assisting you in financial planning include www.mint.com, www.buxfer.com, and www. money.strands.com.

Finding Balance Between Work and Personal Life

The phrase "finding a balance" sounds so simple, yet is a highly complex task for most people. The fact is that the method by which you find a balance between work and personal life may change at different stages of your career and your life. Perhaps you have heard the phrase "you can have it all"—well, one of your authors (REL) prefers a slightly modified version—"you can have it all, just not at the same time." There are so many aspects of life that need your simultaneous attention, it is difficult to imagine "having it all" at the same time; hopefully, sacrifices and dedication in parts of your work life are sowing benefits you hope to reap eventually. If you examine this concept from merely a time-based perspective, you will likely spend about one third of each day (8 hours) on "work"—that is, on nonweekends (and for some industries, the weekend may not always be Saturday and Sunday).

> Work is a major component of the lives of most adults, but clearly not the only component. The interplay of work, love, and play is what we mean by balance; the place of work in one's life has been called its *salience*. (Goodman, Schlossberg, & Anderson, 2006, p. 154; emphasis in original)

We refer to the salience of the work role, with special attention given to resilience and hardiness.

Resilience is the ability to bounce back and weather changes without experiencing major personal turmoil (Goodman et al., 2006)—think of it as operating on an even keel or at one's normal cruising altitude (not too high or too low). Similarly, hardiness is a personality variable characterized by feelings of personal control, active commitment to control the course of one's life, and experiencing challenging and stimulating life events (Mathis & Lecci, 1999). So hardiness may be that trait or quality that gets you through difficult events without much incident, but when you are "thrown off your game," resilience is what helps you get back on track.

Chances are you can readily recall events in your life and probably in college that have required high levels of hardiness, such as persisting in an incredibly difficult course to earn the grade you sought or working hard to make the team. But if you failed in such attempts, it was your resilience that helped you overcome your deep disappointments and return to your normal level of energy and commitment. Hardiness and resilience, if you have them, are excellent qualities when you begin your freshman year in the workplace. Sometimes you'll hear resilience discussed in the context of a different term—*career adaptability* (Goodman et al., 2006). This form of resilience refers to achieving balance between our work lives and personal lives, and it includes our ability to adapt to changing conditions—in other words, the ability to roll with the punches (or, if you prefer a different cliché, making lemonade out of lemons).

When specifically examining career adaptability, Goodman et al. (2006) reported the outcomes of a study indicating seven aspects of adaptation: (1) work values and work salience, (2) autonomy, (3) planfulness or future perspective, (4) exploration and establishment, (5) access to information, (6) decision-making ability, and (7) reflection on experience. It is important to recognize that this is a correlational study, so of course no cause-and-effect conclusions are possible. There is good evidence to suggest that hardiness is a good predictor of mental health and that one's hardiness level is a good longitudinal predictor of college adjustment (Mathis & Lecci, 1999). However, you cannot just "flip the switch" and become hardy or resilient overnight to reap the statistical benefits—you already know that correlational research does not work that way. But what you can do is look to the underlying concepts within resilience and hardiness to see if those are traits and behaviors you can embrace over time. To start you thinking in that direction, complete Item 1 in the "Projects" section, on the S^4 approach to assessing your use of coping strategies and resources.

Closing Comments

Earlier chapters focused on attitudes and motivation (Chapter 8), the role of communications and groups (Chapter 9), and workplace expectations and related dimensions encountered in the first months of a typical job (Chapter 10). Just as Chapter 11 redirected the discussion to personal life issues (social relationships after college), we continued that thread in this chapter by exploring basic dimensions of stress, time, and financial management, along with the importance of seeking work/life balance. You must learn to manage yourself effectively if you want to manage your responsibilities successfully; these two dimensions of your life operate interdependently. In the next chapter, we explore four perspectives on transition; we end this book by examining additional dimensions of workplace readiness from the perspective of your psychology major and what it means to be a Millennial in today's workplace.

Getting Involved

Journal Starters

1. What were the most significant insights you gained about yourself from the material presented in this chapter?

2. Which dimension of self-management are you most in need of improving: stress, time, financial, or balance? Why? Based on what you learned in this chapter, how could you improve?

3. Apply the distinction between needs and wants to your current situation. Assume you will obtain a job that pays much less than you prefer. What kinds of "wants" will be first on your list to modify or give up? By attempting to answer the questions presented below, journal writing can provide clarity (Combs, 2000) and help mold and shape your thought processes. You don't need to answer them all; just write about the two or three items you think are most relevant to you today.

What am I excited about in life right now?

What am I most grateful about in life right now?

What is it I have not yet done that I truly desire to do before I die?

What action could I take today that would lead me to my dream life?

What would I want for myself if I knew I could have it any way I wanted?

What are the most important things in my life?

What are the activities I love and enjoy most today?

What would be my ideal work environment today?

How would my ideal workday go today?

How would I define success today?

What might be my purpose or destiny?

How do I want to be perceived by my friends? Coworkers? Parents? Significant other?

In 10 years, what magazine would I most like to be featured in for my tremendous accomplishments?

What would I like to be the best in the world at?

Who are my heroes and what is it about them that I want to emulate?

What do I really think should be changed in the world?

What do I most want to be remembered for at the end of my life?

Who do I envy and what about them do I envy?

Projects

1. S⁴ Approach: Possible Coping Strategies Survey:

Below is a list of coping strategies based on Goodman et al. (2006). Thinking about any current transition you are currently undergoing, check off the possible coping strategies already in use in the "Now Using" column, and check off any coping strategies you might be willing to try out during this transition in the "Will Try" column.

Because it is difficult to anticipate every coping strategy and everyone's personal preferences for coping strategies, use the blanks at the bottom of the exercise to generate (a) coping strategies you already use that are not on the list and (b) new coping strategies you would at least consider trying that are not on the list.

Describe here, in as much detail as you can, the transition you are currently experiencing

---

Possible Coping Strategies	Check (√) each box regarding the coping strategies described above.	
	Now Using	Will Try
Change/modify situation through problem solving		
Negotiating		
Taking optimistic action		
Seeking advice		
Asserting yourself		
Brainstorming new plan		
Taking legal action (if necessary)		
Other:		
Other:		
Change meaning of situation through reappraisal		
Applying knowledge of transition process		
Rehearsing		
Developing rituals		
Making positive comparisons		

Rearranging priorities		
Relabeling or reframing		
Selectively ignoring		
Using denial		
Using humor		
Having faith		
Other:		
Other:		
Managing reactions to stress		
Playing		
Using relaxation, meditation, prayer		
Expressing emotions		
Doing physical activity		
Participating in counseling/therapy/support groups		
Reading		
Other:		
Other:		

2. Conduct a survey of the industrial–organizational/organizational behavior literature for studies that describe the effectiveness of stress-management techniques and programs on employee satisfaction and productivity, and analyze how those strategies could be applied to a college environment.

3. Visit your campus counseling center and student development/affairs offices and ask about the opportunities or programs they sponsor regarding stress management, time management, and managing finances. Does your school offer any opportunities to develop skills in financial literacy or financial planning? Report the results of your contacts to the class.

4. There is a popular belief that if you want something done, you ask a busy person to do it because busy people generally know how to manage time well. Design a study that permits you to test this hypothesis.

Additional Resources

URL	Brief Website Description
http://www.netwellness.org/healthtopics/wellness/healthylifestyles.cfm	American Psychological Association recommended

- Andrews, A. L. (2011). *Tell your time: How to manage your schedule so you can live free* [Kindle eBook]. Available from http://amylynnandrews.com/tell-your-time/
- Barr, T. L. (2008*). Living well in a down economy for dummies*. Hoboken, NJ: Wiley.
- Gobel, R. (2010). *Graduation debt: How to manage student loans and live your life* [Cliffs Notes]. Hoboken, NJ: Wiley.
- Orman, S. (2007). *The money book for the young, fabulous and broke*. New York, NY: Penguin.
- Palmer, K. (2010). *Generation earn: The young professionals guide to spending, investing, and giving back*. Berkeley, CA: Ten Speed Press.

References

American College Health Association. (2011). *National College Health Assessment II: Reference group executive summary Fall 2010*. Linthicum, MD: Author.

Bahls, S. (2011, June 13). Time to teach financial literacy. *Inside Higher Ed*. Retrieved from http://www.insidehighered.com/views/2011/06/13/essay_on_responsibility_of_colleges_to_teach_financial_literacy

Combs, P. (2000). *Major in success: Make college easier, fire up your dreams, and get a very cool job*. Berkeley, CA: Ten Speed Press.

Covey, S. R. (2004). *The seven habits of highly effective people*. New York, NY: Free Press.

Dell, K. (2011, October 31). I owe you. *TIME*, pp. 41–44.

Ellis, D. (2009). *From master student to master employee: Annotated instructor's edition* (2nd ed.). St. Charles, IL: College Survival/Houghton Mifflin.

Goodman, J., Schlossberg, N. K., & Anderson, M. L. (2006). *Counseling adults in transition: Linking practice with theory* (3rd ed.). New York, NY: Springer.

Greenberg, J. (2010). *Managing behavior in organizations* (5th ed.). Boston, MA: Prentice Hall.

Hamaideh, S. H. (2011). Stressors and reactions to stressors among university students. *International Journal of Social Psychiatry, 57*, 69–80. doi:10.1177/0020764010348442

Helkowski, C. (1998). Passing the stress test. In P. Hettich, *Learning skills for college and career* (pp. 131–163). Pacific Grove, CA: Brooks/Cole.

Holton, E. F., III (1998). Are college seniors prepared to work? In J. N. Gardner, G. Van der Veer, and Associates (Eds.), *The senior year experience: Facilitating integration, reflection, closure, and transition* (pp. 95–115). San Francisco, CA: Jossey-Bass.

Hopper, C. H. (n.d.). *Time management* [PowerPoint presentation]. Retrieved from http://college.cengage.com/collegesurvival/hopper/practicing_college/4e/prepare/ppt/hopper_ch01_scheduling.ppt

Levit, A. (2009). *They don't teach corporate in college* (2nd ed.). Franklin Lakes, NJ: Career Press.

Mathis, M., & Lecci, L. (1999). Hardiness and college adjustment: Identifying students in need of services. *Journal of College Student Development, 40*, 305–309.

Wilner, A., & Stocker, C. (2005). *The quarterlifer's companion*. New York, NY: McGraw-Hill.

CHAPTER 13

Prime Yourself for More Transitions

Life is not divided into semesters. You don't get summers off, and very few employers are interested in helping you find yourself.

—Charles J. Sykes (2007), journalist

The transition from college to post-college life is usually a very dramatic change for the majority of younger students with limited real-world job experiences; Sykes's words just scratch the surface for this group. If, however, you have a full-time job or a family to support, graduation may cause few changes in your routine. In short, the ways students experience transition to post-college life vary widely. Expectations play a major role in workplace transition. If you expect your job to mirror your study routines, your supervisor to act like your teachers, and your company to operate like your school, you are in for culture shock and a potentially miserable transition. Recall from Chapter 3 that the first two recommendations of the "DOs to Pursue" list were a critical assessment of your job and completing internships (preferably in a non-academic setting). In other words, *expect to change your expectations;* we know many supervisors and alumni who strongly concur with this advice.

In this chapter we offer four perspectives on transition to stimulate your awareness of its importance for work and life; they include business (Bridges, 2009), counseling (Goodman, Schlossberg, & Anderson, 2006), phenomenological (Parry, 2009), and college-to-workplace (Wendlandt & Rochlen, 2008). *Webster's New World College Dictionary* (Agnes, 2009) defined transition as "a passing from one condition, form, stage, activity, or place, etc. to another" (p. 1521). You passed from childhood to adulthood, from high school to college, and from less to more mature; you will experience additional transitions in the years ahead. The change from college to post-college life is particularly significant for younger students because it represents, traditionally, a major delineation from dependency on family to independence regarding finances, decision making, and responsibilities. The word "traditionally" is emphasized because many younger college graduates do not achieve the independence they seek until several years in the workplace.

Although we are primarily concerned about college-to-workplace preparedness, the transition to a full-time job is related to other changes that may occur, as Fouad and Bynner (2008) cogently argue:

> Work transitions cannot sensibly be separated from transitions in other life domains, including building a relationship, becoming a parent, and achieving financial independence. Transformation in the labor market and work transitions also influence transitions in these other life domains as well. Thus, extension of the transition to work is likely to delay the commitments involved in long-term partnership and parenthood and to extend the single lifestyle. (p. 244)

Convinced of the merits of these words and aware of the diverse situations our readers reflect and the likelihood they will encounter several transitions throughout life, we offer four contrasting perspectives. If variety is the spice of life, our goal is to whet your appetite for understanding the nature of transitions.

The Three Phases of Transition (William Bridges)

William Bridges was a literature professor in the 1970s who "transitioned" from academia to become a highly respected business consultant, author, and expert on transitions. He distinguishes change from transition.

> It isn't the changes that do you in, it's the transitions. They aren't the same thing. *Change* is situational: the move to a new site, the retirement of the founder, the reorganization of the roles on the team, the revisions to the pension plan. *Transition,* on the other hand, is psychological; it is a three-phase process that people go through as they *internalize and come to terms with* [emphasis added] the details of the new situation that the change brings about. (Bridges, 2009, p. 3)

Beginning graduate school, a new job, or a new relationship is a change from earlier circumstances; your particular reactions to, and interpretation of, such events represent a process or passage from previous to new situations. Because our reactions to events are under *our* control, it is essential for you to understand the processes that make up transition and influence our reactions to change.

Bridges (2009) describes three overlapping phases or processes in transition.

- In the *ending phase,* an individual breaks away from the old identity or ways of doing things.
- In the *neutral zone,* a person is between two ways or habits of doing or being. The old routines are gone, but new habits, beliefs, and attitudes are not yet firmly established.
- In the *new beginning,* an individual is productive and goal oriented in the new environment and possesses a new identity that matches the new situation.

"Because transition is a process by which people unplug from an old world and plug into a new world, we can say that transition starts with an ending and finishes with a beginning" (Bridges, 2009, p. 5).

How does Bridges' model help us understand college-to-workplace transition? You may be tempted to conclude that graduation is your disengagement from college, the time between graduation and your new job is the neutral zone, and the new beginning occurs in the first weeks or months of your new job. Not really. Instead, think of your endings as those specific activities that are directly preparing you for the changes to come. Students generally begin the ending phase during the last two academic terms, when they complete their last required courses, an internship, enroll in basic business or other job- or skill-related courses, disengage from less important social activities, and focus on developing job-search skills (Hettich & Helkowski, 2005), such as those described in Chapter 7. Letting go of the familiar and pleasant aspects of college while anticipating the unknowns of the future often creates ambivalence, anxiety, and even fear, as we'll note later in this chapter. It helps to remember that angst is often part of growth.

> Once you understand that *transition begins with letting go of something,* you have taken the first step in transition in the task of transition management. The second step in transition is understanding what comes after the letting go: *the neutral zone.* This is the psychological no man's land between the old reality and the new one. It is the limbo between the old sense of identity and the new. It is the time when the old way of doing things is gone, but the new way doesn't feel comfortable yet. (Bridges, 2009, p. 8)

When you begin a new job or a new living arrangement, you try to construct meaning (make sense) of the new situation by relying on past expectations and experiences; consequently, the situation can sometimes become confusing and frustrating. Bridges (2009) compared the neutral zone to an emotional wilderness. For example, recall your feelings when you began college: the fear and anxiety of settling into the residence hall after family members departed, attending your first classes, and beginning a part-time job. Chances are you tried to interpret your new experiences by recalling past events and expectations and thought (for instance): Is this what a residence hall is supposed to be? So this is a *college* professor. My new job isn't much different from my old one.

It is important to expect and understand the limbo-like nature and emotional disruptions that often occur in the neutral zone, or else you may suffer three consequences. First, you can become discouraged and blame yourself if matters seem to go wrong during the change. Second, the fears or other discomforting feelings that originate in the neutral zone may prompt you to escape—i.e., to quit your job prematurely or find a new residence elsewhere, actions that could jeopardize the change. Third, if you escape prematurely from the neutral zone, you forfeit the opportunity to learn from this experience (Bridges, 2009). Just as a student matures between the freshman and senior years, you become a freshman again after graduation, perhaps in a new workplace or relationship. Do not be quick to give up if the neutral zone of your transition is uncomfortable or overwhelms you. You have the resources to succeed. If you use them well, sooner or later you will become a senior again.

At the end of the neutral zone is a new beginning, a new and final process when the old habits and attitudes have been replaced with new ones—i.e., when you feel adapted to the new setting or the new relationship, even if there are aspects you are not comfortable with. "Letting go, repatterning, and making a new beginning: together these processes reorient and renew people when things are changing all around them" (Bridges, 2009, p. 9).

In conclusion, Bridges's three-phase model offers one explanation of how we should interpret the effects of changes we experience during transition. Is that all there is to understanding transition?

The Transition Model (Jane Goodman, Nancy Schlossberg, and Mary Anderson)

Transitions can become very complicated, because they are influenced by several factors. During the 1980s, Nancy Schlossberg developed a transition model that was modified in the 1990s and expanded in *Counseling Adults in Transition: Linking Theory and Practice* (Goodman et al., 2006). The Transition Model is intended to provide a systematic framework for counselors and others in the helping professions who assist colleagues, friends, and clients with diverse types of transition. We believe that a thoughtful understanding of its basic features can help you navigate some of your transitions. Recognize, however, that you are not an objective observer in your own transition; you can deceive yourself. If your transition from college seems scary or overwhelming or if you are dealing with other serious issues, seek help from a professional counselor who can help you assess and interpret your thoughts, feelings, and attitudes toward the events you face.

Goodman et al. (2006) defined *transition* in terms that readily apply to recent college graduates: "A transition, broadly, is any event or non-event that results in changed relationships, routines, assumptions, and roles" (p. 33). The dictionary defines *transition* as a passing from one event to another, Bridges describes it as a three-phase process, and now Goodman et al. define it as an event or non-event. Who is correct? As psychology majors, you are no longer surprised that experts disagree on the meanings of abstract terms; read further to discern the similarities and differences among the three definitions.

Approaching Transitions

Transition Identification

The "DOs to Pursue" in Chapter 3 represent much of our advice for planning your transition—that is, actively use the multiple opportunities on your campus to prepare yourself for life after college. As you approach graduation, however, you should also identify and prepare for the *types* of transition you will likely face. *Anticipated* or predicted transitions may include a new job, a move to a different residence, and changed relationships with friends, family, teachers, and others. *Unanticipated* transitions are unpredicted and unscheduled events such as having to move, unwillingly, back home until you find a job; a breakup in an important relationship; an accident or illness rendering you unable to work for months; or unplanned parenthood. *Non-event* transitions are events you expected to occur but did not, such as being rejected from graduate school or not buying the long-anticipated new car because you can't find a job. The particular meaning given to anticipated, unanticipated, or non-events differs from person to person (i.e., it is *relative* and a function of your perceptions). For example, moving back home with parents may be seen as a "good deal" by some students but abhorred by others. The broken relationship may be welcomed by one person and mourned by the other.

Other factors besides *relativity* that influence the approach to transitions are the *context* and *impact* of the transition. Context refers to the setting in which the transition occurs and your relationship to it. For instance, a part-time commuter student will likely leave the campus after graduation with different feelings about it than the person who lived there for 5 years. The transition will more deeply affect the graduating senior than it will classmates who do not graduate. The impact of accepting your first full-time job with little or no preceding work experience will be greater for you than for the graduate who is merely switching jobs. To the extent that the relativity, context, and impact features of a transition affect you strongly, you will need strong resources for managing it. "We may assume that the more the transition alters the individual's life, the more coping resources it requires, and the longer it will take for assimilation or adaptation" (Goodman et al., 2006, p. 37).

The Transition Process

Transition is an active process made up of several dimensions that identify where the person is located in the transition. A transition takes time (from 6 months to 2 years for major transitions), energy, and planning, and during the process, a person's reactions to what is happening can change at different points. A transition should be viewed as an integral, not atypical, part of a person's development and as an experience that may lead to further growth or, sometimes, a step backward. A transition may affect your whole person (mentally, emotionally, and physically) and dominate your daily life.

Similar to Bridges, Goodman et al. (2006) believe transitions occur in stages. *Moving out* is a period of separation, endings, and perhaps anxiety and grieving. In the *moving through* stage, you are "betwixt or between," and in the process of mastering new expectations, roles, and relationships. You may feel challenged by the new situations, question your decisions, ponder new commitments, and seek a new balance in your life. During the *moving in* stage, you become comfortable with, or at least accept, the new roles, rules, norms, and expectations of your surroundings. Depending on your focus, you can be moving out of a situation (e.g., out of college) or moving in (e.g., to a full-time job); consequently, the two terms can be interchanged. At some point, you feel assimilated and adapted to the changes. Goodman et al. summarize their model to this point of our discussion.

> The transition framework is based on the following premises that: adults continuously experience transitions. Adults' reactions to transitions depend on the type of transition, the context in which it occurs, and its impact on their lives. A transition has no end point; rather, a transition is a process over time that includes phases of assimilation and continuous appraisal as people move in, through, and out of it. (p. 53)

Time Out: Reflective Questions

1. Can you identify an example of an anticipated transition, a possible unanticipated transition, and a possible non-event transition you may have to manage during the next 2 or 3 years?

2. How would the concepts of context and impact be applied to each of those transitions to help you understand and successfully manage them?

3. Can you think of each type in terms of moving out, moving through, and moving in?

Taking Stock of Coping Resources: The 4S System

Because transition is a complicated process, it is important to examine the resources you have for coping with changes that occur along the way. View your transition as an ongoing interaction with, and a transaction between, you and your environment. The Transition Model emphasizes the role of four major sets of variables that influence your ability to cope with the events: *situation, self, support,* and *strategies.* Depending on the individual, these factors can serve as potential assets or liabilities you bring to the transition process. The assessment of one's strengths and weaknesses is necessary (e.g., for choosing a career, writing a résumé, and preparing for interviews), complex, and requires an honest self-appraisal of the ratio of your assets (personal strengths, resources) to the liabilities or problems you bring to the transition. For example, do you view this transition as mostly positive or mostly negative? To what extent are you aware of and able to use your resources (e.g., personal and financial supports; opportunities for personal and career counseling) for moving through this transition? An honest appraisal of these issues may require the assistance of a professional helper (e.g., a counselor or family member), but an accurate appraisal of your assets and liabilities will contribute significantly to your success in coping with change (Goodman et al., 2006). The authors address a variety of transitions, from the profound (e.g., death, divorce, or serious illness) to those perceived as normal and "doable." Some of you will perceive your transition to post-college life, realistically or unrealistically, as a daunting challenge; others as unthreatening. Either way, it is important to become aware of specific variables that may operate as assets or liabilities as you navigate through the changes ahead.

Situation

According to Goodman et al. (2006), everyone's situation will vary according to several factors; some factors are more pertinent to certain transitions than are others. For example, assume that you will face two significant transitions upon graduation: finding a satisfying full-time job (or any job, if you are desperate) and returning home to live with your family (but now as a relatively independent young adult). Some situational factors are easy to identify using these examples; others may require a careful analysis of their potential impact. One situational liability is the condition of the national economy, its overall impact on the labor market, and the availability of jobs where you live. For instance, many students who graduate during a recession are unable to find jobs even with careful planning and persistent efforts. Subsequently, an absence of work experience that creates gaps on their résumés during a period of high unemployment exacerbates their attempts to find jobs during economic recovery. Employers do not want to see gaps on résumés. The lesson here is that even if you do everything right (e.g., the "DOs to Pursue" in Chapter 3), you may still encounter a frustrating transition because of circum-stances totally beyond your control. Use the following dimensions to understand (note that we don't say "resolve") the situations that influence your transitions.

Trigger. What set off the transitions? Answer: Completing your degree, being forced to leave campus, moving back home, and needing a job.

Timing. How does the transition relate to your social clock? Answer: You looked forward to college graduation for years, so the timing is good. You may not desire, however, to move back home, because you will lose some independence and return to some level of parental supervision you do not want. On the other hand, while liv-ing at home may become tough at times, you will have a base from which to do your job hunting, likely pay little or no rent, save money for your own place, and enjoy home cooking again. In this situation, the timing of your transitions may be mixed.

Control. What aspects of the transitions can you control? Having worked closely with your school's career counseling office (a decision under your internal control) and feeling confident in your job-search skills, you believe the job-search process is generally under your control, although the job market is highly competitive and you cannot control an employer's hiring decisions (external control). You had no other choice but to move back home, given your lack of income (external controls). How effectively you negotiate living arrangements with your family can be partially under your control.

Role Change. Your role as a student is over, your role as recent graduate in search of a job has just begun, and your role as employee does not yet exist. Your role as a resident will change drastically as you exchange a high level of independence and self-determination for a somewhat dependent role as an adult child living at home under parental expectations. If you are like most students, expect to experience substantial stress due to role changes in each of these situations.

Duration. Are these transitions perceived as temporary or permanent? You want to obtain a satisfying job as soon as possible so you can get on with life, and you want to move away from home as soon as you can afford to. But how long will it be before you are financially independent?

Previous Experiences With a Similar Transition. Most likely, you have not held a full-time job that enables you to apply your college degree, so you have no previous experience with this transition. Although you lived at home before college, you did not live there for an extended period of time as an adult; again, there is no previous experience with this particular transition.

Concurrent Stress. If you graduate without a job and are forced to move back home, you will probably feel highly stressed, at least for a while.

In summary, how well you cope with your job search and move back home is strongly influenced by several situational factors, only a few of which may be under your control; other variables are influenced by your perceptions of the positive or negative impact of the transitions.

Self

Those assets and liabilities *you* bring to your transitions are crucial for determining how well you cope with change. They consist of two groups. First are the personal and demographic characteristics that help shape one's self, including socioeconomic status, gender, age, state of health, and ethnicity/culture. As a college student majoring in psychology, chances are you have acquired knowledge and insights about these characteristics and speculated about how they combine and interact to shape your concept of self. The second group consists of your psychological resources, including the personality characteristics you draw on when challenged or threatened. These qualities include your ego development, maturity, optimism, outlook, self-efficacy, commitments, values, spirituality, resilience, and hardiness. You know from Socrates' admonition to "know thyself" that you possess a certain degree of bias when assessing the extent to which these factors are assets or liabilities for you. Yet, you could ask yourself some of the questions (rephrased) that Goodman et al. (2006) encouraged counselors to ask clients when assessing the strengths and liabilities they possess in a transition.

- Are you able to deal with the world autonomously? Can you tolerate ambiguity?
- Are you an optimist? Is the glass half full or half empty?
- Do you blame yourself for "bad" events that happen to you?
- Do you feel in control of your responses to this transition?
- Do you believe your efforts will affect the outcome of a specific course of action?
- Do you have a sense of meaning and purpose?
- Do you have characteristics that contribute to resiliency?

Your psychology coursework has introduced you to at least some of the concepts and research that form the basis for these questions. In short, to the extent you understand the demographic and psychological qualities that interact to form your "self" (in terms of the strengths or liabilities you possess in these areas), you "own" a set of resources that can help you work through transitions you face after graduation. If these resources are insufficient, seek assistance from a highly experienced, capable helper. Your transition to post-college life occurs but once, and the extent to which it succeeds or fails will affect the rest of your life.

Support

Goodman et al. (2006) maintain that support can be the key to handling stresses precipitated by transition. The types of support they identify include *intimate relationships, family units, networks of friends,* and the *institutions and/or communities* of which you are a member. In Chapter 3, we addressed the roles that campus organizations and volunteer activities can play in establishing relationships and the support your school's counseling services can provide. If you are unable to gain support (remembering that support is not necessarily agreement with your beliefs) from one particular source, seek it wisely from others. Your support systems can function in various ways to provide advice, aid, or simply honest (positive and negative) feedback. Seek a range of supports, ascertain the level of assistance each provides, and determine the extent to which it will be there as you transition into your post-college life (i.e., when family or close friends may be geographically distant from you). Your social-networking skills may become an invaluable resource for you. Many schools offer job-search and career-planning events for alumni. If career or personal counseling is needed, chances are your school can also recommend professional counselors familiar with the issues faced by graduates in transition.

In their book *Not Quite Adults: Why 20-Somethings Are Choosing a Slower Path to Adulthood, and Why It's Good for Everyone,* Richard Settersten and Barbara Ray (2010) drew on numerous sources of data to study today's young adults. One major theme they developed is the distinction (one that often cuts across social classes) between swimmers (who are slowly but thoughtfully moving toward adulthood) and treaders (who rush into adulthood lacking the preparation—e.g., job skills, maturity, or education—needed in a competitive world). In their chapter on the parent–child lifeline, the authors make the following observation:

> Strong relationships with parents are more necessary for a successful launch into adulthood today—at least in the United States. . . . The presence of strong family guidance and support is ultimately the factor that sharply separates those who swim from those who tread or sink in the transition to adulthood. Closeness helps, but closeness alone will not get young people through college and into better-paying and more meaningful jobs and careers. (p. 142)

Strategies

The fourth component of the 4S system is the establishment of strategies for coping with the changes you face. Coping strategies are many and diverse. Beginning with the fourth *S* (strategies) and continuing with the final component of the Transition Model—namely Taking Charge: Strengthening Resources—Goodman et al. (2006) focused on specific examples of transition that call for particular strategies counselors can employ, topics that go beyond our expertise and objectives for this chapter. We addressed selected stress-management and coping issues in Chapter 12. In addition, we encourage you to use your school's opportunities (e.g., workshops or courses) for developing coping skills for the transitions ahead. We remind you again that you paid for such services with your tuition and fees; after graduation, you will pay professionals for developing stress-management skills needed for managing transition.

To summarize: "The transition framework . . . is designed to depict the extraordinary complex reality that accompanies and defines the human capacity to cope with change" (Goodman et al., 2006, p. 55). The model defines the types of transition you may experience (anticipated, unanticipated, and non-event) and the roles that relativity, context, and impact occupy in understanding changes. The process of transition is integral to human development, extends over time, requires your active involvement, affects the whole person, creates changed reactions to events during the process, and is characterized as a three-stage process of moving out (or moving in), moving through, and moving in (or moving out). The four key factors that influence an individual's ability to cope with the changes (factors viewed as an individual's assets or liabilities brought to the transition) include the situation, self, support, and strategies variables.

We devoted a significant part of this chapter to the Transition Model because it is designed to recognize the complexity of diverse transitions and identify variables that promote successful coping, not only for transitioning from college but also for understanding other, perhaps more profound, changes you will encounter. It is easy to dismiss the complexity of transition when you are a graduating senior—"full of yourself," with high expectations and self-confidence, and anxious to get on with life. Your transition from college to post-college life, however, is far more complex than crossing the graduation stage and hoping what comes next will be good. The Sykes quotation that opened this chapter is correct: Your life after college is not going to be divided into semesters, you probably won't get summers off, and your employer is probably not interested in helping you find yourself.

Time Out: Exercise

Identify at least one major transition you will have to manage during the next 2 or 3 years, and analyze its processes or stages. Select one of these components of the Goodman et al. (2006) model: (a) the three types of transition, context, and impact, *or* (b) the elements of the 4S system. Describe how the concepts you chose can be applied to your circumstance to help you understand and successfully manage the transition.

We continue to emphasize that your transition from college to the workplace is likely the most significant transition most of you have encountered to date and that you will encounter many others during future years. We discussed and illustrated at length the concepts of transition with examples of the major components of the Goodman et al. (2006) model, because it provides the depth, breadth, and flexibility to help you comprehend and manage, at least to some degree, the transitions you may face. View this perspective as a conceptual tool you may access when you need to understand the situations you encounter and the ambivalence you feel when change occurs.

The Parable of the Trapeze

Bridges's (2009) three-stage model (endings, neutral zone, and new beginnings) helps us construct meaning for the changes we experience during a transition. Goodman et al. (2006) provided a counterpart to Bridges's stages (moving out, moving through, and moving in), but they also emphasize the importance of approaching transition and examining the potential resources (the 4 Ss) persons can draw on. As psychology majors, you have been taught to value the analytic approach on which these two models are based. You may also appreciate, however, an alternative perspective, one that speaks more to one's affect (especially angst) than intellect. In Danaan Parry's (2009) "Parable of the Trapeze," from *Warriors of the Heart*, we offer a phenomenological perspective on the fear of transformation, a perspective that shares common threads with the other models we explored.

Sometimes I feel that my life is a series of trapeze swings. I'm either hanging on to a trapeze bar swinging along or, for a few moments in my life, I'm hurtling across space in between trapeze bars.

Most of the time, I spend my life hanging on for dear life to my trapeze-bar-of-the-moment. It carries me along at a certain steady rate of swing and I have the feeling that I'm in control of my life. I know most of the right questions and even some of the answers.

But, every once in a while as I'm merrily (or even not-so-merrily) swinging along, I look out ahead of me into the distance and what do I see? I see another trapeze bar swinging toward me. It's empty and I know, in that place in me that knows, that this new trapeze bar has my name on it. It is my next step, my growth, my aliveness coming to get me. In my heart-of-hearts I know that, for me to grow, I must release my grip on this present, well-known bar and move to the new one.

Each time it happens to me I hope (no, I pray) that I won't have to let go of my old bar completely before I grab the new one. But in my knowing place, I know that I must totally release my grasp on my old bar and, for some moment in time, I must hurtle across space before I can grab onto the new bar.

Each time, I am filled with terror. It doesn't matter that in all my previous hurtles across the void of unknowing I have always made it. I am each time afraid that I will miss, that I will be crushed on unseen rocks in the bottomless chasm between bars. I do it anyway. Perhaps this is the essence of what the mystics call the faith experience. No guarantees, no net, no insurance policy, but you do it anyway because somehow to keep hanging on to that old bar is no longer on the list of alternatives. So, for an eternity that can last a micro-second or a thousand lifetimes, I soar across the dark void of "the past is gone, the future is not yet here." It's called "transition." I have come to believe that this transition is the only place where real change occurs. I mean real change, not the pseudo-change that only lasts until the next time my old buttons get punched.

I have noticed that, in our culture, this transition zone is looked upon as a "no-thing," a no-place between places. Sure, the old trapeze bar was real, and that new one coming towards me, I hope that's real too. But the void in between? Is that just a scary, confusing, disorienting nowhere that must be gotten through as fast and as unconsciously as possible?

NO! What a wasted opportunity that would be. I have a sneaking suspicion that the transition zone is the only real thing and the bars are illusions we dream up to avoid the void where the real change, the real growth, occurs for us. Whether or not my hunch is true, it remains that the transition zones in our lives are incredibly rich places. They should be honored, even savored. Yes, with all the pain and fear and feelings of being out of control that can (but not necessarily) accompany transitions, they are still the most alive, most growth-filled, passionate, expansive moments in our lives. (Parry, 2009, pp. 84–85)

Time Out: Reflection Questions

1. What are the two or three most important points you derived from "The Parable of the Trapeze"?

2. To what extent do you identify with the person on the trapeze? Why or why not?

Challenges in the College-to-Work Transition

The fourth perspective on transition addresses essential topics presented in greater depth in other chapters and represents a view critical to successful transition. The three views addressed above provide insights on internal and external factors that influence change and transition processes, but they do not speak to concrete differences between college and workplace environments that we believe are worth repeating. Unfortunately, the literature on the practical aspects of college-to-workplace transition is sparse. In their review of phenomenological studies of transition, Wendlandt and Rochlen (2008) organized the challenges into three categories.

Change in Culture

New graduates must learn to survive the collision between college and corporate cultures. First, interactions with coworkers differ from those with classmates. Coworkers will be older (on the average), are likely to be isolated in their own workspaces, and are focused on different tasks. Second, the workplace often contains less structure, offers less and infrequent concrete feedback, and provides no syllabus of assignments—conditions that create an ambiguous environment that frustrates many new grads. Third, during college, the student focuses on personal development and operates autonomously, but the employee must focus on organizational objectives and often works less independently as part of a team.

Lack of Experience and Skills

Without a record of prior full-time employment or a significant period of time working part-time jobs that generated awareness of organizational culture, chances are the new graduate will be surprised, perhaps shocked, by the differences between college and corporate settings. College students are taught a variety of skills, but when they enter the workplace they are found deficient in some skill sets, especially communications. In addition, graduates often do not know how to apply their skills to workplace settings and tasks. We highlighted skills employers expect graduates to possess in Chapter 2 (Landrum, Hettich, & Wilner, 2010) and in Chapter 6 (National Association of Colleges and Employers, 2011).

Inflated Expectations

The challenges posed by organizational culture and lack of experience, skills, and expectations are interrelated. Without substantial prior work experience, the graduate enters the workplace with high expectations (realistic or unrealistic) and ignorant of what to expect and how to behave in a vastly different organizational culture. Inaccurate and unmet expectations regarding job responsibilities, frequent feedback, and regular supervision can lead to disappointment, job dissatisfaction, and the search for new employment.

Brad provides a good example of these three challenges to workplace transition. Brad graduated as a well-liked human resources major with a 4.0 GPA and low debt (scholarship awards meant he didn't have to work part-time while in school). In spite of working with a personnel service, his early interviews were disasters because he had limited work experience and could not handle hypothetical work situations his interviewers posed with their behavioral questions. He was finally hired by a sourcing organization to recruit employees for finance positions. Brad was excited and confident about his new job and expected the first week of his new job to be special. It was. Brad learned he was in an environment that squelched self-expression and individuality. The job made minimum use of his knowledge. His supervisor dictated what he wore, when he could have lunch, how he answered his phone. His excitement turned to resentment and the resentment to anger. The charisma, creativity, critical thinking, and "personality" that helped him succeed in college now seemed like liabilities. Over the weeks, his impulsiveness and occasional outbursts alienated him from his coworkers, and he was considered a "difficult" employee. After "bottoming out" 2 months into the job, Brad sought support from his family and friends, reevaluated his strengths and weaknesses, and realized that one of his strengths was his ability to relate to his teachers. Gradually, Brad began to reestablish positive relations with those he worked with and ultimately excelled in his responsibilities months later, to the point of receiving performance awards (Hettich, 2009).

Time Out: Reflection Questions

1. What clues in the brief description of Brad would enable you to predict the problems he subsequently encountered in his first job?

2. How representative or unrepresentative do you think Brad's case is of most traditional-aged students?

3. How would you apply Bridges's (2009) three stages of transition to Brad's case?

The challenges Wendlandt and Rochlen (2008) described represent the immediate and concrete situations new graduates face in their transition to the workplace. The models of Bridges (2009) and Goodman et al. (2006) enable us to analyze transition broken down into its components and to see transition from a "big-picture" view: Life contains several serious transitions, of which the transition from college to post-college life is but one significant change. Parry's parable taps into affective reactions, especially fear, many individuals experience. If, however, life continued to be divided into semesters and employers were committed to helping us find ourselves, how little we would grow, how limiting life would become, and how little excitement we would find between the trapeze bars.

Closing Comments

The remarks by Sykes that opened this chapter are accurate, but unless you have solid work experience in typical job settings, you might not grasp their true meaning. The transition from college to career will be the most abrupt change many of you have experienced to date. Yet there are numerous other transitions ahead: from college residence back to home; from home to independent living (with or without a significant other); from single to married and perhaps back to single life again someday (with or without children); from poor or lower socioeconomic class to upper middle class or even wealthy, and possibly back to poor again; from employed to unemployed for long periods of time and employed again; from health to sickness or serious accident; from sober to addicted and perhaps back to sober again; and from emerging adulthood to middle age to old age. Consequently, we end this chapter with but one recommendation. Because transitions, whether gentle or profound, are a fact of life, why not understand the processes and stages involved, especially those aspects you can control; their stages and processes; your resources and constraints; your fears and options; and the expectations (realistic or unrealistic) you will have about each. Understanding transitions is a prescription for understanding a great deal about how to manage your future. If Socrates were your career counselor, he might observe that "to understand your transitions is to know thyself better."

Getting Involved

Journal Starters

1. Bridges (2009), Goodman et al. (2006), and Parry (2009) each invoke a transition process that consists of stages. In what ways are their stages similar, and how do they differ? Which perspective do you most identify with and why?

2. Which specific concepts contained in this chapter do you find may become most helpful in guiding you through transitions you are likely to face in the next 5 years?

3. Recall a critical event in your family or one that occurred to a close friend, such as a death, marriage, serious illness, unwanted parenthood, difficult transition from war, or divorce. How could the Goodman et al. (2006) Transition Model have helped you understand and deal with the changes that occurred as a result of the event?

Projects

1. Search the psychology literature for research on transition. What events or changes does the literature address?

2. As indicated earlier, the research literature on college-to-workplace transition is limited. Is this really true? Given that about 75% of baccalaureate psychology majors enter the workplace each year, why is there not more research on the topic of college-to-workplace transition?

3. Create your own "transition logbook." Try to create a retroactive history of your transitions, and attempt to reflect back on your feelings and emotions at the time. Can you detect any patterns? Were certain types of transitions more or less difficult than other types of transitions?

Additional Resources

URL	Brief Website Description
www.transad.pop.upenn.edu	The Network on Transitions to Adulthood

■ Estrada, A. X., & Benson, W. L. (2010). *Home from deployment: A soldier's challenge.* Washington, DC: American Psychological Association.

References

Agnes, M. (Ed.). (2009). *Webster's new world college dictionary* (4th ed.). Cleveland, OH: Wiley.

Bridges, W. (2009). *Managing transitions: Making the most of change* (3rd ed.). Philadelphia, PA: Da Capo Press.

Fouad, N. A., & Bynner, J. (2008). Work transitions. *American Psychologist, 63,* 241–251. doi:10.1037/0003-066X.63.4.241

Goodman, J., Schlossberg, N. K., & Anderson, M. L. (2006). *Counseling adults in transition: Linking practice with theory* (3rd ed.). New York, NY: Springer.

Hettich, P. I. (2009). College-to-workplace transitions: Becoming a freshman again. In T. W. Miller (Ed.), *Handbook of stressful transitions across the lifespan* (pp. 87–109). New York, NY: Springer.

Hettich, P. I., & Helkowski, C. (2005). *Connect college to career: A student's guide to work and life transitions.* Belmont, CA: Thomson/Wadsworth.

Landrum, R. E., Hettich, P. I., & Wilner, A. (2010). Alumni perceptions of workforce readiness. *Teaching of Psychology, 37,* 96–107.

National Association of Colleges and Employers. (2011, October 26). Job outlook: The candidate skills/qualities employers want. In *Job outlook 2012.* Retrieved from http://www.naceweb.org/s10262011/candidate_skills_employer_qualities/

Parry, D. (2009). *Warriors of the heart* (6th ed.). Earthstewards Network. Retrieved from http://www.earthstewards.org/ESN-Publications.asp

Settersten, R., & Ray, B. E. (2010). *Not quite adults: Why 20-somethings are choosing a slower path to adulthood, and why it's good for everyone.* New York, NY: Bantam Books.

Wendlandt, N. B., & Rochlen, A. B. (2008). Addressing the college-to-work transition: Implications for university career counselors. *Journal of Career Development, 35,* 151–165. doi:10.1080/00986283.2010.488550

CHAPTER 14

What Lies Ahead?

We are nearing the end of our circuitous journey; we've made stops at specific work-related topics, satisfaction with your choice of major, and the skills you'll need in the workplace. Hopefully, you've read about generational issues mentioned previously, but we emphasize those more here. We report on studies of behaviors that lead to promotion and offer suggestions for steps to follow if you lose a job. We close with a review of the book's major themes and a quotation to take with you on your continuing journey through education and your freshman year in the workplace.

Straight Talk About Your Psychology Major

During college, you work to acquire the knowledge, skills, values, and abilities that prepare you for a successful career and life; you chose psychology as the anchor of your higher education. We are biased, obviously, but we believe the psychology major is an excellent choice for many students. According to the National Center for Education Statistics (2010), psychology was the fifth most popular major behind (in rank order) business, social sciences and history, health professions and related sciences, and education. Except for education (which offers several specialized certification programs), the other three fields are composites of traditional disciplines, so the popularity of the single discipline of psychology is likely higher than these rankings suggest. Popularity aside, psychology is simultaneously a liberal arts discipline (with the attendant advantages a liberal arts education offers) and a preprofessional major that prepares students for graduate school and diverse professional programs. In addition, we believe the diversity of psychology program offerings, plus your personal commitment, should generate motivation for becoming an active, lifelong learner. We believe this continual quest for knowledge and self-improvement will only further your successes, both personally and professionally.

You are acquiring a body of information about psychology that includes the content of its many subfields, scientific methodology, and various skills. When you interview for a job, few if any recruiters will inquire about the content of your courses, because they possess a general understanding of what a psychology major entails. Instead, they will ask how you can *apply* your knowledge and skills to their job openings. To be honest, however, assessing one's skills and abilities during college is a tricky proposition for most educators. On the individual course-instructor level, the pattern of teaching and assessing learning using traditional methods occurs continuously each academic term in all disciplines. There is considerable uncertainty and growing concern, however, among educators in all academic disciplines with regard to their capacity to accurately gauge your preparedness for future employment (or graduate school). To be fair, some disciplines are better at assessing student knowledge, skills, and abilities at graduation (e.g., nursing, business, engineering, social work, accountancy) than are others (e.g., psychology and other traditional liberal arts disciplines). Some undergraduate majors have accreditation standards they must adhere to; others have assessment programs specifically targeted at preparedness. However, there appears to be a mismatch between what psychology majors believe they can do (i.e., skills and tasks) by graduation and what they really can do in the workplace.

Borden and Rajecki (2000) surveyed 4,587 alumni who had majored in such fields as health professions, business, social work, education, science and math, public affairs, liberal and fine arts, social sciences, and psychology. Participants were asked to rate their current job in relation to their academic major and whether that major had prepared them for that job and for future prospects. The survey's findings revealed that regardless of the academic major, the alumni's perceptions of the *relatedness* of their major to their job predicted alumni's judgment of their *preparedness* for their job, and their perceptions of preparedness predicted their judgment of future *job prospects*. Two thirds of the psychology alumni in this sample were full-time employees in a wide range of occupations, with the larger proportions classified (in rank order) as administrative support, social worker, counselor, administrator or manager, personnel and labor, marketing and sales, researcher or technician, general manager, executive or owner, and computer science or programmer. Psychology alumni "who gave high ratings of relatedness were also likely to give high ratings of preparedness. . . . For these persons, a sense of preparedness was associated with perceptions of future prospects" (p. 167). The authors noted that these general findings also held for all the other academic majors surveyed in their study. However, about 37% of the psychology alumni "indicated that their current jobs were not related to their major" (p. 165), placing psychology as the second highest in the distribution of alumni who believe their major was "not at all" related to their job. Only 23% of the psychology alumni rated their job as "directly related" to their major. In addition, about 25% of the psychology alumni believed they were "not at all" prepared for their job (the highest level in that distribution), whereas 16% indicated they were "very much" prepared. Finally, about 9% of the psychology alumni believed their education enhanced their future prospects for advancement "not at all," but 34% believed it did (Borden & Rajecki, 2000).

In a replication and extension of this study, Rajecki and Borden (2009) surveyed 1,760 alumni from the 2003 to 2006 graduating classes of a university sample regarding *first-year* employment in connection with major, necessity of the degree for the job, preparedness, and salary and raise issues. Alumni were grouped into 10 academic categories: business, education, engineering/technology, fine arts, general studies, human/public services, humanities/social sciences, natural sciences, nursing/allied health, and psychology. Full-time employment of respondents ranged from a low of 54% (natural sciences) to a high of 89% (nursing). Psychology alumni reported the second-lowest level, with 61% in full-time jobs, but 40% were also enrolled in a postgraduate degree program, exceeding all other major groups except natural sciences, at 49%. Of the psychology alumni, 31% indicated their job was not related to the major, ranking fifth of the 10 academic major groups; 49% believed a degree was not needed for their job, a value surpassing all but three of the groups. When queried about job preparedness, only 12% reported "not at all prepared" (ranking fourth lowest). Respondents were also asked if their annual salary was $30,000 or below. Those who worked for their employer 6 months or more prior to graduation were also queried about receiving a raise or promotion. Overall, 48% of the psychology alumni (rank = second highest) were earning less than $30,000 annually (33% of the men and about 51% of the women). About 44% of this group (rank = fifth highest) reported receiving a raise or promotion. The overall results of this study shows that preprofessional degree graduates (nursing, business, engineering, and education) ranked in higher tiers (i.e., a comparatively favorable status) and liberal arts graduates (including psychology) in the lower tiers in first-year employment outcomes, consistent with Borden and Rajecki (2000).

Do not become discouraged about studying psychology after studying this data. Recall from Chapter 3 that we strongly encourage you to elect a minor or a second major in areas that are connected to business, allied health, and technology fields to add an edge to your academic credentials. Depending on your time, resources, and prior commitments, this advice may or may not be feasible, or absolutely necessary. In their discussion, Rajecki and Borden (2009) made an important distinction. Their data focuses on *first-year* employment outcomes; they also cite studies suggesting that in subsequent years, liberal arts graduates (including psychology) can expect upward mobility, defined as an increasing percentage of a cohort having jobs that require a college degree.

> That is, psychology alumni are likely to have higher qualifications than demanded by some of their first-year jobs. A positive shift in the quality of occupations eventually held by such graduates illustrates the distinction between *employment* versus *employability*. Employability, or employability profile, refers to capacities: the generic attributes, competencies, and skills associated with the completion of a given academic major or course. (Rajecki & Borden, 2009, pp. 27–28)

In short, don't judge the long-range value of a baccalaureate psychology degree by your first postgraduation jobs. While your first year or two of employment might not be satisfying, your long-term employability is likely to rise. Recall also the important statistic that 40% (the second-highest percentage of the 10 groups) of those psychology alumni who held full-time jobs were simultaneously enrolled in a degree program—they were on their way to carving a path to upward mobility beyond a bachelor's degree.

In their earlier study, Borden and Rajecki (2000) suggested that the psychology graduates in this study may have entered the job market holding *expectations* that were similar to those of graduates from the more occupationally oriented programs, such as nursing and business. We believe this point is worth elaborating. Although there is a direct connection, for example, between what a nursing student studies and what a nurse does and between what an accounting major studies and what an accountant with a baccalaureate degree does, there is not that direct connection for liberal arts baccalaureate graduates, including psychology majors. But there may be advantages and disadvantages to this situation: On one hand, the psychology baccalaureate has several options (see Chapter 2) and is not as restricted to a specific occupation as are nurses and accountants; on the other hand, the psychology graduate should not expect to find an identifiable *professional* occupation with a bachelor's degree. You have been told since your first introductory psychology course that if you want to be called a psychologist, you must have at least a master's degree, if not a doctorate.

Borden and Rajecki (2000) recommended that students increase their awareness of the practical and professional skills the undergraduate psychology major provides; you are acting on that suggestion by reading this book. Because of the preparedness mismatch observed by Borden and Rajecki, one reviewer lamented that "the low level of relatedness between the psychology major and a particular job is not surprising. The problem is that students apparently do not expect this" (p. 168). Studying successful psychology alumni in the workforce, with specific attention paid to preparation and readiness (Landrum, Hettich, & Wilner, 2010), can provide both faculty and students with concrete suggestions on how to make the most of the undergraduate psychology major experience, with reasonable expectations of the jobs and careers it can lead to.

You should be aware, however, that not all educators agree with this viewpoint—or, to be more precise, some educators would like to see stronger evidence supporting the notion that academic skills and job opportunities are positively linked. Rajecki and Borden (2010) refer to this general belief as the meritocracy hypothesis, meaning that the higher the level of skills (implying the higher the GPA) a psychology graduate possesses, the better the employment outcomes for that graduate. These authors point out that there is very little empirical support for this hypothesis, although many, if not most, educators believe that a high level of skill acquisition is important for students' future success. In our opinion, when teachers devote all or nearly all of a course to *content* (the long-standing tradition of liberal arts disciplines) and limit the time spent on articulating specific course-related *skills* transferable to the workplace, a positive linkage between skills and workplace is difficult to demonstrate.

So if we do not have support for the linkage between skills and workplace success, does that mean these outcomes (skills and success) are not linked? What is perhaps a more likely outcome is that psychology educators (like educators in other liberal arts disciplines) are not particularly well versed in the assessment of transferable skills (it is not part of their training) and are more inclined to assess content knowledge. Once valid and reliable assessments of skills are established and used on a consistent basis, we will be better able to see if the meritocracy hypothesis can gain support.

We acknowledge, however, that the success of any college graduate in the workplace is undoubtedly more complicated than just measuring one's skill level at graduation. In the meantime, teachers and students could collaborate to identify the skills that specific course assignments strengthen, such as writing and critical thinking for written reports, and public speaking, group skills, and technology skills for class presentations, just to name a few. Students are also encouraged to work with career counseling professionals who can help them translate academic work into an electronic portfolio for job searches. Finally, the five student learning outcomes, part of the program benchmarks described in earlier chapters (Dunn, McCarthy, Baker, Halonen, & Hill, 2007), are a starting point for exploring skills assessment. In the meantime, students should view every course assignment not only as an occasion for mastering content but also as an opportunity to identify specific transferable skills such as those described in Chapters 2, 3, and 6.

Career Choices: How Far Do You Want to Distance Yourself From Psychology?

Recall the earlier example of the direct connection between nursing and accounting programs to practicing the professions of nursing and accountancy, respectively: The match or "distance" in content and methodology between coursework and practice is very close. In contrast, consider viewing the application of your psychology major to a career as analogous to taking a road trip (after all, life is a journey). For example, if you have lived most of your life in the Midwest, a drive over the hills and flatlands to a Midwestern city or town is through somewhat familiar territory (some would say "dull"). The Midwesterner would encounter unfamiliar territory, however, if he or she drove west across the plains, over the Rocky Mountains, across semi-arid regions of Utah and Nevada, and over the Sierra range to California. And a long, long drive is not only through highly unfamiliar and distant territory but also becomes an adventure with more potential risks and rewards than the other trips entail.

Similarly, your psychology baccalaureate prepares you for relatively familiar and "close-to-home" occupations where you directly apply a substantial part of your coursework to jobs such as social services or human resources, occupations that can become very satisfying. Choosing an occupation in social media or marketing might be equivalent to that journey to California. And finding yourself in an unusual occupation you would never dream could connect to psychology is analogous to that long and daring drive to Alaska. In short, we speculate that the farther you travel from the familiar content and methodology of your psychology major to occupations seemingly less connected to psychology, the more likely you will encounter risks, but also some rewards, as they relate to workplace preparedness, relatedness, and future prospects. When celebrities (just to name one group who chose roads less traveled by psychology students) such as NBA championship coach Phil Jackson, actresses Katharine Hepburn and Natalie Portman, and Facebook founder Mark Zuckerberg (Halonen, 2011) were studying psychology during college, they may not have seen themselves in the occupations that made them famous. Perhaps they envisioned that road trip to California but probably not a drive to Alaska that subsequently became an exciting high-adventure journey (their celebrity careers).

In contrast, psychology majors who enter graduate school are also on a journey with risks and rewards. It is a journey to higher levels of knowledge, critical thinking, social skills, professional development, and other challenges more demanding than what they faced as undergraduates. Students who enter the workplace with a baccalaureate degree are on a journey that carries them away, sometimes far away, from the familiar topics of psychology, familiar relationships with teachers and peers, and familiar environment of a university into different realms. If our journey analogy has merit, should we be surprised by the Borden and Rajecki (2000) and Rajecki and Borden (2009) findings regarding the dissatisfaction with relatedness, preparation, and prospects that many of the sample's psychology alumni expressed?

Satisfaction with one's liberal arts undergraduate major in subsequent occupations is a highly complex, multivariate issue; much thought and research are needed to understand the numerous interrelationships. The findings of the three studies conducted by Borden and Rajecki (2000; Rajecki & Borden, 2009, 2010) should not create undue anxiety about your psychology major (your friends in other liberal arts disciplines face similar concerns). Nevertheless, it is important that you enter the world of work with "eyes open," especially during periods of protracted economic and labor problems—not only with realistic expectations but also with an open mind to the potential applications of your college education in general and your psychology major in particular. Again, we advise you to explore your identity and the many career options available; to monitor your expectations as you go; and, like the person on Danaan Parry's trapeze (Chapter 13), to be ready to grab the bar that is flying toward you with confidence—and be sure to hang on.

Time Out: Reflective Questions

Has our "straight talk" caused you to think about your future? We hope so. We are raising serious issues about your academic choices and long-range planning, issues you may not encounter in your coursework or discussions with advisors; these issues contain implications of importance to you.

1. What are the implications of the findings in the Borden and Rajecki (2000) and Rajecki and Borden (2009) studies on relatedness, preparedness, and prospects?

2. What are the implications of the Rajecki and Borden (2010) findings on the meritocracy hypothesis as they might apply to you?

Why not discuss these issues with your academic advisor, family, teachers, counselors, and in your psychology club/Psi Chi meetings?

More Straight Talk About Skills

The topic of skills has been a primary theme throughout this book, so it is fitting that we include one last survey in this closing chapter, a study that sounds the alarm over a skills gap emerging during the second decade of 21st century America. According to Hanneman and Gardner (2010), the gap is caused by the loss of jobs resulting from outsourcing and the retirement of baby boomers, combined with a new, interdisciplinary-based, knowledge-intensive work environment. The situation has caused companies to seek young adults who must come prepared with higher levels of skills and abilities than their predecessors of 5 years ago. Although the study was inspired by concerns in the technical fields, it focused on all academic majors and types of employers across the job spectrum. These authors observe that changes in skill requirements are not so much a matter of adding new skills but of taking the essential skills (such as those we have discussed throughout this book) to a higher level of competency across nearly all sectors of the economy. Of the 950 employers surveyed, 897 provided usable data. Table 14.1 lists the relative importance of abilities new college hires are expected to possess in an entry-level job.

"We consider these skills and competencies to transcend job specific abilities and should be considered meta-competencies. Meta-competencies transcend a specific situation and can be applied across different situations depending on the context of the assignment or task" (Hanneman & Gardner, 2010, p. 2). When the data were analyzed to identify differences among the academic majors, researchers discovered that the top-three skills in Table 14.1 were the same among employers for all majors; similarly, the greatest shifts over the past 5 years in the skills needed were among the same three skills. When the data were analyzed for non-engineering internship and co-op positions, the five skills most sought after by employers were communication, team work, planning, project management, and analytical skills. Employers are expecting a higher level of these skills from their current interns than they did 5 years ago. In fact, "Today's employer expectations of co-ops and interns are comparable to their expectations of entry level employees just five years ago" (p. 8).

What does this daunting analysis mean for you? A review of Table 14.1 suggests the following: (1) Your psychology major is a good place to gain a conceptual understanding involved in building relationships, but you will probably have to gain practical experience with these concepts (and implied skill sets) outside most of your coursework, in challenging internships, jobs, and extracurricular activities. (2) Skills involved in data analysis, evaluation, and interpretation of data are the core methodology of your psychology major! You can *excel* in these skills if you work at them. (3) Your willingness to engage in continuous learning and global

Table 14.1   Importance of Selected Abilities in Starting Positions for New College Hires

Ability	Average Rating*	Essential, Highly Important, or Important (%)
Building working relationships	4.11	97
Analyzing, evaluating, and interpreting data	3.93	92
Engaging in continuous learning	3.87	91
Oral persuasion and justification	3.46	81
Planning and managing a project	3.22	72
Creating new knowledge	3.20	73
Global understanding	3.03	66
Building a successful team	2.87	57
Mentoring others	2.84	47

Source: Adapted with permission from Hanneman and Gardner (2010).
* where 5 = *Essential* and 1 = *Not at all important*

understanding emanates from intrinsic motivation and the opportunities you *actively* pursue. (4) Skills in oral persuasion, justification, planning and managing a project, building a successful team, and mentoring can be established to an extent (but in general, not highly) in your coursework, jobs, and extracurricular activities, but recognize that those activities are only a start to establishing proficiency. (5) Creating new knowledge derives from your motivation, abilities, and the coursework and teachers you select. In summary, we believe the skills gap survey indicates that more competence will be demanded of college graduates than ever before in the skills and characteristics they must bring to a satisfying and challenging job, and graduates will be operating in an economic climate where good jobs are hard to find.

Time Out: Reflective Questions

If Hanneman and Gardner (2010) are correct about the importance of these skills, what skill sets should you make a priority to develop and strengthen? What activities should you pursue to accomplish that goal?

Millennials in the Workplace

As psychologists, we have focused on the individual—you. But, as your sociology friends will remind you, you also function as part of many larger groups, each of which influences your beliefs, feelings, and behaviors. As you enter the workplace, most of you will discover that most supervisors and coworkers perceive and judge you, in part, by your age. Each generation has opinions of other generations.

Ask your parents, uncles and aunts, and grandparents what they think of younger (and previous) generations, and you are likely to get an earful—quickly and passionately—perhaps with surprising comments.

Twentieth century American generations have been grouped by varying dates and labeled with many names. For example, Howe (2010) identifies six generations of Americans: G.I. Generation (born 1901–1924), Silent Generation (1925–1942), Boom (or Boomer) Generation (1943–1960), Generation X (1961–1981), Millennial Generation (1982–2004), and Homeland Generation (2005 and later). You may find variations on these age groupings in other sources, such as the label Generation Y used for Millennials. Most likely, you are a Millennial.

As you know from your psychology courses, labels are often assigned to group individuals with similar qualities. Often, these qualities overlap categories rather than representing dichotomous differences between them, and considerable variation may exist within groups. We advise you to view these categories from that perspective. Whether you learn about Boomers, Gen X-ers, and Millennials (or Gen Y-ers) through television, Internet, newspaper, or scholarly sources, you are likely to discern diverse attitudes toward these groups, especially toward Millennials. The popular and research literature on Millennials is vast, but we summarize main points from a few primary resources as they relate to work so you can develop a sense of how this issue may apply to you. So who are you, and what are your strengths and weaknesses?

The Generation of Destiny

Howe (2010) identified seven core traits of the Millennial Generation: special, sheltered, confident, team oriented, conventional, pressured, and achieving. For each trait, Howe discusses the implications for educators, employers, and the public sector. In general, he speaks positively about Millennials and predicts they will become a "generation of destiny" who will most likely create several major social shifts in our culture, including

> a powerful new sense of national community, . . . greater emphasis on avoiding economic, lifestyle and career risks, . . . greater group cohesion in families, neighborhoods, and the workplace, . . . more female leadership, yet more cooperation between gender, [and] . . . a unified, big-brand technology landscape. (pp. 241–242)

Howe's predictions reveal a high level of confidence in Millennials. Can your generation do this? Jean Twenge (2006) might not agree.

"Generation Me"—Anxious and Ambitious

In *Generation Me: Why Today's Young Americans Are More Confident, Assertive, Entitled—and More Miserable Than Ever Before,* Twenge (2006) explores cultural changes in American young people using 12 studies on generational differences and data from 1.3 million young Americans. Twenge uses the label Generation Me (Gen Me) to include those born between the 1970s and 1990s (she was born in 1971). Gen-Me adults puts themselves first. They are not necessarily self-absorbed as much as they are self-important and independent. They have been told they are special and they should follow their dreams and not be constrained by social expectations. When their expectations are not met in an increasingly competitive world, however, they tend to blame others for their problems and experience stress, anxiety, and depression. For this, Twenge blames a decline in social norms and parental discipline and the impact of the self-esteem movement emphasizing that a child can do anything and become anyone.

To avoid or counteract Gen-Me problems, Twenge (2006) recommended that young adults establish realistic goals, get involved in community or service projects (to construct meaning in their lives), value their social relationships, avoid television programs that focus on the lifestyles of the fortunate few, reduce depression naturally (e.g., through sufficient sleep, diet, sunlight, and exercise), and avoid overthinking or brooding over problems. Twenge told employers that young adults will work hard but are not motivated by a sense of duty; they expect to be praised and appreciated. In addition, Gen-Me adults appreciate directness over abstraction, do not respect authority automatically, are frank with others, and are willing to share private or sensitive information. They learn best by doing but do not take criticism well (recall our remarks on criticism from Chapter 9). Gen-Me adults are accustomed to dealing with diversity but may need guidance in dealing with older people. They value salary and good benefits, and they are ambitious (Twenge, 2006).

Twenge and Campbell (2009) attempted to diagnose, identify root causes and symptoms of, and address the prognosis and treatment of narcissism. They also addressed a key component of narcissism—entitlement, which they define as "the pervasive belief that one deserves special treatment, success, and more material things" (p. 230). Entitlement is common on campus (e.g., students who believe they are entitled to a high grade or special treatment, in spite of minimal or no effort on their part). Entitlement corrodes personal and work-related relationships. At work, entitlement is reduced to the equation of "less work for more pay" or "ask not what you can do for the company but what the company can do for you." "Entitled people often confuse working hard with actually producing something good" (p. 233).

Twenge and Campbell (2009) reported that in a 2007 survey of 2,500 hiring managers, "87% agreed that younger workers 'feel more entitled in terms of compensation, benefits, and career advancement than older generations'" (p. 235). To deal with entitlement, Twenge and Campbell recommended that individuals should learn to become grateful for what they have—gratitude as the opposite of entitlement. How many of you who spent just a few hours in a soup kitchen or homeless shelter returned home grateful for what you have? These authors also recommend that supervisors assign employees a job that gives them some humility—an easy prescription in today's job market, especially since most jobs contain some boredom and grind.

Swimmers and Treaders

For a third perspective on young adults, we turn to the MacArthur Foundation's Research Network on Transitions to Adulthood, which used two dozen large and representative data sets, nearly 500 in-depth interviews across the country, and a multidisciplinary team of social and behavioral scientists to track trends in the lives of young adults (ages 18–34). The Research Network's results are reported by Settersten and Ray (2010). These authors noted an alarming trend in the data that divides young people into two categories, including the *swimmers* who "are taking their time launching into adulthood, but doing so in a careful and calculated way" (p. xi). Swimmers are willing to take on debt to obtain an education that creates the building blocks for a successful career. They delay marriage and children until they get their lives in order, and along the way, they typically receive strong family support. In contrast is a large group of young people who are "treading water" (*treaders).* They have embraced the responsibilities of adulthood (job; parenthood, with or without marriage) too quickly and without the educational preparation needed to succeed in a competitive environment. Settersten and Ray believe, however, that young adults have been misperceived regarding their lack of work ethic and their desire to succeed without paying their dues.

> Where some see a self-indulged, entitled worker, we see an adaptive response (with a small dose of self-entitlement) to a gutted workforce. In this downsized and globalized economy, job-hopping is not necessarily a sign of restlessness or fickleness. It is a smart professional strategy for the well credentialed. It is job-*shopping.* (p. xiii)

Remember, however, although the swimmers have the credentials for job-shopping, the treaders do not, and, as we noted earlier, job-shopping may arouse the suspicions of employers.

Settersten and Ray (2010) stated that young adults are unjustifiably criticized for their lack of commitment to marriage. As we noted above, the swimmers delay marriage and family until they have the education, job security, and maturity to make commitments; in contrast, treaders take on these responsibilities without sufficient preparation. Settersten and Ray interpret their data in a framework of support and understanding for young adults—swimmers and treaders. Nevertheless, their observations poignantly address characteristics of young adulthood that many older adults, including supervisors and managers, will strongly agree with.

> Many parents today have fostered a sense of invincibility in their children. Young people often do not understand how much time and effort they must invest if they are to get the grades they need or the jobs they want. . . . The mentality of young people today is often that they are consumers of higher education, buying their degrees to ensure a certain kind of future. Many even feel entitled to degrees in exchange for expensive tuition. The growing

corporate climates of universities also exacerbate the student-as-consumer mentality. . . . Many members of this generation have been reared to believe that their potential is limitless. If young people are to be successful, they should have plans for education and work that are detailed and realistic. Not everyone can be at the top. High ambitions cannot be met if clear plans and solid skills are absent. (p. 178)

Time Out: Reflective Questions

Some of your classmates would agree and others disagree with this somewhat critical judgment of young adults. What parts of this quotation do you agree with, and what statements do you disagree with? Why?

Looking Ahead (But Maybe Not That Far)

We have attempted throughout this book to address the diverse issues of workplace preparedness as related to psychology majors. However, in a volatile economy with high unemployment and low job security, even a thorough understanding of the issues, involvement in activities that promote preparedness, personal maturity, and mastery of the skills that employers seek may be insufficient for finding or keeping a job.

Becoming an Invaluable, Recession-Aware Employee

Given the ebbs and flows of any economy, the phrase "recession-proof employee" has almost become a cliché. To be fair, it is not possible to completely protect any job in any economy, as there are so many factors in the external domestic and international environment beyond our control, even beyond the control of business and government. You cannot make yourself recession-proof, but you can educate yourself to become recession-aware, perhaps recession-resistant. There is plenty of advice about making yourself invaluable (Crenshaw, 2010), indispensable (Griffin, 2011; Minnick, 2009), recession-proof (Cohen, 2010; Sander, 2009), or the linchpin (Godin, 2010).

We believe you can become invaluable and indispensable to your future employers and to yourself during college. In Chapter 6, we created an exercise based on a survey by Gardner (2007) that identified those qualities and behaviors of new hires that lead to discipline or termination. Behaviors that were the cause of termination included (in rank order of relative frequency) unethical behavior, lack of motivation/work ethic, inappropriate use of technology, failure to follow instructions, being late for work, and missing assignment deadlines. In this survey, Gardner collected another set of data that we saved for this closing chapter—namely, the behaviors, qualities, and skills that lead to promotions and new assignments. From a pool of about 1,500 characteristics identified by employers, 10 were mentioned by at least 5% and are shown in Table 14.2.

Table 14.2   Characteristics That Lead to Promotions and New Assignments

Behavior	*% Employers*
Taking initiative	16
Self-management	13
Personal attributes	9
Commitment	9
Leadership	8
Show and tell	7
Technical competence	7
Organizational savvy	5
Learning	5
Critical thinking	5

Source: Gardner (2007). Adapted with permission.

You likely have read some of these general terms often in this book, so you should also know how they were defined in this particular study. Essentially, they are transferable qualities and skills you should be practicing in your academic and non-academic experiences during college.

- *Taking initiative* means accepting responsibility beyond one's regular tasks, volunteering, promoting new ideas, and being a self-motivated, self-starting person.
- *Self-management* includes managing time, stress, work commitments (priorities), and change, and demonstrating accountability and a customer-service orientation.
- *Personal attributes* include friendliness, dependability, patience, flexibility, reliability, and respect for diversity.
- *Commitment* means working with passion, a positive attitude, enthusiasm, dedication, and a strong work ethic.
- *Leadership* is described as building consensus for and reaching common goals, displaying management skills, and recognizing the need to develop the abilities of others.
- *Show and tell* is the ability to present one's ideas persuasively, both orally and in writing.
- *Technical competence* means the person possesses the core knowledge and competence in his or her area of study and demonstrates mastery of the position, including its technical requirements.
- *Organizational savvy* indicates the individual can navigate competing interests; works well with others, including in conflict situations; and is able to fit in and promote the organization.
- *Learning* in this context refers to an eagerness to learn and pursue new ideas, including a willingness to learn about the next position.
- *Critical thinking* includes cognitive abilities such as critical, analytical, and creative thinking, and the ability to evaluate data, innovativeness, and open-mindedness (Gardner, 2007).

As true skills, these characteristics would be established habits, not occasional manifestations in your courses, job, or extracurricular activities. You will need to refine these qualities through practice and feedback if you plan to hone them into marketable skills that make you an invaluable or indispensable employee. Consider taping this list of definitions where you can view it regularly to remind yourself that if you want to rise above the routine tasks in a job and become an invaluable employee, you must proactively create or use current opportunities (such as those described in Chapter 3) in which the 10 characteristics can be developed.

No matter how well prepared you become for the workplace or how valuable to your supervisor, there may be a time when you are laid off or terminated due to outside factors beyond your control. Then you will want to reread Chapter 7 (by John Jameson) in this book and conduct a new job search. Allerton (2009) offered her top-10 list of points of action for restarting a job search (see Table 14.3). You may want to take special note of this list for possible future use.

Table 14.3   Job Search Strategies to Pursue After a Layoff

Jane Allerton describes her experience of being laid off and her immediate launch into a job search:

1. **Don't Ignore an Opportunity:** The day I was let go, I walked out with a job lead and name at 4:30 p.m. by simply chatting with a coworker about my layoff, who said, "I know XYZ Company is hiring and I know someone there." I asked, "May I have that name please?" By not being overwhelmed with job-loss news, you can realize the potential of a next step.

2. **Get Your Résumé Ready and Out There:** I updated my résumé the night I was let go. . . . I live by the Girl Scout motto: Be prepared.

3. **Network Into Action:** I updated my LinkedIn network that night, too . . . [and] also posted the short message out to my network—you never know who knows whom. Having a strong network is critical for successful networking.

4. **Proactively Plan Ahead:** I wrote up a daily logbook of job activities and tasks to do, planning out into the future months. It is vital to me to establish a solid routine in writing early on in my job search so I honor the commitments made to myself for my action plan. I include networking events, contact calls, career counseling and next steps.

5. **Volunteer Your Expertise:** I found one conference right in my backyard being orchestrated by a fellow sports friend. This volunteer work allows me to use my marketing skills to promote the event, liaison with key speakers and interact with the C-level participants in a dynamic business setting.

6. **Establish a Healthy Regimen:** I consciously decided that from now on, I will either go jogging or to the gym every morning at 8 a.m. A healthy body lends to a healthy mind. In short, feeling physically good enables me to focus on an effective job search.

7. **Find a Professional Home for the "Work of Finding Work":** I also committed to myself to either be at the outplacement office or library as my work office from 9 a.m. to 4 p.m.

8. **Keep a Routine in the Home Life:** Having a routine on the home front is reassuringly normal. . . . Job searching is stressful enough without . . . the family being impacted.

9. **Apply Extra Effort:** From 9 p.m. to midnight, I do more job search work, so that's 10 hours of job search work a day. I committed the extra time to maximize my effectiveness. While they are tough hours, it is tougher the longer you are unemployed.

10. **Create Your Own Support Group from Those Who Know You Best:** Given many months of previous layoffs at my firm and the ensuing national press, I was bound to receive panicky emails from friends asking me if I was alright. To sidestep that, I proactively texted a brief note on my cell that said, "yes, I was let go and yes, I am doing well and have action plans in place." One text to 30 friends resulted in a sort of controlled, private Twitter network and supportive group feedback.

Source: Allerton (2009).

Finally, part of becoming a valued and recession-aware employee is understanding the national and international events that influence our economy, conditions that ultimately affect your job. Take time to engage *intelligent* media through television, Internet, newspapers, and/or weekly magazines. As you approach graduation, you should be motivated to search beyond the somewhat sheltered world of your college campus for in-depth information that will affect your future as a citizen, employee, and taxpayer. Regardless of your political affiliation, seek contrasting views on major issues—no political party is always right or always wrong. And don't mistake media style and persuasiveness for substance. If you have not yet completed a course or two in economics, know that its theories and concepts have powerful influence on domestic and international events and politics that may determine whether your organization will show red or black on the next quarterly report. Knowledge of current events, the economy, and politics provides personal enrichment (a primary reason for being in college), builds professional acumen, and accrues respect from those you work with, friends, and family. Try to grasp the relationship between your company's objectives and financial position and the economic climate in which it operates. To the extent you want to become an invaluable and recession-aware employee, knowledge of the "big picture" is a likely prerequisite.

Closing Comments

Someplace in your introductory psychology book, you learned basic concepts of perception, one of which was the principle of closure. We are in the last pages of this book, and our paperback mentoring is drawing to a close. However, to provide you with some closure on *Your Undergraduate Degree in Psychology*, we identify major themes that coursed their way through these 14 chapters. If you forget many of the details we presented, be sure to remember these themes, for they serve as guidelines for your freshman and perhaps sophomore years in the workplace.

1. Your transition from college to the workplace is a critical period in your life for which you must be prepared in order to achieve early career and life stability and success.

2. Several tools exist for identifying numerous occupations that enable you to succeed in the workplace with a baccalaureate in psychology, but at some point in your future, you may seek a graduate or professional degree to enhance your professional and personal success.

3. Become actively engaged in the diverse and enriching opportunities college offers beyond coursework in order to improve your readiness.

4. Engage also in the process of mature self-reflection as a means of exploring your identity, pursuing the career planning process, understanding psychosocial development, and establishing successful job-search strategies.

5. Establish, practice, and be able to clearly articulate the numerous skills you are expected to acquire from your total college experience, and learn how to transfer them to the workplace.

6. The cultures of college and companies are so distinct that you must adapt quickly to the differences and enter the workplace with the appropriate attitudes, motives, and communication skills.

7. Expect to change whatever expectations you now hold of the workplace, unless you currently possess a high degree of work experience.

8. Expect also your personal life to change in many ways after graduation, including your relationships and the ways you go about managing your time, stress, personal finances, and the achievement of balance.

9. If you have a strong work ethic, value this quality and be willing to work even harder to succeed in your freshman year on the job. If your work ethic is weak and if you have limited work experience, take strong steps now to change this situation.

10. Study the quotation below that ends this chapter. We believe it reflects key values we have tried to communicate.

We have done our best in this book to identify important areas of workplace preparedness. We may have omitted certain topics, but we have attempted to provide you with breadth and depth regarding key issues you will face in your post-college employment, especially if you enter it with limited work experience.

We did not open Chapter 14 with our usual short quotation because we wanted you to remember at least the spirit of the quotation below, if not many of the words. At the time your authors wrote the later chapters of this book, the eminent technology inventor and founder of Apple, Inc., Stephen Jobs, was in his last months; he passed away on October 5, 2011. We believe that many remarks he gave at the 2005 Commencement address at Stanford University represent the best advice we can offer to close this book. At the point where the quotation begins, Jobs was describing his resilience and the professional and personal accomplishments he achieved after he was fired at age 30 from his job as the CEO of Apple, the company he founded.

> I'm pretty sure none of this would have happened if I hadn't been fired from Apple. It was awful tasting medicine, but I guess the patient needed it. Sometimes life hits you in the head with a brick. Don't lose faith. I'm convinced that the only thing that kept me going was that I loved what I did. You've got to find what you love. And that is as true for your work as it is for your lovers. Your work is going to fill a large part of your life, and the only way to be truly satisfied is to do what you believe is great work. And the only way to do great work is to love what you do. If you haven't found it yet, keep looking. Don't settle. As with all matters of the heart, you'll know when you find it. And, like any great relationship, it just gets better and better as the years roll on. So keep looking until you find it. Don't settle. (Jobs, 2005, para. 15)

Getting Involved

Journal Starters

1. Describe the most significant insights you gained from reading this chapter.

2. Which aspects of the information we presented about generational issues do you most identify with? What aspects do you question or disagree with?

3. Review the journal entries you have written since beginning the book. What have you learned about yourself that might guide future actions you pursue to prepare for the workplace?

Projects

1. Compare work by Twenge (2006) or Twenge and Campbell (2009) with that of Settersten and Ray (2010) on persons from younger generations. To what extent might different methodological approaches influence their findings?

2. Review individually or in either combination of authorship studies performed by Rajecki and Borden regarding career and preparedness issues in relation to psychology majors, and report the findings to the class. Are there similar studies linking college and workplace preparedness, relatedness, and professional advancement in the literature?

3. Consider the possibility that soon after you finish this book, there will be an examination on all or most of the chapters. Choose the four chapters you deem most important to you, and write two short essay questions and two long essay questions for each chapter.

Additional Resources

There are a number of books on becoming a recession-proof/invaluable/indispensable/essential employee, including the following:

- Cohen, J. (2010). *The complete idiot's guide to recession-proof careers.* New York, NY: Penguin/Alpha Books.
- Crenshaw, D. (2010). *Invaluable: The secret to becoming irreplaceable.* San Francisco, CA: Jossey-Bass.
- Godin, S. (2010). *Linchpin: Are you indispensable?* New York, NY: Penguin.
- Griffin, J. (2011). *How to say it: Be indispensable at work—winning words and strategies to get noticed, get hired, and stay ahead.* Upper Saddle River, NJ: Prentice Hall.
- Minnick, D. J. (2009). *Survive downsizing: How to keep your job and become indispensable to your company.* Bloomington, IN: iUniverse.
- Sander, P. (2009). *What to do when the economy sucks: 101 tips to help you hold on to your job, your house, and your lifestyle.* Avon, MA: Adams Business.

References

Allerton, J. (2009, June 2). My top 10 points of action in kicking off an organized job search after a layoff. *Monster Blog.* Retrieved from http://monster.typepad.com/monster-blog/2009/06/my-top-10-points-of-action-in-kicking-off-an-organized-job-search-after-a-layoff.html

Borden, V. M. H., & Rajecki, D. W. (2000). First-year employment outcomes of psychology baccalaureates: Relatedness, preparedness, and prospects. *Teaching of Psychology, 27,* 164–168.

Cohen, J. (2010). *The complete idiot's guide to recession-proof careers.* New York, NY: Penguin/Alpha Books.

Crenshaw, D. (2010). *Invaluable: The secret to becoming irreplaceable.* San Francisco, CA: Jossey-Bass.

Dunn, D. S., McCarthy, M. A., Baker, S., Halonen, J. S., & Hill, G. W., IV (2007). Quality benchmarks in undergraduate psychology programs. *American Psychologist, 62,* 650–670.

Gardner, P. (2007). *Moving up or moving out of the company? Factors that influence the promoting or firing of new college hires* (CERI Research Brief 1-2007). East Lansing: Michigan State University Collegiate Employment Research Institute.

Godin, S. (2010). *Linchpin: Are you indispensable?* New York, NY: Penguin.

Griffin, J. (2011). *How to say it: Be indispensable at work—winning words and strategies to get noticed, get hired, and stay ahead.* Upper Saddle River, NJ: Prentice Hall.

Halonen, J. S. (2011, February 5). *Are there too many psychology majors?* White paper prepared for the Staff of the State University System of Florida Board of Governors. Retrieved from http://www.cogdop.org/page_attachments/0000/0200/FLA_White_Paper_for_cogop_posting.pdf

Hanneman, L., & Gardner, P. (2010). *Under the economic turmoil a skills gap simmers* (CERI Research Brief 1-2010). East Lansing: Michigan State University Collegiate Employment Research Institute.

Howe, N. (with Nadler, R.). (2010). *Millennials in the workplace: Human resource strategies for a new generation.* Great Falls, VA: Life Course Associates.

Jobs, S. (2005, June 14). "You've got to find what you love," Jobs says. *Stanford Report.* Retrieved from http://news.stanford.edu/news/2005/june15/jobs-061505.html

Landrum, R. E., Hettich, P. I., & Wilner, A. (2010). Alumni perceptions of workforce readiness. *Teaching of Psychology, 37,* 97–106. doi:10.1080/00986281003626912

Minnick, D. J. (2009). *Survive downsizing: How to keep your job and become indispensable to your company.* Bloomington, IN: iUniverse.

National Center for Education Statistics. (2010). *Digest of educational statistics 2010.* Washington, DC: Department of Education. Retrieved from http://nces.ed.gov/programs/digest/d10/tables/dt10_282.asp

Rajecki, D. W., & Borden, V. M. H. (2009). First-year employment outcomes of US psychology graduates revisited: Need for a degree, salary, and relatedness to the major. *Psychology Learning and Teaching, 8,* 23–29.

Rajecki, D. W., & Borden, V. M. H. (2010). Liberal arts skills, psychology baccalaureates, and first-year employment: Notes on a meritocracy hypothesis. *Teaching of Psychology, 37,* 157–164. doi:10.1080/00986283.2010.488550

Sander, P. (2009). *What to do when the economy sucks: 101 tips to help you hold on to your job, your house, and your lifestyle.* Avon, MA: Adams Business.

Settersten, R., & Ray, B. E. (2010). *Not quite adults: Why 20-somethings are choosing a slower path to adulthood, and why it's good for everyone.* New York, NY: Bantam Books.

Twenge, J. M. (2006). *Generation Me: Why today's young Americans are more confident, assertive, entitled—and more miserable than ever before.* New York, NY: Free Press.

Twenge, J. M., & Campbell, W. K. (2009). *The narcissism epidemic: Living in the age of entitlement.* New York, NY: Free Press.

Author Index

Agnes, M., 190, 245

Alexander, Michael, 198

Ali, Muhammad, 209

Allerton, Jane, 274

American College Health Association (ACHA), 228–229

American Psychological Association (APA), 13, 27, 166

American Society of Training and Development, 99

Anderson, Mary L., 239, 240, 245, 248–251, 253-255, 258, 259

Andrews, A. L., 244

Appleby, D. C., 13, 21, 44, 104, 105–107, 182

Arnett, Jeffrey, 81, 83, 84, 85–87, 88, 90, 153, 210

Aronica, L., 71

Association of American Colleges and Universities, 40, 97

Austin, D. R., 105

Badger, S., 217

Bahls, S., 236

Baker, S., 52, 265

Baldwin, T. T., 48–49, 183

Barr, T. L., 244

Barry, C. M., 217

Bauer, T. N., 193

Baumann, K., 193, 194

Baxter Magolda, Marcia D., 209, 210, 217

Bendat, W., 116

Bennington, E., 204

Benson, W. L., 260

Berglund, P., 221

Bergmann, M., 193

Bialik, C., 4

Blake, William, 227

Bok, Derek, 153

Bommer, W. H., 48–49, 183

Bonior, Andrea, 212, 214, 219, 222

Borden, V. M. H., 24, 262–264, 266

Bradt, George, 192, 193

Brewer, C. L., 104

Bridges, William, 245, 246–248, 255, 258, 259

Bureau of Labor Statistics, 210

Bynner, J., 246

Campbell, John, 200–201

Campbell, Joseph, 72

Campbell, W. K., 270

Cappelli, P., 4

Carducci, Bernardo, 182

Carnegie, Dale, 126

Carnevale, A. P., 4, 5, 6, 99

Carroll, J. S., 217

Carson, A. D., 16, 17

Caruso, D. R., 176–177

Cautin, R. L., 104

Chao, G. T., 89, 90, 147, 158, 160, 161–162

Cheah, B., 6

Ciarrochi, J., 177

Clay, R. A., 38

Clough, J., 99

Cohen, J., 272, 278

Collegiate Employment Research Institute (CERI), 40, 43, 45

Combs, P., 101, 241

Consortium for Research on Emotional Intelligence in Organizations, 177
Coplin, B., 96
Cote, J. E., 80
Covey, S. R., 234–235
Cowman, Shaun, 173
Crenshaw, D., 272, 278
Cross-Tab, 128
Cruaz, Huma, 174
Csikszentmihalyi, Mihalyi, 72, 157

D'Aurizio, P., 193
Davis, S. F., 39, 40, 104, 105–107
Dawis, R. V., 16, 17
de Cervantes, Miguel, 3
Deci, E. L., 156, 157
Dell, K., 237
Demler, O., 221
Dickens, Charles, vii
Dikel, M. R., 75
Drucker, Peter F., 165
Dunn, D. S., 51, 104, 265

Edwards, J., 99
EI Skills Group, 177–179
Elison-Bowers, P., 25
Ellis, D., 95, 103, 123, 124, 195, 236
Erdogan, B., 193
Erikson, Erik, 78, 80–81, 88, 213
Estrada, A. X., 260

Farber, H. S., 82
Farr, R. J., 49, 51
Ferazzi, K., 127
Fitzpatrick, M. D., 82
Forgas, J. P., 177
Fouad, N. A., 246
Fox, D., 30
Frankl, Victor, 72
Fretz, B. R., 29
Frink, S., 174
Fritz, K., 193
Furstenberg, F. F., Jr., 210, 220

Gabhauer, M., 44
Gainer, L. J., 99
Gallagher, R. G., 50
Gardner, P., 52, 89, 90, 109–110, 147, 158, 160, 161–162, 181, 189, 190, 267, 268, 272, 273
Gates, Bill, 157

Gitomer, Jeffrey, 113, 127
Gladwell, M., 157
Gobel, R., 244
Godin, S., 272, 278
Goleman, Daniel, 176
Goodman, Jane, 239, 240, 245, 248–251, 253-255, 258, 259
Gordon, L. P., 220
Greenberg, 186
Greenberg, J., 144, 145, 146, 148, 149, 150, 151, 154, 166, 168, 169, 171, 173, 197, 230, 231
Griffin, J., 272, 278
Gurung, R. A. R., 104
Gysbers, N. C., 68

Hafferty, F. W., 105
Hageman, W., 65
Halonen, J. S., 52, 265, 266
Hamaideh, S. H., 229
Hammersley, M. J., 21, 44
Hanna, S., 118, 122
Hanneman, L., 267, 268
Hardy, S. A., 213
Harris-Bowlsbey, J., 75
Harris, Sydney J., 77
Harris, T. E., 169, 175
Harrold, R., 99
Harwood, L., 114, 121
Hayes, N., 99
Helkowski, Camille, 9, 72, 231, 247
Heppner, M. J., 68
Hess, A. K., 2
Hettich, P., 24, 40, 47, 49, 53, 72, 83, 104, 105–107, 159, 166, 167, 173, 247, 257, 262
Hill, G. W., IV, 52, 265
Hodge, H., 24
Holland, John L., 18
Holton, E. F., III, 186–187, 189, 194, 195, 203, 233
Hopper, C. H., 235, 236
Howe, N., 269

Institute for College Access and Success, 152

Jacobsen, M. H., 60, 61
Jameson, John, 10, 124, 133
James, William, 143, 162
Jensen, L. A., 88
Jin, R., 221

Jobs, Steve, 15, 64, 276–277
Johnson, M., 194
Johnston, J. A., 68
Jung, C., 70

Kaestner, M., 193
Kamenatz, A., 16
Kanchier, Carole, 32
Kane, Kathy, 165
Kantrowitz, Mark, 237
Keil, J., 78, 145, 156, 167
Keith, K. D., 104
Keith-Spiegel, P., 27
Kennedy, S., 210, 220
Kessler, R. C., 221
Korschgen, A. J., 13
Kracen, A. C., 27
Kruger, D. J., 100
Krumboltz, John, 68–69
Kuther, T. L., 13, 27

Landrum, R. E., 24, 25, 39, 40, 99, 104,
     105–107, 166, 257, 262
Latham, Gary, 154
Lawford, H. L., 213
Lawler, E. E., 151
Lecci, L., 239, 240
Lee, J., 210
Leibow, D. M., 51
Levin, A. S., 68–69
Levin, B., 193
Levit, Alexandra, 82, 146–147, 182, 198,
     215, 235
Levitt, J. G., 114, 121
Light, J., 26, 32
Light, R. J., 38
Lineberg, S., 204
Littlepage, G., 24
Locke, Edwin, 154
Losey, S., 193
Lumina Foundation, 97
Lunneborg, P. W., 30

MacArthur Foundation's Research
     Network on Transitions to Adulthood,
     153, 220, 271
Madsen, S. D., 217
Magnuson, S., 61
Malin, J. T., 7
Malott, K. M., 61
Marcia, James, 78, 80–81

Maslow, A., 150
Mathis, M., 239, 240
Mayer, John, 176–177
McAdams, D. P., 78–79, 80
McCall, William A., 95
McCann, L. I., 104
McCarthy, M. A., 52, 265
McCloyd, V. C., 210, 220
McCormick, B. P., 105
McGinty, J., 119
McGregor, L. N., 104
McGuinness, C., 100
McIlvaine, A. R., 166
McIntyre, M. G., 198–199
McKay, D. R., 17
Meeker, F., 30
Meister, J. C., 204
Meltzer, A. S., 99
Merikanges, K. R., 221
Michalski, D. S., 27
Miller, Abby (Wilner), 11, 87
Millspaugh, B. S., 21
Millspaugh, D. S., 44
Minnick, D. J., 272, 278
Mitchell, K. E., 68–69
Mobray, K., 124
Morgan, B. L., 13
Morgan, R. D., 13
Mulvey, T. A., 27

Naquin, S., 186, 189, 194, 195
National Association of Colleges and
     Employers (NACE), 24, 37, 40, 42, 46,
     47, 48, 49, 65, 95, 96, 114, 128, 166,
     189, 190, 199, 202, 257
National Center for Education Statistics, vii,
     5, 6, 261
National Commission on Writing, 101
National Institute for Mental
     Health, 222
National Opinion Research Center, 83
Nelsen, L. R., 39
Nelson, L. J., 217
Newman, R., 5

O'Hare, L., 100
Oliver, Mary, 59
Olsen, J. A., 213
Orman, S., 244
Orwell, George, 128
Osborn, D. S., 75

Palmer, K., 244
Palmer, Parker, 63
Pancer, S. W., 213
Parks, Dirk, 173
Parks, McLean, 173
Parry, Danaan, 245, 255–256, 258, 259, 264
Partnership for 21st Century Skills, 97
Perlman, B., 104
Perry, S., 24
Peters, R. L., 27
Pew Research Center for the People and the Press, 210
Pfeffer, J. A., 144
Pink, Daniel, 69, 156–158, 163
Pollack, L., 102, 125
Pollak, L., 40, 43
Porter, L. W., 151
Pratt, M. W., 213
Puymbroeck, M. V., 105

Radtke, D., 118, 122
Rajecki, D. W., 21, 25–26, 262–264, 266
Raufman, L., 116
Ray, Barbara, 84, 153, 253, 271
Raz, T., 127
Robbins, A., 209, 221
Robinson, K., 71
Rochlen, A. B., 257, 259
Rogers, Fred, 63
Rose, J., 125
Rose, S. J., 6
Rossi, Alice, 222
Rubenstein, C., 222
Rubin, R. S., 48–49, 183
Rumbaut, R. G., 210, 220
Russell, J. E. A., 101
Ryan, R. M., 156, 157

Salancik, G. R. A., 144
Salovey, Peter, 176–177
Sampson, J. P., 75
Sander, P., 272, 278
Satterfield, C., 16
Scharf, R. S., 68
Scheef, D., 67
Schlossberg, Nancy K., 239, 240, 245, 248–251, 253-255, 258, 259
Schultheiss, D. E. P., 13
Senges, M., 194

Settersten, Richard A., Jr., 84, 153, 210, 220, 253, 271
Shaffer, S. M., 220
Sherblom, J. C., 169, 175
Skillicorn, J., 105
Smith, K., 99
Smith, T. W., 24
Snell, A., 193
Stang, D. J., 29
Stocker, C., 200, 219, 221, 222, 237, 238
Strapp, C. M., 49, 51
Suggett, R., 118, 122
Sukiennik, D., 116
Super, Donald, 67, 73
Sykes, Charles J., 245

Tanner, Jennifer L., 82, 83, 84, 85–87, 88, 153
Thielfoldt, D., 67
Thoreau, Henry David, 35
Thorndike, Edward L., 95
Timmreck, C., 7
Turner, S. E., 82
Twenge, Jean, 222, 269–270

U. S. Census Bureau, 6

Vander Ven, T., 55
Voight, M. J., 104
Vonnegut, Mary, 192

Wahlstrom, C., 13
Walfish, S., 28
Wallace, I. J., 27
Walters, E. E., 221
Ware, M. E., 97, 99
Wear, D., 105
Wendlandt, N. B., 257, 259
Whitley, B. E., Jr., 30
Wicherski, M., 27
Wiederman, M. W., 27
Williams, B. K., 13
Willyerd, K., 204
Wilner, A., 24, 166, 200, 209, 219, 221, 222, 237, 238, 257, 262
Wilson, L. O., 105
Wilson, V. M., 30

Yena, D. J., 121

Zechmeister, Eugene, 38, 100

Subject Index

Academic success, 30, 49

Academic tourism, 52

Adjusting to work environment, 191–192
    See also Organizational culture
        compared to college culture

The Adventures of Johnny Bunko (Pink), 69

Assessments, career
    interest inventories, 17
    job satisfaction, 147–148
    occupational alternatives, 16–17
    online services, 16, 18
    overview of, 16–17
    Self-Directed Search (SDS), 18–20 (box)
    self-evaluations, 17, 60–65

Attitude, importance of, 32, 143–147

Authentic life, 70–71

Balance, work/life, 239–240

Bridges's three phases of transition model, 246–248

Bucket list, 59, 65–66

Bullying, 230

Burnout, job, 145

California Psychological Inventory, 16

Campus jobs, 37–39

Campus organizations, 49

Campus resources, 53
    See also Career centers

Career adaptability, 239–240

Career centers
    assessment opportunities, 16–17
    college/university, 16, 50–51
    for occupational research, 44
    See also Career counselors

Career choices
    career genogram, 60–61, 62
        (figure), 74
    chance, role of, 68–69
    desirable job characteristics, 88–90,
        89 (table)
    effect of economy on, 67–68
    familial influences on, 60, 84
    generational effects on, 67, 161

Career counselors, 42, 50–51

Career Decision Scale, 17

Career Explorer, 16

Career Factors Inventory, 17

Career growth quiz, 32–33

Career Maturity Inventory, 16

Career planning
    assessment tools, 16–20, 63–66
    familial influences on, 60–61
    making a career genogram, 60–61, 62
        (figure), 74
    and research, 64–65
    tips, 70–71
    unpredictable events, 66–69

Career preparation
    internships, 40–43
    part-time work during college,
        35–36, 85
    skill sets, 11–12, 36
    temporary employment, 38
    transitioning from college,
        97–99
    work-study programs, 37–38
    See also Skill set development

Career satisfaction. *See* Job satisfaction

Career Thoughts Inventory, 17
Careers/job diary, 32
"CERI Thought Piece: Internships as High Stakes Events" (CERI), 43
Certificate programs, 26–27
College culture compared to organizational culture, 185–192, 187 (table), 233 (table)
College education, advantages of, 6, 6 (table), 7, 88, 153
Communication skills
    organizational expectations, 166–167
    in teamwork, 169–175
    types of media, 167–168
    See also Emotional Intelligence; Skill set development; Teamwork
Conflict, managing, 172–175, 230
Constructive criticism, 173–174
Consumer Reports, 238
Coping strategies, development of, 50, 241–243, 250–255
Counseling Adults in Transition (Goodman et al.), 248
Counseling services, seeking, 50–51, 223
    See also Mental health
Coursework, advantages from, 38–39, 47–48, 51–52, 264–265
Cover letters, 119–120
    See also Résumé
Covert curriculum, 104–107
Credit cards, 236–237
Criticism, constructive, 173–174

Dating dos and don'ts, 217–219
Debt, student, 152–153, 237
    See also Financial management
Degree Qualifications Profile (DQP), 97
Depression. *See* Mental health
Dictionary of Occupational Titles, 21, 44
Digital footprint, 128–129
DISCOVER (assessment), 16

Economy, effect of, 67–68, 90, 272
Elective courses, 47–48
The Element (Robinson and Aronica), 71
E-mail etiquette, 102
    See also Communication skills
Emerging adulthood
    age of instability, 83
    age of possibilities, 84
    characteristics of, 85–88
    and dating, 217–219

feeling in between, 83–84
identity exploration, 82–83
recentering, 86–87
self-focused age, 83
transitional issues, 209–211
Emotional intelligence
    four-branch model, 177–180, 177 (figure)
    importance of, 176
    and teamwork, 179–180
Emotional Intelligence (Goleman), 176
Employee assistance programs (EAPs), 231
Employee traits, desirable, 273 (table)
Employment statistics, 4, 82
Entry-level positions, 4, 267–268, 268 (table)
Erikson's stages of human development, 78–81
Expectancy theory, 151–153
Extracurricular activities, benefits of, 20, 46, 48–50

Facebook, 215
Familial influences. *See* Career choices, familial influences on
Financial advantages (college graduates), 6, 6 (table), 153
Financial management, 236–239
FindAMentor, 198
First-day strategies, 195–196 (table), 197
Flow, establishing, 157

4S coping system, 250–255
Friendships
    post-college experiences, 211–214
    and roommates, 216, 219
    significance of, 87, 212
    and social media, 215
    social outlets, 212–213
    in the workplace, 214–215

Gen Me, 270
Generation Me (Twenge), 269–270
Generation of destiny, 269
Generational effects on careers, 67, 161, 268–272
Goals, setting
    for job search, 121–122, 135
    motivation and, 153–155
    receiving feedback, 155
    S.M.A.R.T. technique, 121–122, 155
Graduate school, 26–28, 28–29 (table), 265–266

Groupthink, 170–171, 182
Groupwork
    See Teamwork

Happenstance, 68–69
*Highlights of the National Survey of
    Counseling Center Directors 2010*
    (Gallagher), 50
Holland codes. *See* Self-Directed Search (SDS)

Identity development, 78–80
Identity exploration, 82–83
Identity status theory, 78–81
Informational interviewing, 44–45
Initiative in the workplace, taking, 190–192
INROADS Guide to Corporate Survival
    Training Module, 199, 202
Interest inventories, 17
    See also Assessments, career
Internet career assessments, 16, 18
Internet job searches, 121
Internships, 38, 40–43, 41 (table)
Interpersonal skills, development of, 47–48,
    48–49
    See also Skill set development
Interview skills, 129–133
Inventories. *See* Assessments, career

Job-characteristics resources, 21
Job Choices 2012 (NACE), 199, 202
Job culture. *See* Organizational culture
Job Outlook 2012 (NACE), 37, 46, 48
Job performance, 200–202
Job satisfaction
    assessment survey, 147–148
    and attitude, 144–147
    benefits, ranking of, 88–90, 89 (table)
    and centrality of work, 160–161
    and change, 66–67
    first-year graduates, 24
    and organizational justice, 148–150
    rankings for American workers, 25
        (table)
    salary data, 24–25
    social information processing model of,
        144–145
    value theory, 144
Job-search strategies
    cover letter, 119–120
    creating a plan, 122–123, 274–275
    desirable job characteristics, 88–90,
        89 (table)

    and identity exploration, 82
    Internet sites, 121, 126–127
    interview skills, 129–133
    job fairs, 125–126
    networking, 123–127, 136
    online job boards, 121
    selecting references, 123
    setting goals, 121–122, 135
    tips, 274–275 (table)
    See also Networking; Résumé; Skill
        set development
Job shadowing, 43–44
Job skills. *See* Skill set development
Job statistics, U.S., 4
Job termination, reasons for, 109 (table)
Journal prompts, 241
Jung Career Indicator, 16

Layoffs, 272–275
Let Your Life Speak (Palmer), 63
Life changes, 63–64, 78–81
Life list, 65–66, 74
Lifelong learning, 104–107
"Life-Span Life-Space Approach to Career
    Development" (Super), 67–68
LinkedIn, 121

Math skills, 103
Mental health, 50–51, 85, 221–223
Mentors
    faculty members as, 39
    importance of, 71–73
    "paperback" mentor, 4, 7–8
    tips for success, 197–198
Military training, 53–54
Millennial generation, 268–270
MonsterTRAK, 89, 160
Motivation, work
    expectancy theory and, 151–153
    Maslow's hierarchy and, 150
    Motivation 2.0 system (Pink), 156–158
    Motivation 3.0 system (Pink), 156–158
    and performance, 151–152
Motivation 2.0 system (Pink), 156–158
Motivation 3.0 system (Pink), 156–158
My Vocational Situation, 17

National Association of Colleges and
    Employers (NACE), 24, 42
Negativity. *See* Attitude, importance of
Networking
    benefits of, 123–124

building a network, 124–125
Internet sites, 126–127
job-search events, 125–126
networking events, 46
networking map, 136
and social media, 127–129
New hires. *See* Entry-level positions; First-day strategies; Onboarding programs
1984 (Orwell), 128
Not Quite Adults (Settersten and Ray), 253

Occupational alternatives (assessments), 16–17
Occupational choices (for psychology majors), 21–23 (table)
Occupational Outlook Handbook, 44
Office of Teaching Resources in Psychology, 44
Office politics, 198–200
Onboarding (Bradt and Vonnegut), 192
Onboarding programs, 192–195, 193 (table)
O*NET Occupational Information Network, 21, 44
Online career-planning assessments, 16, 18
Online job boards, 121
An Online Resource to Enable Undergraduate Psychology Majors to Identify and Investigate 172 Psychology and Psychology Related Careers (Appleby et al.), 44
Organizational culture compared to college culture, 185–192, 187 (table), 233 (table)
Organizational justice, 148–150
Organizational Research Grid, 129, 137
Outsourcing, 5

"Parable of the Trapeze" (Parry), 255–256
Performance feedback, 200–202
Persistence, 72
Positive psychology, 72–73
Preparation. *See* Career preparation
Psychological problems, 50–51, 86
    See also Mental health
Psychology major
    career outcomes of, 261–265
    career satisfaction, 24–26
    certificate programs, 26–27
    skills sets gained, 11–12, 51–52, 99–100, 276
    See also Coursework, advantages from; Graduate school

Psychosocial development, 78–81
Purpose, finding, 72–73

Quarterlife crisis, 209, 216, 222–223

RA, 38–39
Recentering, 86–87
Research assistant (RA), 38–39
Resilience, 90, 239–240
Résumé
    chronological, example of, 117
    cover letter, 119–120
    format of, 115–116, 118–119
    functional, example of, 117
    purpose of, 114–115
Roommates, 219

SDS, 18–20 (box)
Self-Directed Search (SDS), 18–20 (box)
Self-evaluation
    and defining success, 30–31
    and job searches, 114
    performance of job tasks, 202
    of skill sets, 20
    S.M.A.R.T. technique, 121–122, 155
    of stress on academic performance, 228 (table)
Self-management
    coping strategies, 241–243
    and finances, 236–239
    finding balance, 239–240
    and stress, 231–232
    and time, 232–236
Sexual harassment, 230
Skill set development
    benefits of internships, 40–43
    for career preparation, 36–38
    characteristics of good employees, 273 (table)
    comparison of skill sets, 96 (table)
    Degree Qualifications Profile (DQP), 97
    lifelong learning skills, 104–107
    math skills, 103
    of psychology majors, 11–12, 99–100
    transferable skills, 95, 98 (table), 201–202, 264–265, 273–274
    work-content skills, 95, 201–202
    written communication skills, 101–102
Skills diary, 12
Skills gap, 267–268
Small-group communications, 47–48

S.M.A.R.T. approach (goal setting),
121–122, 155
SOAR technique, 130, 131, 132
SOC codes, 21
Social media, 126–129, 215
Socializing, post-college, 212–214
Standard occupational classification (SOC)
codes, 21
Stress
during college years, 228–229
reduction strategies, 231–232
transitional, 227–228
in the workplace, 229–230
Study abroad, benefits of, 20, 52
Success, definitions of, 30–31
Support networks, 49, 253–254

Teaching assistant (TA), 39
Teamwork
and cohesiveness, 170–171
establishing roles, 169–170
resolving conflicts, 171–176
Temperament and Values Inventory, 16
Temping. *See* Temporary work
Temporary work, 38
Terminations, reasons for, 109 (table), 272
They Don't Teach Corporate in College
(Levit), 146
Time management
adjusting to 8-hour workday, 220–221,
232–233
Covey Time Management Matrix, 234–235
and efficiency, 235–236
and prioritizing tasks, 235
The Transition Model (Goodman et al.)
4S coping system, 250–255
identifying type of transition, 249
stages of transition, 249–250

Transition models
Bridges's three phases of transition,
246–248
"Parable of the Trapeze" (Parry),
255–256
The Transition Model (Goodman et al.),
249–255
Wendlandt and Rochlen's college-
to-work transition perspective,
257–258
Transitional periods
changing roles, 210
college-to-workplace, 247
coping with change, 221–223,
241–243
and friendships, 211–214
quarterlife crisis, 209–210, 222
See also Transition models
Twitter, 121
2011 Internship & Co-op Survey
(NACE), 42
Type I (Intrinsic) behavior, 156–157
Type X (extrinsic) behavior, 156–157

Unemployment rates, 5

Volunteering, benefits of, 45–46

Warriors of the Heart (Parry), 255
Webster's New World College Dictionary
(Agnes), 245
Work culture. *See* Organizational culture
Workplace readiness. *See* Career prepara-
tion; Skill set development
Workplace romance, 214, 216
See also Dating dos and don'ts
Workplace violence, 230
Work-study programs, 37–38
Writing skills, 101–102

ⓈSAGE research**methods**

The essential online tool for researchers from the world's leading methods publisher

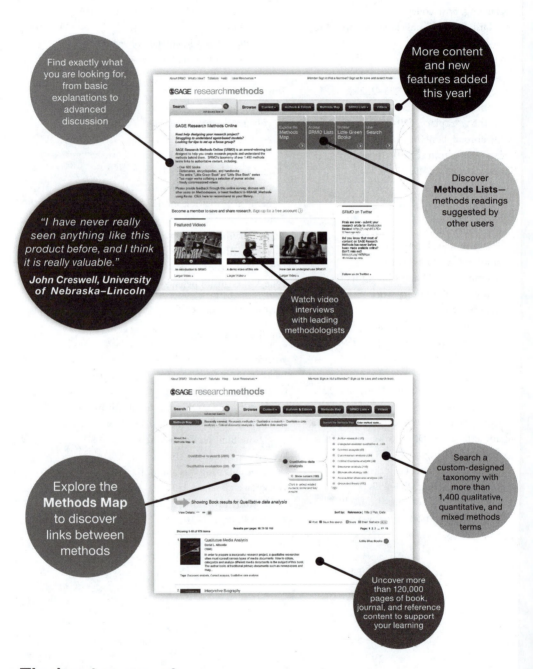

Find exactly what you are looking for, from basic explanations to advanced discussion

More content and new features added this year!

"I have never really seen anything like this product before, and I think it is really valuable."

John Creswell, University of Nebraska–Lincoln

Discover **Methods Lists**— methods readings suggested by other users

Watch video interviews with leading methodologists

Explore the **Methods Map** to discover links between methods

Search a custom-designed taxonomy with more than 1,400 qualitative, quantitative, and mixed methods terms

Uncover more than 120,000 pages of book, journal, and reference content to support your learning

Find out more at
www.sageresearchmethods.com